BENDER GESTALT SCREENING
FOR BRAIN DYSFUNCTION
SECOND EDITION

Bender Gestalt Screening
for Brain Dysfunction

Second Edition

PATRICIA LACKS

John Wiley & Sons, Inc.

New York • Chichester • Weinheim • Brisbane • Singapore • Toronto

Library of Congress Cataloging-in-Publication Data:

Lacks, Patricia.
    Bender Gestalt screening for brain dysfunction / Patricia Lacks. —
2nd ed.
      p. cm.
    Includes bibliographical references and index.
    ISBN 0-471-24257-8 (cloth)
    1. Bender-Gestalt Test.   2. Brain—Diseases—Diagnosis.
  I. Title.
    [DNLM: 1. Bender-Gestalt Test.   2. Delirium, Dementia, Amnestic,
Cognitive Disorders—diagnosis.   WM 145.5.B4 L141b 1999]
RC386.6.B46L3   1999
616.8'0475—dc21
DNLM/DLC
for Library of Congress   98–7635
                                                         CIP

Printed in the United States of America.

10 9 8 7 6 5 4 3 2 1

To my always loving and supportive husband,
Paul Gawronik

Preface

In the clinician's assessment battery, the Bender Gestalt Test (BGT) continues to be a popular test more than 60 years after its introduction. Even with the growing practice of more extensive and sophisticated neuropsychological evaluation, the BGT's brevity, simplicity, and demonstrated effectiveness in the diagnosis of brain impairment make it a useful assessment tool.

My book is not about how to use the BGT as a *single test* of "organicity," a long outdated practice. Instead, the focus is on neuropsychological assessment as a continuum. The screening process is at one end, comprehensive neuropsychological assessment is at the other. All along this continuum, the BGT can be used, along with other tests, to evaluate an individual for brain impairment. This test belongs in the domain of perceptual-motor brain function or visuo-constructive skills. However, success on this test also appears to require good *executive* skills. Research has shown that the BGT is useful in detecting disorders due to diffuse brain damage or impairment in the parietal and frontal lobes.

Since 1984, when the first edition of this book was published, much has changed in the field of psychological assessment. Clinical neuropsychology is now a healthy specialty. The older adult population has grown dramatically. Psychologists are often called upon to evaluate forensic cases. Computers are now used to assist in many aspects of assessment. One thing that has not changed, however, is the continued popularity of the BGT. Surveys of psychologists still show that they rank it among their most used and valued instruments.

If you use the BGT within a battery of psychological tests, this book will teach you to use it well: to administer it in a standard way, to note relevant behavioral observations that aid in analysis of the test, to score the test accurately with a well-developed scoring system, to take into account variables that have the potential to affect the number of errors, and to apply an eight-step interpretation to the results.

Sometimes I have been frustrated by purchasing a revision of a book and finding that not all that much has been changed. The reader can be assured that a great deal of this book is different from the 1984 edition. Over half the references appeared later than 1984. The new references include updates of the research, neuropsychological topics, and information about new subjects in the book. There are five added chapters covering new material. Because of the explosion of information about neuropsychological assessment, I have included a chapter that reviews neurophysiology and neuropathology and discusses how the BGT can be used in screening for brain impairment. Included in this chapter is a lengthy discussion of the problem of discriminating brain damage from schizophrenia, a frequent dilemma for psychologists. It also addresses the question of what the BGT measures and describes appropriate ways to use the test in different assessment situations.

The first version of this book focused on teaching administration and scoring of the BGT. This edition, however, adds a chapter on the systematic interpretation of the results and how to use computer software to assist in this process. Because the population of older adults has increased greatly since 1984, I have added a chapter on this group, including discussion of the cognitive implications of normal aging and special issues for assessment of this age group. The BGT also continues to be very popular for work with children. Although the scoring used in this book is only for adults and adolescents, there are many complicated issues that are covered in a new chapter about using the BGT with children. Finally, recent research has shown that the scoring approach used here is applicable for adolescents age 12 to 16. Therefore, a new chapter that includes norms for this age group and two case examples has been prepared. One chapter also includes a lengthy new section on how to detect malingering on the BGT. Finally, this edition includes 18 new practice cases on which to hone your scoring skills.

My work with the BGT began in 1962 with my master's thesis (in the name Brilliant) under the direction of Malcolm D. Gynther. The study compared the diagnostic accuracy of three screening tests for brain damage: the Bender Gestalt, the Benton Visual Retention, and the Graham-Kendall Memory for Designs. The latter two tests have detailed scoring instructions incorporated into their test manuals. However, the BGT does not; over the years a number of scoring systems have been developed for it. Before 1960, most psychologists used the Pascal and Suttell instructions for scoring. However, these procedures are cumbersome, time-consuming, and do not apply to older and less educated individuals.

In 1960, Max Hutt and Gerald Briskin published a book on the Bender Gestalt that focused on personality interpretation. Mentioned almost in passing was a list of 12 *essential discriminators* for organic brain dysfunction. A major appeal of their evaluation method was its brevity. Test protocols are inspected for the presence or absence of these 12 *errors* (compared to 105 screening decisions in the Pascal-Suttell system), a procedure that with practice takes only 1 to 3 minutes (compared to as much as 20 minutes for the Pascal-Suttell method). This greatly lowered time makes the scoring more realistic for clinical usage.

The chief drawbacks to Hutt and Briskin's method, however, are the lack of detail in the description of the 12 errors and the absence of examples of each type. To allow me to evaluate the protocols in my early study consistently, I developed a detailed scoring manual based on the 12 essential discriminators. The results of that research demonstrated that the BGT, scored with this manual, could discriminate very effectively among psychiatric patients with brain dysfunction and those with other disorders.

This scoring manual has consistently been used in a number of research studies, with generally favorable results. In recognition of Hutt and Briskin's original work and in acknowledgment of my own contribution, I originally called the procedures presented in this book the Lacks adaptation of the Hutt-Briskin scoring system. I continue to use this term in the revised edition, but in the interests of brevity also sometimes use the terms *Lacks methods* or *procedures.*

The first edition of this book was written to reproduce the training procedures I have used with my research assistants and clinical trainees. Briefly, this tutorial method includes a detailed scoring manual with many examples of the errors, as well as examples of when not to score an error. It also provides a series of 12 cases with the scoring explained and 10 additional practice cases with feedback provided at the end. I often receive requests to check the BGT scoring being used in research projects. Some researchers do an excellent job; they are very accurate in their scoring. Others show low scoring accuracy. Whenever I read results from a study that are out of step with other research on the topic, I wonder about the accuracy of the scoring in that study. I am confident that clinicians who devote 3 to 4 hours to following this training sequence will develop high levels of scoring accuracy.

Although this book is essentially a manual of practical clinical use, the reader will also find a good deal of information about the reliability, validity, and diagnostic accuracy of the BGT in general and of this scoring system specifically. Included is information about the relative effectiveness of evaluation through clinical judgment, as opposed to use of objective scoring schema; the effect of level of experience on diagnostic accuracy; and a comparison of this test with other neuropsychological tests and neurological procedures. In addition, there is a lengthy discussion of the utility of this test as a preliminary screening instrument, as compared to its use as a measure of visuoconstructive abilities within a complete battery of neuropsychological tests.

Extensive norms are provided for psychiatric patients and nonpatients, including college students, adults, and older adults. A new section adds normative data for adolescents.

At this time, I would like to acknowledge the large number of individuals who have helped me in this work. First, I want to thank Malcolm Gynther, whose original idea developed into my first work on the Bender Gestalt Test. He served as my research mentor for many years. He also taught me that research can be fun.

A number of former students, very talented research assistants, colleagues, researchers, and clinicians have been very generous in sharing their time, moral support, knowledge, and the results of their own work. Many were thanked by name in the first edition of this work; I will confine my gratitude here to those who helped with this second edition. With their help, this book is more interesting and helpful.

Finding so many clinical BGT examples that illustrate points about the test and help to teach various aspects of the scoring was a very time-consuming task. Seven psychologists took precious time to go through their files to locate BGT protocols that would make a contribution. Some are academic psychologists who shared cases from their research; some are clinicians who provided cases from their practice. One person is a forensic psychologist who spent a great deal of time looking through his files of known malingerers to provide a case that would illustrate the special diagnostic issues with this population. In the interest of taking maximum precautions to protect the identity of the clients or patients whose BGTs are published in this book, the providers of the protocols and I agreed that it would be better not to name the psychologists. They did make a tremendous contribution to this book, and I am greatly appreciative of their selfless and anonymous efforts.

I also received much assistance from researchers with the Memory and Aging Project (National Institution on Aging grant numbers AG 03991 and AG 05681) at Washington University Medical School, especially Martha Storandt and Emily La Barge. They provided several cases of older adults, both those with Alzheimer's type dementia and those with no brain impairment. Additional thanks go to Dr. Storandt, who allowed me to reproduce some of her normative data for older adults.

Another group of psychologists allowed me to reproduce their published normative data on the BGT with adolescents: Ronald Belter, Julia McIntosh, Garry Edwards, A. J. Finch, Conway Saylor, and Lee Williams. Dr. Belter also served as a consultant to me on various matters about testing adolescents. Jerome Sattler generously agreed to let me reproduce one of his cases from his book on psychological assessment of children.

In 1996, I worked with Psychological Assessment Resources (PAR) to develop computer software that would facilitate the interpretation and report writing of BGT results. R. Bob Smith, the President and CEO of PAR, has allowed me to reproduce the scoring summary sheet from the software and a sample report produced through the use of this software. Also, Gary Groth-Marnat has served as a valuable colleague.

The publishers of the work of Lauretta Bender and of Elizabeth Koppitz have also been very helpful in letting me reprint part of their material in my book. Finally, I am grateful to Kelly Franklin and M. R. Carey for their very skillful and responsive assistance in the production of this book.

Writing a book is a stressful act; it also has an impact on your family and close friends and colleagues. For six months, whenever they asked me about how my life was going or what I was doing, the answer was always, "the book." The response became a mantra of sorts. I am particularly grateful to my husband, Paul Gawronik, and to my children Jeffrey and Amy Lacks for their cheerful acceptance of the effects of this project on their lives and for their constant support of my efforts.

If Hutt and Briskin had not published their original scoring system, I might not have developed my interest, which has led to many years of challenging and rewarding research. Also, if the several thousand psychiatric patients and community members had not volunteered to participate in my research on the Bender Gestalt Test, there would have been no book to write.

PATRICIA LACKS
Santa Barbara, California

Contents

Tables

Figures

CHAPTER 1

Introduction to the Bender Gestalt Test

One of the most popular tools in the armamentarium of the clinical psychologist is the Bender Gestalt Test (BGT). It consists of nine figures, mostly familiar geometric designs, that are presented one at a time to the person being evaluated. The usual procedure requires the individual to copy these figures as accurately as possible on one or more blank sheets of paper. There is no time limit.

The result is a very brief (and therefore inexpensive), nonverbal, standardized, *perceptual-motor* test. Other descriptive terms for this type of measure are *visuospatial, visuoconstructive,* and *visual-motor.* In this book, the BGT will be variously referred to in all these ways. Generally, this test is placed in the broad category of *neuropsychological* assessment tools.

The BGT also entails little risk or discomfort. These characteristics can be especially valuable when testing individuals who may be unable or unwilling to cooperate on a longer task: children, the deaf, individuals of low intelligence, and psychiatric inpatients with low motivational and aspirational levels. Because it requires minimal amounts of communication and cooperation, the BGT is also useful for identifying mental deterioration in older adults. The nonverbal response mode may also minimize test differences due to cultural or socioeconomic factors.

CLINICAL USAGE OF THE BGT

With these many useful qualities, it is not surprising that the BGT is so popular for use across all age groups: children, adolescents, adults, and older adults. In surveys of clinical psychologists over the past 40 years, it has usually been listed as among the top four or five most-used tests and as among those that clinicians most advise students of clinical psychology to learn (Piotrowski, 1995).

Most recently, Watkins, Campbell, Nieberding, and Hallmark (1995) surveyed 412 "assessment-active" licensed psychologists, randomly selected from American Psychological Association membership rolls. They found an identifiable core of assessment tools most often used by the majority of clinical psychologists across seven types of work settings. Overall, the BGT was ranked seventh most frequently used procedure after clinical interview, Wechsler Adult Intelligence Scale—Revised (WAIS-R), Minnesota Multiphasic Personality Inventory (MMPI-2), sentence completion methods, Thematic Apperception Test, and Rorschach. Only 20% of their sample had never used this test.

1

The BGT was used somewhat more often by psychologists from psychiatric hospital and private practice settings and less often in university departments and medical schools. Other neuropsychological tests and their ranks were: Wechsler Memory Scale (12), Benton Visual Retention Test (22), Halstead-Reitan Battery (23), Graham-Kendall Memory for Designs (28), and Luria-Nebraska Neuropsychological Battery (32).

In 1989, Piotrowski and Keller found very similar results with 413 psychologists working in outpatient mental health facilities. The BGT was the third most used test, below the MMPI-2 and WAIS-R. The other five neuropsychology tests previously listed appeared in exactly the same order and nearly the same ranks as found by Watkins et al. (1995). The long neuropsychology batteries, such as the Halstead-Reitan and the Luria-Nebraska, were either infrequently used or administered only in part.

Supporters of the widely used BGT advocate it for a variety of purposes (Piotrowski, 1995). It is often suggested as a buffer or warm-up procedure because it is relatively innocuous or nonthreatening. It may also help to establish rapport or calm an uneasy client. Many clients even enjoy taking the BGT. This test has also been used to estimate nonverbal IQ. Or it may serve as a transition between the objective and the more emotion-laden projective techniques. The BGT is used by some as a projective personality measure for the psychodynamic understanding of an individual's needs and conflicts. With children, this test is given to assess developmental maturity, which is then frequently utilized to predict school or reading readiness or to identify learning problems. However, the widest use of the BGT has been as a *screening test of brain dysfunction* administered within a battery of tests that generally includes the WAIS.

The most recent chapter in the life of the BGT is the growth of the subspecialty of neuropsychological assessment. In the past 20 years, there has been a great increase in psychological knowledge about brain function, methods to measure it, and activities for remediation of cognitive disorders. Neuropsychologists now can deploy a wide repertoire of measures to assess many aspects of brain function.

The very early practice of giving a single test to screen for brain impairment is no longer defensible, and in fact has not been evident for many years. Now evaluators use a continuum of neuropsychological assessment varying in thoroughness and amount of effort and expense. At the least extensive end of the continuum, a psychologist may administer a *general screening battery* to assess both cognitive and emotional functioning. The results of any of the tests in this battery, including the BGT, might suggest that there is brain impairment that requires further investigation (e.g., WAIS Performance IQ significantly lower than Verbal IQ). At a midpoint on this continuum, a clinician might include a *neuropsychological screening battery* that is more focused on identifying brain impairment but is, of necessity, less thorough and time-consuming than a full neuropsychological battery of tests. Here, the general screening battery might be supplemented with other brief neuropsychological measures, such as the Wechsler Memory Scale, Benton Visual Retention Test, or the Rey-Osterrieth Complex Figure. The most extensive evaluation would be a *comprehensive clinical neuropsychological evaluation* by a highly trained specialist working in a multidisciplinary setting. The latter provides a thorough assessment of cognitive strengths and weaknesses. It also allows formulation of an extensive intervention plan involving professionals from various disciplines.

This great sophistication of neuropsychological assessment, however, does not mean that the BGT no longer serves a function. This test is still often included in assessment batteries at all points along the just-described continuum. A survey completed by 614 members of two national associations of neuropsychologists (Seretny, Dean, Gray, & Hartlage, 1986) revealed that up to 44% utilize the BGT, which was ranked fourth in usage. Butler, Retzlaff, and Vanderploeg (1991) found large variability in the choices of tests used by a sample of 50 neuropsychologists. The BGT was endorsed by 27% of this group. However, further analysis of the results (Retzlaff, Butler, & Vanderploeg, 1992) showed that BGT usage among neuropsychologists varied from 14% to 50% depending upon their theoretical orientation.

The BGT continues to be useful for a variety of reasons that will be described in later sections. For example, most neuropsychologists recommend that both a screening battery and a full-fledged neuropsychological evaluation include at least one measure from each of the major cognitive *domains*. Perceptual-motor ability is always included as one of the cognitive functions (Lacks, in press) and many psychologists use the BGT as their preferred choice to measure this skill (e.g., D'Amato, Rothlisberg, & Rhodes, 1997). Other frequently mentioned cognitive domains are attention, memory and learning, verbal and motor performance, and executive functions (e.g., Groth-Marnat, 1997, in press). More detailed discussion of the BGT as a neuropsychological test is presented in Chapter 2.

HISTORY OF THE BGT

The BGT was developed by Lauretta Bender (1938) as a test to study the relationship of perception to various types of psychopathology. She adapted its nine figures from a larger number of designs used by Wertheimer (1923) in his studies of principles of visual perception. During these early years, the BGT stimulus cards were unavailable in a standardized form and were distributed only informally. In 1946, Bender did, for the first time, make the test stimuli and instructions for their use commercially available. At the same time, she published a summary of responses for each year of age from 4 through 11 years and for adults. Lauretta Bender was a child psychiatrist; her interest in this test was primarily maturational or developmental. As such, her work is covered in more detail in Chapter 11 on use of the BGT with children.

From 1938 until 1946, when the figures were first published for general use, most BGT literature was descriptive, mainly emphasizing a developmental approach. Little or no attention was given to issues of reliability or to the empirical substantiation of BGT interpretations. Starting in the mid-1940s, Hutt introduced a psychodynamic or projective orientation, emphasizing the BGT as a nonverbal, projective personality test (Hutt & Briskin, 1960). In 1945, he had printed his own set of stimulus cards, which he believed were more faithful to Wertheimer's (1923) original gestalt principles. Today, psychologists can use either the figures employed by Bender or those slightly modified by Hutt.

During the period from 1946 to 1960, the BGT went from a relatively obscure measure to the rank of third most popular test, employed by the majority of experienced clinicians (Tolor & Brannigan, 1980). As more psychologists included it in their skills, they began to recognize a need for some kind of reliable, objective scoring system. With the publication of the earliest scoring systems (e.g., Pascal & Suttell, 1951), the psychometric approach to the BGT was initiated, resulting in several hundred publications. In contrast to the earlier work, most were empirical studies on such topics as scoring systems, reliability, validity, norms, and perceptual maturation. The research also focused attention on the BGT as a neuropsychological test for the differential diagnosis of brain impairment in psychiatric patients.

DETERMINANTS OF BGT PERFORMANCE

Since the invention of this test, psychologists have questioned which psychological abilities or functions account for competent performance on the BGT. It has been assumed that performance on this test is a function of either perceptual ability, motor ability, or the integration of perceptual and motor functions.

Much of the evidence regarding the determinants of test performance comes from early research on maturation in children. In two studies done by Allen (1968, 1969) with mildly retarded adolescents, the quality of test performance was found to be directly related to the level of visual-perceptual maturation. The latter was measured by the Frostig Developmental Test of Visual Perception. For a group of children with neuropsychiatric diagnoses, BGT scores were significantly correlated with Frostig subtests of eye-motor coordination and spatial relations but not with subtests measuring figure-ground, form constancy, or position in space (Culbertson & Gunn, 1966).

Koppitz (1975) sees BGT performance as the culmination of a complex series of processes (see Figure 1.1). The first of these is vision—the design stimulus impinges on the retina and is transmitted to the brain. Assuming normal vision, the person sees the design. However, seeing is not perceiving. First there must be a process of visual association involving recognition and recall of the stimulus. Then, there is the process of visual perception or interpretation of the design. The person must be able to label the design in some way (e.g., circle and tilted diamond of about equal size touching each other).

Before the design can be copied, other processes must come into play. The test taker must have certain graphomotor abilities, that is, motor coordination. And finally, he or she must be able to integrate the perceptual with the motor to achieve accurate reproduction of the stimulus design.

Koppitz (1975) believes that this last skill, the integrative function, is not present, even among normal children, until the age of 8 or 9. For her, the majority of school-age children with deviant reproductions do not have visual perception or motor coordination problems. Instead, they have difficulty with this higher-order integrative function.

Another useful paradigm for understanding this complex visual-motor functioning was developed by Williams (1983) and is also covered in detail by Cummings and Laquerre (1990). Stimulus reception and processing are followed by sensory integration where the new material is compared with information previously stored in long-term memory. For example, the child may perceive that the stimulus is a geometric design, then interpret it, and recognize it as a figure he or she is familiar with and may even know the name of. For the next step, the child makes a decision to act and then implements the motor behavior, that is, drawing the design. As the child draws, the motor movement triggers information feedback, multiple signals that can influence the motor activity. Signals can come from such sources as movement, position in space, touch or pressure, and verbal feedback.

Other studies have used a Multiple-Choice Bender Test or a Tracing Bender Test to study the contributions of visual and motor functions to BGT performance. Wedell and Horne (1969) found that good test results were correlated

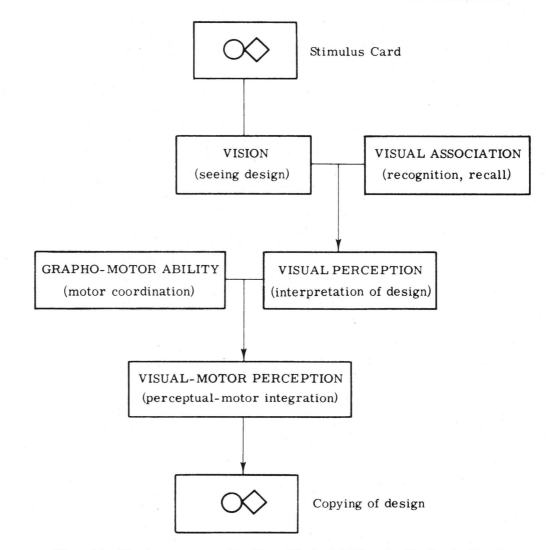

Figure 1.1 Visual-motor perception. (From Elizabeth M. Koppitz, *The Bender Gestalt Test for young children, Volume II: Research and application 1963–1973.* Copyright © 1975 by Allyn and Bacon. Reprinted by permission.)

with good visual perception and motor coordination. However, poor results did not have a consistent relationship with impairment of either of these components. These two alternative skills are not well correlated with each other but each is correlated with the standard copying method. Visual perception and motor coordination appear to be independent functions but both are key ingredients of visual-motor perception.

Stoer, Corotto, and Curnutt (1965) studied the question of perceptual versus motor skills through a BGT matching test consisting of six deviant reproductions taken from illustrations of the Pascal-Suttell scoring system, each participant's own drawing, and the original stimulus. All were hand drawn for each of the nine designs.

Participants for this study were four groups of 14 each: psychiatric technicians serving as nonpatient controls, inpatients with neurological pathology, patients hospitalized for the first time with acute schizophrenia, and patients with prior hospitalizations for chronic schizophrenia. Groups were matched for gender, age, and intelligence.

Participants were presented first with the BGT stimulus card. Then they were shown the eight choices of the same design all at once, lined up in a random order. Next they were asked to pick the card most like the stimulus card, and then that card was removed. Next they were asked to select the one least like the original. The remaining six choices were then ordered by participants from most to least like the original design. Two scores were calculated for total accuracy of matching: one based on three judges' rankings of similarity and one based on Pascal-Suttell scores. These scores were regarded as a measure of the perceptual component of the test. The individuals' own reproductions of the designs, as scored by Pascal-Suttell, were regarded as a measure of the reproduction component of the test.

In terms of reproduction of the designs, nonpatient and pathological groups differed significantly. Although patients with diagnosed brain pathology had more deviant scores than patients with schizophrenia, these differences did not achieve significance. No significant differences were found among the four groups on the matching or perceptual aspect of the task whether scored by the ranking or by the Pascal-Suttell method.

The authors conclude that there are no differences in visual discrimination between nonpatient and disturbed individuals. All four groups generally had very similar scores on this measure. Deviant reproductions are due to factors other than visual perception, such as motor or integrative skills. The authors point out that a situation may exist where the person perceives the design correctly but can see that the reproduction is incorrect. In other words, "sensory feedback may lead to an experience of incongruence between perception and reproduction. This phenomenon, clinically referred to as perplexity or impotence, is observed frequently in the performance of patients with neurological disorders" (p. 478).

Arbit and Zager (1978) took a factor-analytic approach to analyzing the functional determinants of the BGT. Their data consisted of scores on a battery of neuropsychological tests, including the WAIS, Wechsler Memory Scale, Graham-Kendall Memory for Designs, and the BGT. The data were from 144 neurological patients from a university hospital. Results were analyzed through factor analysis (linear) and hierarchical cluster analysis (nonlinear).

For the principal component factor analysis, three factors emerged: memory, perceptual performance, and verbal intellectual ability. The hierarchical cluster analysis revealed three clusters: learning, verbal and perceptual intelligence, and memory. For both these analyses, the BGT loaded most heavily on the factor of memory ability (.879 and .838, respectively) even though the Memory for Designs Test loaded most heavily on perceptual-motor ability.

Most research on the functions behind BGT reproduction have examined perception, coordination, or the integration of both. Another group of skills that influence BGT performance is the *executive functions.* Lezak (1995) conceptualizes the executive functions as having four components: volition or intentional behavior, planning, purposive action, and effective performance. Specific skills include reasoning, cognitive flexibility, goal setting, decision making, and many others. There are few formal measures of these functions.

Instead, psychologists are often reduced to using their own clinical observations and judgment about how patients handle standard neuropsychological tests. Many neuropsychological tests leave little opportunity for patient discretionary behavior that would demonstrate these executive functions. Adequate performance on the BGT, however, requires the use of many of these skills: planning behaviors like efficient use of space, logical sequential placement of drawings, deciding whether to count elements of the designs before drawing them, and persistence even in the face of difficulty. In Chapter 13, Figures 13.1, 13.9, and 13.15 (Cases A, H, and N) illustrate a haphazard approach to planning on the BGT. Figures 10.1 and 13.18 (Case Q) show good organization. Figure 13.19 (Case R) is generally well ordered but the patient left insufficient room for design 6 and showed poor judgment by deciding to put it into too small a space. Figure 13.17 (Case P) is an example of some planning problems even when few drawing errors were made.

Yulis (1970) examined the effect on BGT performance of what may be another executive function, level of drive. Level of drive in this study varied along four points of a continuum. The lowest drive level was produced by repeating the standard administration of the BGT. The second drive level consisted of the standard BGT administration followed by Canter's (1966) Background Interference Procedure (BIP), where a person is asked to draw the BGT figures on a page with a background of wavy lines. To obtain the third level of drive, Yulis added a second BIP administration, but this time under threat of shock. The final drive level added the actual application of a single electric shock prior to another BIP administration. Participants were 30 patients diagnosed with brain damage and 60 nonpatients receiving vocational evaluation. Groups were matched for age, education, and IQ. They were divided evenly among the drive conditions; however, patients with brain damage were not assigned to the actual shock group.

For nonpatients, there was a U-shaped relationship between drive and BGT performance. Lower levels of increased drive served to improve performance but higher levels of drive resulted in decrements in performance (mean adjusted D scores were 20.00, 14.13, 26.80, and 28.80 for the four drive-level conditions; higher scores indicate worse performance). For the patients with brain damage, a linear function was obtained between drive and performance. All increases in drive level resulted in greater decrements in BGT reproduction (mean adjusted D scores for three drive levels were 21.40, 36.00, and 43.10). At a low level of drive or arousal, patient and nonpatient participants (used as their own controls) showed no differences in their D scores (between first and second standard BGT administration). Only when drive level was increased through the use of the BIP or threat of shock did significant differences appear between the two groups. These results do not shed much light on standard BGT performance but do aid in an understanding of the BIP effect (for more detailed description of the BIP, see Chapter 4).

From this research a number of psychological functions are implicated as contributing to the reproduction of the BGT designs: spatial relations, visual-perceptual maturation, memory, eye-motor coordination, planning, and level of drive. In one study, visual perception was ruled out as an explanation of deviant reproduction. More research is needed before the complex determinants of BGT performance can be fully known. More studies such as the one by Yulis that tie performance to new concepts are desirable.

DIFFERENTIAL DIAGNOSIS

The purpose of this section is to acquaint the practicing clinician with the current status of the Bender Gestalt as a neuropsychological test for adults, especially in terms of diagnostic accuracy. Using this test for personality assessment is controversial and will not be covered in this book. For the clinician who wishes to use the BGT as a projective test for the description of personality dynamics, Hutt's work is the definitive source (Hutt & Briskin, 1960; Hutt, 1985). The primary focus of this book is on use of the BGT with adults, not with children. However, because this measure is widely employed with children, Chapter 11 does explore this aspect of its use. Extensive additional coverage about the BGT with children can be found in Koppitz (1963, 1975) and Tolor and Brannigan (1980).

The BGT is used most frequently by clinicians to aid in the differential diagnosis of psychiatric patients, especially of the cognitively impaired from the psychotically disturbed. The fact that many psychiatric inpatients, regardless of diagnosis, do more poorly on psychological tests than nonpatients is well documented and well known. Anxiety, depression, and psychosis can all impair psychological functioning in areas such as the ability to pay attention and concentrate. To be clinically useful as a screening test for brain dysfunction, a test must demonstrate its ability to discriminate reliably between patients with organic brain pathology and those who have serious emotional disorders but no cerebral impairment. For this reason, only those BGT studies that make comparisons among neuropsychiatric groups are included in this book, not those comparing the cognitively impaired with nonpatients.

In studies before 1960, there were many reports of the ability of the BGT to discriminate between patients with organic brain dysfunction and nonpatients as well as between those with diagnoses of brain pathology and other diagnoses, in particular schizophrenia. However, even though significant group differences were reported, there was so much overlap of the distributions of scores between groups that successful individual patient identification was not possible.

Research after 1960 addresses the clinical *utility* of the test, meaning its ability to predict the diagnosis of individuals with accuracy. In this chapter, only those studies in which diagnostic accuracy could be discerned are reported. Where it was not stated by the researchers, it has been calculated using procedures advocated by Meehl and Rosen (1955).* For discussion of other BGT validity studies not meeting this criterion, the reader may consult Hutt (1985) or Tolor and Brannigan (1980).

Methodological Shortcomings of BGT Research

The absence of information about the clinical utility of this test is only one of the methodological shortcomings of BGT research. Other problems have been discussed by Garb and Schramke (1996), Heaton, Baade, and Johnson (1978), Parsons and Prigatano (1978), and Wedding and Faust (1989). In a review of 94 studies on various neuropsychological tests, Heaton et al. (1978) found that 63% of the studies did not indicate whether their data were representative of

---

* In the example of organic brain dysfunction, Meehl and Rosen calculate diagnostic accuracy for brain impairment by dividing the number of individuals that the test *correctly* identified as having brain damage by the total number of individuals that the test labeled as having brain damage. Accuracy for the absence of brain damage is the number *correctly* called nonimpaired by the total number called nonimpaired. Total accuracy is the total number of individuals correctly identified divided by total *N*.

any particular population. For example, were cases taken from a general psychiatric hospital population or were they representative of patients referred for psychological testing? Were they taken retrospectively from clinical files where results of the measure under study or of other tests may have already influenced the assigned diagnosis? When cases are taken from files, there is also no assurance of uniform administration of the test under investigation.

A related matter is the absence of information about diagnostic base rates for the patient population. For proper assessment of the predictive power of a psychological test, a comparison must be made with the accuracy one could achieve by prediction from the base rate alone (for further discussion of this issue see Chapter 7 and Meehl & Rosen, 1955). Also, the diagnostic accuracy of a test may vary as a function of the base rates of certain diagnoses groups (e.g., brain damage or psychosis) in the population in question. Heaton et al. (1978) estimate at least a 30% base rate for diagnosed brain pathology in most populations of psychiatric inpatients referred for psychological assessment. It is difficult in many studies to know how closely the patients studied approximate typical base rates of the populations from which they were drawn.

Another difficulty has to do with the adequacy of the criteria used to assign diagnoses to participants. In 85% of the studies they reviewed, Heaton et al. (1978) found no mention of whether neurological exams or lab tests had been used to rule in or rule out brain dysfunction. The specific criteria for diagnosis and the professional expertise of the diagnosticians, and whether the diagnosis was made at discharge or some earlier point, were often not reported.

In terms of scoring the tests, some studies use *standard* (i.e., cross-validated) cutoff scores for the test diagnosis of brain impairment, and others use cutoff scores that are *optimal* (i.e., achieve the best possible diagnostic discrimination) for the specific study. Results using optimal cutoff scores must be interpreted much more conservatively. Heaton et al. (1978) found that optimal cutoffs on the average provided a median hit rate that was 14 percentage points above that achieved in studies using standard cutoff scores.

Other frequently uncontrolled research factors are chronicity of disorder, medication dosage and length of usage, and age and education of participants. The results of the following empirical investigations should be weighed against these methodological deficiencies. Remember also that not all the shortcomings serve to influence the results in the same direction; some will facilitate test validity, some will reduce discriminative ability, and some have an unknown influence. Further discussion of methodological issues for research on neuropsychological tests will be found in Chapter 7.

Diagnostic Utility of the BGT

The following studies (presented in chronological order) are all attempts within psychiatric settings to determine the diagnostic accuracy of the BGT for the differentiation of patients with organic brain disorders from those with other psychiatric diagnoses. Some of this research is presented in more detail in Chapter 7. Each study has one or more shortcomings, although some were more carefully done than others.

The first study demonstrates the pitfalls of using optimal cutoff scores and the need for cross validation of results. In 1964, Hain developed a system for scoring BGT protocols for brain dysfunction. He tested all admissions during 3 months to a university neurology ward ($N = 20$) as well as 38 selected patients with mild diagnoses from the psychiatric ward. Most classifications were made at discharge and were the result of complete and careful psychiatric, neurological, and medical studies. The neurological patients were significantly older than the psychiatric patients, although they were similar on IQ. Using an optimal cutoff score, he found an accuracy rate of 86%. Upon cross-validation of this cutoff score, however, this figure dropped to 62%.

In 1966, Canter compared the BGT performance shortly after entry of 86 consecutive admissions to a university psychiatric hospital: 30 with brain impairment, 22 with psychosis, and 34 with neither brain impairment nor psychosis. Whereas the three groups were similar in years of education, the brain-injury group was older than the other two patient groups. The latter difficulty is a common one in this type of research. It is also a pertinent issue because BGT performance declines with increasing age. Using standard cutoff scores for the Pascal-Suttell system, the BGT showed an overall diagnostic accuracy of 70%.

Kramer and Fenwick (1966), using a standard cutoff for the Hain scoring system, found a BGT overall diagnostic accuracy of 76%. They compared 42 patients with cognitive disorders to 24 mixed psychiatric inpatients (using final hospital diagnoses based on psychiatric and neurological exams). Those with cognitive deficits were considerably older than the patients without brain injury, although they were more closely matched on IQ. A BGT expert using clinical judgment achieved a rate of 80%.

Johnson, Hellkamp, and Lottman (1971) tested 240 inpatients from a large state mental hospital. Of these, 120 were diagnosed with chronic brain disorder based on the presence of one or more of six specific criteria (e.g., history of epilepsy). The remaining half of the sample consisted of patients with non-brain-damage disorders. Patients were matched for IQ. Using the Hutt-Briskin system (with standard cutoffs), these researchers found overall hit rates to be 64%. This study is discussed further in Chapter 7. One difficulty is the inclusion of a large number of epileptics in the brain-impairment group; there is some evidence that the BGT is not reliably sensitive to the presence of epilepsy.

Butler, Coursey, and Gatz (1976) did a study comparing 72 African American and white inpatients classified as having either brain damage or no brain damage and individually matched by ethnic group, age, education, and IQ. They were chosen from the VA hospital folders of 250 male patients with brain damage and 500 psychiatric patients. Patients with brain damage had to have a neurological report that specified a diagnosis based on at least one neurological procedure. It is difficult to know the effect of choosing this small number of participants from the much larger pool. The more accepted procedure is to test consecutive admissions. Of the 36 patients with brain damage, 14 or 39% had epilepsy. The BGT protocols were scored by a skilled psychometrician using both the Pascal-Suttell and the Hain methods; however, neither system could reliably differentiate between the patients with and without brain damage. For both scoring systems, the patients with brain damage received much lower error scores than had been reported for such a group in previous studies, perhaps because of the high number of cases with epilepsy. A neuropsychologist who is an expert with the BGT achieved an overall accuracy level of 69% using clinical judgment.

Lacks and Newport (1980) selected 50 patients from a larger sample of 200 consecutive admissions to the acute psychiatric treatment unit of an urban community mental health center. Diagnoses were made by senior supervising psychiatrists after several weeks of observation, interviews, and physical and neurological exams and tests. The subsample was chosen to match hospital diagnostic base rates (34% brain damage, 30% psychosis, 16% personality disorder, 20% chronic alcoholism), and to match groups on ethnicity, gender, age, education, and IQ. Patients were tested within 3 days of admission to minimize effects of hospitalization and medication. Using the Lacks adaptation of the Hutt-Briskin system with standard cutoffs (which matched optimal cutoff scores) and three scorers of varying levels of experience, they found the BGT hit rate to range from 82% to 86% with a mean of 84%. Using other scoring systems generally lowered the diagnostic accuracy. See Chapter 7 for more detailed discussion of these results.

In 1984 in South Africa, McCann and Plunkett studied 30 patients with Korsakoff's syndrome, 30 patients with paranoid schizophrenia, and 30 nonpatient controls. The BGT was administered in four ways: (a) a tachistoscopic method, where designs were drawn after a 10-second exposure; (b) the standard administration; (c) use of the nonpreferred hand to draw the designs; and (d) the "perfect" method, where participants were asked to compare their drawings from the standard method with the stimulus cards. They were asked to identify any errors of reproduction and to redraw the figures, eliminating any errors. Diagnoses were made by resident psychiatrists. BGTs were scored by clinical psychologists trained in the Pascal-Suttell system.

Although an attempt was made to match participants on relevant demographic variables, the patients with brain impairment were older than the other two groups, and the nonpatients had a higher level of intelligence than the patient groups. Optimal hit rates were used to compare the three groups over four types of test administration. The cutoff was maximized for each different comparison, an unacceptable practice. On the standard administration, as would be expected, the highest diagnostic accuracy was achieved in comparing patients with brain damage to nonpatients (hits = 87% for both groups). Diagnostic accuracy for the more relevant and much more difficult comparison of individuals with brain damage versus psychosis showed much lower hit rates (77% versus 63%). Results were similar for these two groups using the tachistoscopic and the nonpreferred hand methods. However, the perfect method showed considerable increase of the hit rate for diagnosing brain damage but a large reduction in the rate for psychosis (87% versus 53%). Unfortunately, this work was not cross-validated; success using optimal cutoffs is often reduced with further study.

The researchers posed several theories to account for the improved accuracy of the perfect method: increased task complexity, task-related stress, or "cerebral excitation-inhibition balance" requirements. Unfortunately, no other researchers have continued this line of investigation.

Another study used the BGT to diagnose 112 male felons (59% African American) incarcerated in a state forensic facility (Friedt & Gouvier, 1989). These cases were selected through chart review and independently classified into three diagnostic groups: personality disorder or no psychiatric diagnosis ($N = 38$), schizophrenia ($N = 34$), or brain damage ($N = 40$). The latter group consisted of cases with various diagnoses (including epilepsy) who were significantly older and less educated than the other two groups. The BGTs were scored with the Lacks adaptation of the Hutt-Briskin method. Using the standard cutoff score of 5 errors, highest hit rates were achieved in identifying those without brain damage (85%), not surprising because some of this group did not even have psychiatric diagnoses. The hit rate for brain damage was 55% and the overall rate was 74%. Using a cutoff score of 4 errors increased correct identification of patients with brain damage to 63% but lowered it for cases without brain damage to 76%; overall hits were 71%. No cross-validation was provided on the use of an optimal cutoff. Problems with the study include the use of chart review to select cases; the inclusion of epileptics; and the participants being much different on many variables, including their prisoner status, than the typical neuropsychiatric sample. Additional research will have to be done to ascertain whether the BGT can be used for accurate assessment of a forensic population. Further analysis of this study can be found in Chapter 7.

Lownsdale, Rogers, and McCall (1989) compared the BGT scores of three groups of 15 patients each, diagnosed with schizophrenia, depression, and brain damage, respectively. These cases were selected from the records of 1500 discharged patients from a midwestern private psychiatric hospital. Records were chosen only if the psychologist and the psychiatrist had agreed about the patient's discharge diagnosis, forming an atypical group. Unfortunately, these cases included psychological tests as part of the diagnostic workup. Ten of the 15 patients with brain damage had at least one medical test confirming brain disease. This group also was much older and had much lower IQs than the other two groups. The BGTs were scored with the Lacks method. Diagnostic hits were 77% for presence of brain damage and 84% for absence of brain damage. These rates were slightly lower than, though not significantly different from, those using Hutt's Configurational Analysis method.

Another study (Marsico & Wagner, 1990) compared the Lacks and the Pascal-Suttell methods of scoring the BGT on a sample of 104 outpatients, half of whom were diagnosed with brain damage. Patients were selected from the files of outpatients referred for psychological evaluation. Diagnoses of brain damage were based on such medical confirmation as neurosurgical reports, neurological tests, or a history of substantial head trauma. Patients without brain damage had diagnoses of neurosis, personality disorder, or psychosis. The researchers acknowledged some possible contamination of their sample due to selecting patients who had previous psychological testing that contributed to the final diagnosis. In order to conform to the needs of the Pascal-Suttell system, only patients between the ages of 15 and 50 years with at least 9 years of education were included. The two patient groups were matched on age, education, gender, and ethnicity. The sample was relatively young (overall mean age of 25 years).

Using this 50/50 brain damage/no brain damage split with optimum cutoff scores led to the following hit rates. For the Lacks method, hit rates were 69% for brain damage, 67% for absence of brain damage, and 65% overall. For the Pascal-Suttell method, hit were 60% rates for brain damage, 89% for absence of brain damage, and 74% overall. The analyses were redone based on a 31/49 split that matched their agency's base rates (by removing the last 21 patients with brain damage and the last 3 without brain damage). With this new configuration, and using the standard cutoff scores, the Lacks procedures resulted in mean errors of 5.39 ($SD = 2.11$) for the group with brain damage and 2.82 ($SD = 1.45$) for the nonimpaired group. Hit rates were 65% for brain damage, 88% for absence of brain damage, and 79% overall. The mean errors for the Pascal-Suttell method were 116.71 ($SD = 14.67$) for the group with brain damage and 71.16 ($SD = 20.19$) for the nonimpaired group. Hit rates for brain damage were 58%, for absence of brain damage were 96%, and overall were 81%. Correlation between the two systems was .83.

The researchers concluded that overall the two systems were comparable but the Lacks method was easier to learn and use, less time-consuming, and applicable to a wider range of individuals. With both systems, a higher percentage of those with "true" brain damage were missed. Methodological problems in this study include initial use of nonstandard cutoff scores and use of file cases. The study does vividly demonstrate the differences between results achieved with standard versus optimal cutoffs and using artificial versus actual base rates.

For these four studies that used the Lacks scoring method with psychiatric patients, mean overall accuracy was 79% (median = 81%). Accuracy for identifying brain damage averaged 69%; for absence of brain damage, it was 80%. For three studies done by Lacks (described following and in Chapter 7), the respective accuracies were: overall, 84% (median = 82%); for brain damage, 77%; for absence of brain damage, 87%. These more recent results compare favorably with those found by Heaton et al. (1978). In their review of eight BGT studies that used various scoring methods, the median overall hit rate for eight classification attempts was 76%.

The BGT versus Other Single Neuropsychological Tests

Table 1.1 presents a summary (from Heaton et al., 1978) of hit rates for the five (at that time) most frequently studied single neuropsychological tests with psychiatric patients (omitting patients with process schizophrenia). The BGT alone or with the BIP modification resulted in the highest accuracy of classification. However, these tests were all used in separate studies, not compared directly against each other.

There have been a few attempts to show more directly the relative diagnostic accuracy of the BGT in comparison with other neuropsychological tests by using more than one test with the same group of patients. For example, Brilliant and Gynther (1963) compared the predictive accuracy of the BGT to the Benton Visual Retention Test (BVRT) and the Graham-Kendall Memory for Designs Test (MFD). The sample was composed of 120 consecutive admissions to an urban mental health center and matched the annual diagnostic base rates for the hospital, including 30% with brain damage and 22% with schizophrenia. As is often the case, patient groups were comparable on IQ, but those with brain damage were older. Patients were tested within 3 days of admission to minimize drug effects. Final discharge diagnoses were made by a supervising psychiatrist using multiple sources of information that usually included EEG results. Using the standard cutoff score of 5 errors (which was also equal to the

Table 1.1 Hit Rates of Frequently Studied Screening Tests for Cerebral Dysfunction

Test	Classification attempts	Median % correct
Bender Gestalt	8	76
Bender Gestalt-BIP	11	84
Benton Visual Retention	4	73
Memory for Designs	9	68
Trail Making	4	71

Source: Heaton, R.K., Baade, L.E., and Johnson, K.L. (1978). "Neuropsychological test results associated with psychiatric disorders in adults." *Psychological Bulletin, 85,* 141–162. Copyright 1978 by American Psychological Association. Reprinted by permission of the author.

optimal cutoff score), they found that the BGT (with Hutt-Briskin scoring) had an overall diagnostic hit rate of 82%, compared to 81% for the BVRT and 78% for the MFD.

Another study compared the BGT with the Trail Making, MFD, and Spiral Aftereffect tests (Korman & Blumberg, 1963). Participants were 40 VA inpatients and outpatients (mostly males) with cerebral damage; they were matched in age, education, and gender with 24 patients of mixed psychiatric diagnoses and 16 nonpsychiatric medical patients. Brain dysfunction diagnoses were made by neurologists using an average of four neurological techniques. The overall diagnostic accuracy of the BGT (using the Pascal-Suttell method) was 74%, compared with 90% for uncorrected MFD, 83% for MFD corrected for age and education, 83% for Spiral Aftereffect, and 70% to 83% for various combinations of scores on the Trail Making Test. Results of all tests were based on optimal cutoff scores.

In a study of drug effects upon tests, Owen (1971) gave the BGT and the BVRT to 45 inpatients with mixed schizophrenic disorders (omitting 15 patients receiving acute drug therapy) from an urban community mental health center. The diagnosis was made by a supervising psychiatrist, and only patients to be treated with chlorpromazine were included. With the standard cutoff for the Hutt-Briskin method, the BGT correctly classified 73% as not having brain damage. The BVRT produced 64% and 53% accuracy for number correct and number of errors, respectively.

Single versus Multiple Neuropsychological Tests

Another issue is whether to give a single test or several measures for detection of brain damage. Many researchers (e.g., Bigler & Ehrfurth, 1981; Parsons & Prigatano, 1978) appear perplexed by the continued interest of clinical psychologists in single neuropsychological tests such as the BGT when much more extensive and sophisticated batteries of neuropsychological tests are available. These critics generally base their criticism on two main points. First, the use of a single test to detect the presence of brain dysfunction suggests that the examiner subscribes to a unitary concept of brain function that predicts that most forms of brain dysfunction will produce a general lowering of all aspects of functioning. If this were so, then a single test sensitive to brain dysfunction would be sufficient to detect any impairment. These psychologists criticize this unitary concept of *organicity* as naive, with little recognition of the complexity and heterogeneity of neuropathology, including such factors as its extent, progression, location, duration, and cause. They believe, instead, that specific damage will lead to specific deficits, requiring a wide range of different tests tapping a variety of functions to make an accurate diagnosis.

Albert (1981), however, indicated that some single tests are multifactorial measures; that is, adequate performance requires the normal functioning of many different parts of the brain and abilities (e.g., attention, psychomotor skill, visual-spatial accuracy, memory, and organization). Such a test, like the BGT, can be useful as a *marker* for dysfunction per se even though it does not indicate the precise source or degree of impairment.

Nemec (1978) found evidence that supports both these points of view. He studied the general and lateralized effects of background interference on verbal and perceptual-motor tasks with 30 control patients without brain damage, 30 patients with right hemiplegia (left hemisphere damage), and 30 patients with left hemiplegia (right hemisphere damage). These groups were given a word-naming task and the BGT under noninterference and background interference conditions. Nemec found that for the patients without brain damage, background interference did not cause significant lowering of performance on either the verbal task or the BGT. However, verbal interference on the verbal task significantly lowered the performance efficiency of both groups with brain damage, with the group with left hemisphere damage showing more impairment than those with right hemisphere damage. On the perceptual task, the reverse pattern was found. Again, perceptual interference significantly lowered the performance of both groups with brain damage, but more so this time for those with right hemisphere damage.

These findings show that individuals with brain damage are rendered more distractible in general than individuals without brain damage, supporting the general-effect viewpoint. However, Nemec's results also support a specific-effect viewpoint in that verbal and perceptual distractibility had a differentially greater effect on those patients with left and right hemisphere damage, respectively.

Research indicates that a single screening test probably has as much success in terms of general diagnostic accuracy as multiple combinations of such tests (Parsons & Prigatano, 1978). Spreen and Benton (1965), in a review of the literature, found that the average diagnostic accuracy for single neuropsychological tests, when comparing nonpatients and those with brain damage, was 71%. When several tests were used, this rate rose to 80%. Korman and Blumberg (1963) found only a 2% increase in hit rate when two or three tests were used in combination as compared to their most successful single test of cerebral dysfunction. Heaton et al. (1978) found a median hit rate of 75% for single tests in discriminating those with cortical impairment from those with other psychiatric disorders (omitting those with chronic schizophrenia).

Single tests and combinations of tests appear to give similar results. Smith (1975) found that the seven individual tests of the Halstead-Reitan Battery (HRB) each produced about the same hit rate as the composite index of all seven tests. In fact, for differential diagnosis, the very brief BGT has demonstrated greater diagnostic accuracy with psychiatric patients than the lengthy HRB (Lacks, Colbert, Harrow, & Levine, 1970). Of course, the HRB does provide much additional and detailed diagnostic information.

The second focus of criticism of the continued popularity of the BGT is that this single test does not allow for a thorough description of an individual's brain dysfunction, including the type of damage, location, severity, and specific functions that are impaired. This is an accurate portrayal of the BGT. However, for many clinical psychologists, the typical assessment request is for differential diagnosis in a neuropsychiatric facility where 30% of referrals ask questions about central nervous system involvement (Craig, 1979). In other words, the psychologist is asked to *screen* for brain dysfunction as a part of an evaluation for differential diagnosis. In such a setting, the typical brain dysfunction base rates are 30% (Heaton et al., 1978), and the base rate for schizophrenia is also high. In most instances, larger batteries of neuropsychological tests (e.g., Halstead-Reitan or Luria-Nebraska) were designed and have been used to differentiate patients with impaired brain functions from groups of primarily medical, nonpsychiatric patients, very often in neurology clinics. This diagnostic task is very different and more simple than that typically facing the clinical psychologist in an inpatient psychiatric setting. In the more typical settings, the elaborate test batteries have generally not shown high discriminative ability in comparisons between those with diagnosed brain pathology and those with schizophrenia (Klonoff, Fibiger, & Hutton, 1970; Watson, Thomas, Anderson, & Felling, 1968).

For example, Lacks et al. (1970) compared the usefulness of the BGT to that of five tests from the HRB. Participants were all white males (mainly VA inpatients), 19 with impaired brain functions, 27 with schizophrenia, and 18 general medical patients matched on age, education, and IQ. All patients with impaired brain functions had a diagnosis made by a neurologist. Using standard cutoff scores, the researchers found that a composite HRB score correctly diagnosed 84% of the brain-impaired patients (versus 74% for the BGT) and 62% of the nonimpaired patients (versus 91% for the BGT).

Some studies with the Luria-Nebraska and Halstead-Reitan Batteries have found higher diagnostic accuracies rivaling those previously accomplished with the BGT (e.g., Kane, Sweet, Golden, Parsons, & Moses, 1981). However, administration of an elaborate battery of neuropsychological tests in these settings does not seem realistic or cost efficient. It may be somewhat like trying to kill a fly with a cannon. Why give expensive 3- to 8-hour procedures if you have a 5-minute test that serves the same *screening* purpose?

In summary, there continues to be controversy over the appropriate use of the BGT; however, many psychologists find it to be a valuable tool for a number of purposes. It continues to enjoy wide usage. For the purpose of screening for the presence of brain damage in a differential diagnostic evaluation, there seems little reason to give more than one or two screening tests within a larger battery of psychological tests including the WAIS. Single reliable and valid tests provide almost the same level of diagnostic accuracy as combinations of tests. The results with the BGT compare favorably to those found in a major review of 94 studies (1960 to 1975; Heaton et al., 1978) of neuropsychological test results with psychiatric patients (including some of those just reviewed in this book).

Heaton et al. (1978) concluded that clinicians can use these tests with confidence for the task of assessment of brain dysfunction except where patients with chronic or process schizophrenia are concerned. They found that psychiatric groups other than those with chronic or process schizophrenia showed greater skill on neuropsychological tests than patients with brain damage. Diagnostic accuracy decreased steadily, however, with increased severity of pathology of the group with which those with cognitive disorders were being compared (see Table 1.2). Omitting patients with chronic or process schizophrenia, the overall median hit rate for all tests was 75%, a figure comparable to that found in a review of 36 studies contrasting neuropsychological test performance of the cognitively impaired with nonpatient controls, a much simpler comparison (Spreen & Benton, 1965). This figure is also comparable to hit rates generally found for EEG and neuroradiologic techniques that entail more risk and cost (Malec, 1978).

It may be that the difficulty of differentiating between brain damage and chronic schizophrenia is due in part to the presence of neuropathology in some patients with psychosis, perhaps from some biological etiology for their disorder (Goldman, Axelrod, & Taylor, 1996). Chapter 2 discusses in more detail the important issue of differentiating between schizophrenia and the traditionally conceptualized brain damage.

Table 1.2   Median Diagnostic Accuracy for Neuropsychological Test by Diagnosis of Comparison Group

Diagnosis of comparison group	Median diagnostic accuracy
Nonpsychotic disorders	82%
Mixed psychiatric disorders	77%
Affective disorders	77%
Mixed psychotic disorders	70%
Acute or reactive schizophrenia	77%
Mixed schizophrenic disorders	69%
Chronic or process schizophrenia	54%

Source: Lacks, P. (1979). "The use of the Bender Gestalt Test in clinical neuropsychology." *Clinical Neuropsychology, 1,* 29–34, Table 1, p. 32. Reprinted by permission of *Clinical Neuropsychology.*

This book is written for those psychologists who wish to use the BGT as a visuoconstructional test either for screening for brain dysfunction or to assess a particular cognitive domain. Regardless of the purpose for using the BGT, this book provides the information necessary to use the test well: administration, scoring, validity and reliability, and interpretation.

CHAPTER 2

Neuropsychological Screening

The topic of neuropsychological screening is a complex one, much of it beyond the scope of this book. Many issues have been raised about the practices of neuropsychology, such as which methods are appropriate in what settings. In this book, however, our primary concern is to identify the role of the Bender Gestalt Test (BGT) in this type of assessment. Even though the BGT is one of the most used instruments, some psychologists have expressed a number of concerns about its use and misuse as a neuropsychological test. For example, many claim that the BGT is unable to perform one of the most frequently requested diagnostic tasks, that is, to discriminate between brain damage and schizophrenia.

Before turning to these important topics, however, let us begin with a rudimentary review of brain functions and neuropathology simply to provide a context for the material on neuropsychological assessment. It is difficult to discuss neuropsychology outside of this context. For those who would like more comprehensive information about this topic, there are many excellent resources (e.g., Joseph, 1996; Kolb & Whishaw, 1990; Lezak, 1995).

ORGANIZATION OF THE CENTRAL NERVOUS SYSTEM

The focus of study for neuropsychology is the extremely complex and only partially understood central nervous system and its relationship to human behavior. Through various sources of direct and indirect evidence, facts and theories have evolved that guide the practices of the neuropsychologist. For example, we know that the brain is organized in many different ways. One gross, anatomical differentiation is the three brain regions of hindbrain, midbrain, and forebrain.

The *hindbrain* is the earliest-developed and lowest part of the brain, regulating the more primitive and simple life functions, such as breathing and heart rate. The *midbrain* contains the center for integration of the major sensory and motor activities. The most complex and elaborate region is the *forebrain,* which accounts for the most developed functions, such as reasoning, concept formation, and problem solving. The largest part of the forebrain is the *cerebrum.* Its exterior layer is called the *cerebral cortex* and it is responsible for the highest level of brain functions: vision, hearing, motor activity, and cognition. In general, disorders of the forebrain and midbrain are most often diagnosed and treated by neurologists. The tools of the neuropsychologist were specifically developed to evaluate functions of the forebrain (Gregory, 1996).

Another often-employed partition of the brain is into its two *hemispheres*. The left hemisphere, for most people, is the region where language is produced and comprehended; the right hemisphere is the source of nonverbal spatial and tactile activity as well as the understanding and expression of emotion.

Yet another useful division for understanding the working of the brain is that of the four major lobes of the cerebral cortex: occipital, temporal, parietal, and frontal. The primary function of the *occipital region* is visual perception and interpretation; the *temporal lobes* encompass auditory perception as well as long-term memory storage and modulation of certain biological drives. The *parietal lobes* process visual-spatial and kinesthetic information. *Frontal lobes* are responsible for what are called *executive functions*, those high-level activities such as planning, intentional behavior, judgment, and decision making.

The character of any cognitive or behavioral disruption will depend on which side of the brain is disabled and in which very specific location. Determining which side of the cortex is injured or malfunctioning is referred to as *lateralization*. Determining which lobe is responsible for the dysfunction is called *localization* (e.g., posterior right parietal). *Caudality* refers to whether the injury is toward the front (or *anterior*) part of the brain area or toward the rear (or *posterior*).

Of particular interest to the user of the BGT are the *parietal lobes*. A very simplified version of the overall function of the parietal lobes is the integration of cues from many senses (e.g., touch, hearing, and vision) to give us a sense of spatial relationships and the orientation of our bodies. Examples of the kind of cues used by the parietal lobes are movement of the eye, position of the hand, feedback from the lips and tongue, kinesthetic information, and much more (Joseph, 1996).

Damage to the parietal region can produce a wide variety of deficits, including disturbed body image, visual-spatial impairment, sensory deficits, loss of orientation, and difficulty tracking moving objects (Joseph, 1996). Constructional disorders, such as difficulty with drawing and assembling, are among the most common products of parietal damage. More specific types of constructional disability depend upon whether damage is primarily on the left or the right side of the brain. For example, with a drawing task, left-sided damage can cause difficulty with motor programming, resulting in impoverished drawings that lack detail but preserve the general shape. The person may be able to recognize the errors he or she has made. Also, the larger the left-side lesion, the more extensive the behavioral deficit (Benson & Barton, 1970; Lezak, 1995).

With right-sided parietal injury, construction deficits are likely to be more severe (Benson & Barton, 1970; Benton & Tranel, 1993), especially if the impairment is in the right posterior region (Black & Bernard, 1984). Right-sided parietal damage involves more of a perceptual problem; the person cannot integrate parts into a whole to maintain the gestalt of the object. As a result, drawings are likely to be grossly distorted even though the patient may be unaware of any drawing errors. Generally, the size of a right parietal lesion has little bearing on the degree of perceptual deficit (Black & Bernard, 1984; Lezak, 1995). The reader can consult Lezak for many more details about the relationship between brain lateralization and constructional ability.

NEUROPATHOLOGY   *Brain dysfunction* or *brain damage* refers to anatomical or physiological changes in the brain's structure or function as the result of injury, tumor, infection, disease, insufficient oxygen, metabolic or endocrine disturbance, exposure to alcohol, drugs, or toxic substances, and many other conditions. Besides the cause of the brain impairment, many other aspects are necessary for the full description of such a complex phenomenon as brain dysfunction. For example, how extensive is the damage? Brain impairment may be either *focal* (limited to a specific brain site, such as the right temporal lobe) or *diffuse* (affecting most or all of the brain). The latter condition is much more debilitating because it can affect almost every facet of behavior, including ability to concentrate and perform complex mental operations, alertness, mood, and energy (Fantie & Kolb, 1991). Traditionally, psychologists working in neurological settings concentrate more on focal damage but those in psychiatric settings are more interested in diffuse brain problems, probably because of the different types of cases seen in these two settings. Other aspects important to the diagnosis of brain damage concern whether the damage is continuing to increase (progressive) or has stabilized (static). Where is the problem located in the brain? Is it a recent occurrence or long-standing (acute versus chronic)? What specific abilities are impaired, and how do the present abilities compare to those before the impairment?

In her comprehensive text, Lezak (1995) describes the major disorders of the nervous system that are typically seen in hospitals and clinics. She cautions that the presence of one of these brain disorders does not preclude any others or, for that matter, one of the *functional* disorders, such as depression. In fact, some cognitive disorders seem to regularly precede or be a risk factor for others, such as head trauma with Alzheimer's disease.

NEUROPATHOLOGY ASSOCIATED WITH PERCEPTUAL-MOTOR DEFICITS

Because the BGT is thought in large part to measure perceptual-motor skill, let us look more closely at a number of neuropathological disorders that characteristically demonstrate deficits in perceptual-motor ability.

Alcohol Abuse

One of the most common psychiatric disorders in this country is chronic abuse of or dependence on alcohol. It is estimated that 50% of alcoholics have mild to moderate neuropsychological impairment that can affect their daily functioning, employment, and treatment compliance. This degree of impairment is found even though testing is typically done with the patient in a detoxified state (2 to 4 weeks after hospitalization) to avoid influence from the effects of withdrawal and from the medications administered during detoxification. Another 10% of alcoholics meet criteria for a severe cognitive disorder from the neurotoxic effects of persistent alcoholic intake. Alcoholics are also susceptible to a number of events and illnesses that further compromise brain function, such as head injuries, diabetes, liver malfunction, poor nutrition, and withdrawal seizures (Rourke & Loberg, 1996). Grant (1987) constructed a complex model of variables that may interact to produce the pattern of alcohol-associated cognitive deficits. He has also made a strong case for the gradual recovery of many of these abilities with long-term abstinence.

Rourke and Loberg (1996) reported that the typical profile of chronic detoxified alcoholics shows intact verbal skills but impairment in many other areas: "problem solving and abstract reasoning, learning and memory, visual-spatial analysis, complex perceptual-motor integration" (p. 430), simple motor skills, and executive functioning. For example, Tarbox, Connors, and McLaughlin (1986) compared neuropsychological performance of 297 binge and daily alcohol abusers. They found that binge drinkers had fewer cognitive deficits than daily drinkers on short-term memory, internal scanning, visual-spatial conceptualization, and visuomotor performance. Younger drinkers (<40 years) consistently performed better on neuropsychological tests, including the BGT, than those who were older (>40 years).

Dementia   Another disorder associated with significant cognitive deficits is *dementia*. Although Alzheimer's disease may account for as much as 50% of cases of dementia, there are at least 50 different causes, including cerebrovascular disease (Brown, Baird, Shatz, & Bornstein, 1996), Parkinson's disease (McPherson & Cummings, 1996), HIV infection/AIDS (Kelly, Grant, Heaton, Marcotte, & the HNRC Group, 1996), and even cancer (Davis et al., 1987).

Recent research on dementia caused by *Alzheimer's disease* suggests that the "hippocampus and entorhinal cortex are involved in the earliest stage of the disease and that frontal, temporal, and parietal association cortices become increasingly involved as the disease progresses" (Bondi, Salmon, & Kaszniak, 1996, p. 167). For Alzheimer's disease, striking memory problems are usually accompanied by significant other cognitive deficits, including impairment in language, executive functions, attention, and constructional and visuospatial skills.

In contrast, individuals with *Parkinson's disease* show only moderate memory deficits but frequent impairment on visuospatial and visuoconstructive tasks; executive functions are the earliest and most consistently disrupted skills (McPherson & Cummings, 1996). As for dementia from *Huntington's disease,* impairment of attention and memory skills, executive functions, and visuomotor ability, even with simple geometric designs, are apparent from the early stages of the disease (Brandt & Butters, 1996). In fact, the BGT was one of several tests used to identify potential victims of Huntington's disease before its usual onset in midlife (Lyle & Quast, 1976).

Repeated measures of these specific cognitive domains can aid in tracking the progression of mental decline during the course of dementia. In fact, Bondi et al. (1996) note that because memory deficits reach floor performance at an early stage of the dementia, measures of the decline of other abilities are better suited for determining severity of the disorder. Further discussion of the assessment of dementia can be found in Chapter 10, which covers the evaluation of older adults.

HIV Disease/AIDS   HIV disease affects the immune system, resulting in a variety of serious medical diseases. However, it is also a neurobehavioral disorder that can result in subtle cognitive impairment all the way up to full-blown HIV-associated dementia. Incidence of dementia is relatively rare (5% to 7% of symptomatic HIV-infected individuals). More common is the mild neurocognitive disorder that involves impairment in at least two cognitive domains, including complex perceptual-motor performance. Kelly et al. (1996) thoroughly review the connection between neuropsychological deficits and this disease. In a longitudinal neurobehavioral study of 500 HIV-infected males, each successive stage of the disease showed a higher rate of overall brain impairment: asymptomatic (31% with cognitive deficits), mild symptoms (44%), and severe immunodeficiency (56%). With disease progression, the brain impairment was also more severe, affecting more areas of ability. The areas of cognitive ability most often impaired were attention (61%) and learning of new material (57%). Psychomotor deficits were found in 32% of affected persons.

Hypoxemia Another area of interest to neuropsychologists is brain impairment associated with oxygen deprivation or hypoxemia. Sleep apnea, chronic obstructive pulmonary disease, living at a high altitude, and cerebral vascular accidents are all conditions that reduce the supply of oxygen to the brain. Rourke and Adams (1996) review the research on neuropsychological effects of acute and chronic hypoxemia. They describe a number of studies that document multiple deficits in cognitive abilities in hypoxemic individuals, including impairment of intellectual efficiency, attention and concentration, perceptual-motor organization and efficiency, and executive functioning. A number of these studies have used the BGT, including Krop, Block, and Cohen (1973) and Greenberg, Watson, and Deptula (1987). The latter researchers gave a battery of 14 neuropsychological tests to 14 patients with sleep apnea, 10 patients with disorders of excessive somnolence, and 14 healthy volunteers. Sleep-apnea patients performed worse than the other two groups on half of the tests, including the BGT. Results could not be attributed to either daytime sleepiness or aging. This topic of oxygen-deficiency disorders is explored in more detail in Chapter 10.

SCREENING FOR BRAIN IMPAIRMENT Since 1980, there has been an increasing demand for clinical neuropsychological services for the assessment and treatment of a wide variety of patients. This kind of evaluation can range across a continuum from briefer screening procedures through comprehensive neuropsychological assessment. Furthermore, assessment practices, diagnostic questions, and the base rates of these types of patients vary greatly across different clinical settings. Discrimination between brain damage and schizophrenia remains one of the psychologist's most difficult diagnostic challenges.

The Diagnostic Setting Diagnostic settings range from inpatient psychiatric hospitals (both private and government supported) to neurological, medical school, and outpatient psychiatric clinics. These settings vary widely on many factors, such as the available financial and personnel *resources,* the most *common diagnoses,* and the *base rates* of brain disorders and such psychiatric diagnoses as schizophrenia. The psychiatric setting (especially when government funded), in contrast to a neurological facility, tends to have limited funds and staffs of clinical psychologists rather than neuropsychologists. The psychiatric setting also has a high base rate of brain disorders, typically 30% or more of largely diffuse problems, such as alcohol abuse or dementia, that usually do not have clear signs of anatomical damage and often mimic the symptoms of depression or schizophrenia. Neurological settings have a low rate of schizophrenia and a higher number of such disorders as severe head injuries, strokes, and epilepsy, disorders that are generally not confused with schizophrenia. It is unlikely that the same approaches to neuropsychological assessment would be equally effective in these two very different types of diagnostic milieus.

Discrimination of Brain Damage from Schizophrenia It has become fashionable to dismiss as misguided any attempts to discriminate between individuals with brain damage and those with schizophrenia because, of course, schizophrenia *is* a brain disease. Although it is true that there are some shared symptoms between schizophrenia and the cognitive disorders, it is also true that schizophrenia has a unique, diverse, and often episodic pattern of symptoms, unlike other forms of brain damage. Its clinical picture and etiology are still unclear and are the subject of constant debate among scientists. The reader should consult Heinrichs (1993) for a thorough discussion of this topic, which will be reviewed only briefly here.

In terms of clinical picture, some patients with schizophrenia show such *positive* signs as delusions or hallucinations; for some, symptoms gradually appear but for others, onset is sudden. Over time, some show deterioration but others maintain their abilities. Some respond to medications, although the symptoms of others are resistant to or even made worse by such treatment. Some patients with schizophrenia show a family history or signs of neurological damage, but most do not. Attempts to delineate reliable subdivisions of schizophrenia have been largely unsuccessful. Furthermore, as of now, schizophrenia has not been reliably linked to any specific neuropathology of brain structure, physiology, or chemistry. The abnormalities that have been noted do not seem to produce the types of deficits that we see in other neurological cases (Heinrichs, 1993). In short, evidence for a neurological cause of schizophrenia has mostly been inconsistent, contradictory, and unreplicated.

There has been some criticism of the use of tests like the BGT to identify brain damage in a population that includes persons with schizophrenia, on the basis that those with schizophrenia and those with brain damage perform alike on these tests. A few studies do show that patients with chronic or process schizophrenia perform more like patients with cognitive disorders than do patients with acute or reactive schizophrenia (e.g., Horine & Fulkerson, 1973). Lilliston (1973) reported that schizophrenics who performed in the brain-impaired range on all of three neuropsychological tests had the most *process* scores on a prognostic rating scale. Those patients with schizophrenia who did not perform in the brain-damaged range on any of the three tests had the most *reactive* scores.

But patients with schizophrenia generally look different from those with brain damage on most tests, including the WAIS, MMPI, Rorschach, and the BGT. In a normative group of 349 carefully chosen, diagnosed, and evaluated psychiatric inpatients (discussed in detail in Chapter 7), comparisons of BGT performance show that the group with psychosis looks more like those with personality disorders, not like those with diagnosed brain damage. The two groups without brain damage made similar numbers and types of errors. As for diagnostic accuracy, the following percentages were found for correctly identified status (i.e., brain damage or not brain damage): 76% of personality disorders, 73% of psychoses, and 82% of brain disorders. These figures may, in reality, be underestimates of diagnostic accuracy because it is highly likely, given their lifestyle, that some of the patients with personality disorders or schizophrenia also had some brain damage from alcohol or substance abuse, accidents, poor nutrition, and other causes.

Heaton et al. (1979) found that although patients with schizophrenia showed some impairment on neuropsychological tests compared to nonpatients, their impairment was not nearly so severe as that of patients with acute or chronic brain disorders. These results were achieved, however, when the schizophrenics were recently hospitalized and drug effects were minimized. Also, those schizophrenics who were more clinically paranoid showed less impairment. Most reports of patients with psychosis who have serious deficits on neuropsychological tests concern patients with chronic schizophrenia who have had lengthy stays in institutions. In addition, they usually have had lengthy courses of treatment with large amounts of potent antipsychotic medications, perhaps leading to drug-induced cerebral pathology. More about the effects of psychotropic drugs and ECT upon BGT results can be found in Chapter 7.

Furthermore, there may be some subset of schizophrenia that includes brain damage. Some researchers suggest that there may be two syndromes of schizophrenia. One shows structural damage to the brain, *negative* signs, poor drug response, and progressive deterioration. Patients with this pattern may have an organic basis and may also be the ones who produce deficits on neuropsychological tests. The second group has fluctuating symptoms due to dysfunctional dopamine operation, *positive* signs, good response to drugs, and a lack of deterioration. They may perform adequately on these tests. As a rule, however, most patients with schizophrenia do not show brain anomalies (Goldstein, 1986).

Perhaps one reason that many patients with schizophrenia (73% in this normative sample) are often able to perform well on the BGT is that they are less likely to have impaired constructional ability (Goldman et al., 1996; Saykin et al., 1991). Goldman et al. (1996) indicate that the functional domains most pertinent to schizophrenia are attention, executive functions, and memory. Perhaps because the BGT is a relatively brief and nondemanding test, most schizophrenics can handle it. It may be that patients with brain damage have ability deficits whereas most with schizophrenia have deficits of attention, motivation, and comprehension. To emphasize the perceptual-motor aspects of the BGT, it is essential for the examiner to keep disruptions from other factors, like attention, memory, and psychotic ideation, to a minimum. Testing a patient with schizophrenia requires special skills. The examiner must be very patient, encouraging, and persistent; he or she must also give clear and concrete instructions with frequent reminders of the directions. One explanation for the patient with schizophrenia who does poorly on the BGT is a less than ideal administration of the test.

Other researchers speculate that brain injury leads to deficits on both simple and complex tasks but schizophrenia only produces deficits on complex tasks. Complex tests require sustained attention, abstract reasoning, and freedom from distraction. More patients with schizophrenia do poorly on longer and more complex tests, such as the Halstead-Reitan (HRB) and Luria-Nebraska batteries, than they do on the BGT (Strauss & Silverstein, 1986; Watson et al., 1968). Lacks et al. (1970) found that for a group of 27 schizophrenics and 18 general medical patients, the HRB Impairment Index correctly identified only 62% of the group as without brain damage, compared to a 91% correct diagnosis from the BGT scores. Yet another theory is that the schizophrenia deficit involves the left hemisphere but the BGT measures more strongly the function of the right hemisphere (Goldstein, 1986).

Identifying schizophrenia is one of the most important diagnostic tasks in the majority of inpatient psychiatric settings. Treatment for schizophrenia is complex and usually involves specific drugs that have dangerous side effects. When a clinical psychologist is asked to make this discrimination, it is not so important whether schizophrenia has a basis in brain dysfunction. What the clinical psychologist is being asked to do is separate these patients into two groups. One group contains those with conditions of traditionally defined brain damage, such as chronic alcohol abuse or dementia. The other group is made up of those with schizophrenia, who may well have some kind of "partially genetic, partially acquired disorder, marked by intermingled episodes of disorganized behavior and quiescent phases" (Goldstein, 1986, p. 149). It is this disorganized behavior that is the usual trigger for admission; therefore, upon admission to a neuropsychiatric hospital, patients with schizophrenia and those with brain damage may look alike. Psychologists are often the ones called upon to differentiate between them using a balanced battery of tests that includes a visuoconstructive measure such as the BGT.

Neuropsychological Screening as a Continuum

Think of neuropsychological assessment as a continuum. The *screening* process is on one end of the continuum, full neuropsychological assessment is at the other end. Why not give every person who has any kind of psychological, psychiatric, or neurological difficulty a comprehensive battery of psychological tests? Because lengthy testing for all would be much too costly of money and personnel. Also, it would waste resources because such a large amount of information is not necessary to classify and treat every case. Hutt (1985) says that screening takes place early in the process of diagnosis and should not be equated with final diagnostic decisions. He means that screening is a *preliminary* step, and once brain disorder has been suggested or established, further investigation should be done to delineate the disorder more fully. Screening consists of administering a brief battery of tests to aid in diagnosis and treatment planning, especially in cases deemed confusing or urgent. Lezak (1995) calls it an *early warning system*.

The focus of screening will vary with the goals of the treatment center and the typical kinds of patients seen there. In many instances, the goal of screening is to detect whether the patient has brain damage. This type of screening is especially used at inpatient neuropsychiatric centers where there is a high base rate of cognitive disorders and psychoses, typically as much as 30% each of their populations. Because patients in these two diagnostic categories often share many symptoms and because their treatment is very different, it is essential to distinguish between them soon after admission.

Typical questions for neuropsychological screening are:

Does the person have brain damage?

If so, does this knowledge explain the person's history, symptoms, and deficits?

If brain damage is present, what are the behavioral, intellectual, social, and occupational consequences for the person?

If the diagnosis is unclear, should the person be given more neuropsychological screening tests?

Once brain damage is established, should the person be referred for comprehensive neuropsychological testing to obtain a fuller picture of the problem and recommendations for treatment?

Which patients get screened? Some institutions require that a brief screening battery be given to all new patients. Others will use screening only when the clinical picture is unclear or when the patient's history, behavior, or referral questions raise suspicion of brain impairment. Examples of patients more at risk for brain dysfunction are older adults and those with a history of alcohol or drug abuse or HIV infection. Diagnostic questions are also raised by patient complaints of changes in cognitive ability, speech, vision, or memory and symptoms of confusion, clumsiness, headaches, seizures, and other characteristics of potential brain involvement.

What is the difference between a screening battery of tests and a screening test? The latter is a test that is brief, has objective scoring with good validity and reliability, and is not too narrow—that is, too specific—in what it measures. It has a research history of being able to identify persons who have some type of brain dysfunction, but it is not able to indicate the specifics of the person's disorder. A screening test is never used alone but always in the context of a screening battery. A screening battery should be composed of an interview, measures of intellectual ability (usually all or part of the WAIS), of personality (often the MMPI), and of brain damage. Measurement of the latter should include at least two tests that measure different aspects of brain function.

About 14% of psychologists take a formal and relatively inflexible approach to neuropsychological screening (Sweet, Moberg, & Westergaard, 1996). The largest group (60%) has a core set of tests to which they add individual tests tailored to the specific patient. For another group, neuropsychological screening is done as a "rolling" activity where tests are chosen based on questions raised from initial information, such as patient complaint, referral question, and first impression. This approach is used by 25% of neuropsychologists. As new questions or hypotheses are raised, data can be collected from other sources, such as additional tests, ward observations, chart review, and interviews with significant others (Cummings & Laquerre, 1990). Hammainen (1994) reports on a computer program (NADIA) developed to facilitate the hypothesis-testing approach. During the testing session, the program rapidly provides test results, allowing a step-by-step selection of tests based upon patient-specific criteria. Practitioners of this flexible or individual approach use measures that tap a wide range of abilities from various *domains,* such as those listed in Table 2.1. The table also includes tests that are often associated with each domain. It was compiled from the ideas of Bondi et al. (1996), Chouinard and Braun (1993), D'Amato et al. (1997), Gregory (1996), Groth-Marnat (1997, in press), and Lezak (1995). Difficulty with any of these functions *may* indicate brain impairment. Note that the standard BGT is listed in the visual-spatial domain; the recall version is listed in the learning and memory domain.

When assessing patients on these domains, neuropsychologists prefer tests with high *specificity.* However, note that none of the measures in Table 2.1 purely assess a particular ability; most measure two or more functions. Although psychologists largely agree on the content of the functional domains, there is little consensus on the appropriate measures to be used.

The BGT is a good example of a screening test for brain impairment and is one of those most often included in screening batteries for adults (Groth-Marnat, 1997, in press; Gregory, 1987; Berg, Franzen, & Wedding, 1994) and children (Franzen & Berg, 1989; Sattler, 1992). Drawing tasks have traditionally been used for screening because they are sensitive to many different kinds of brain impairment (Lacks, in press). Note that in this context screening means *identifying* a person likely to have a cognitive disorder. It does not mean that the test will be able to describe specific details of the brain impairment, such as location, extent, and cause.

The BGT as a Screening Test

Even though the BGT has been shown to be useful for identifying persons with a wide range of cognitive impairment, it primarily assesses disordered perceptual-motor and executive functions. Someone with diffuse brain damage, or with dysfunction in the area of the brain tapped by the BGT, is likely to be identified by it. However, some patients with impairment in other parts of the brain may be able to do well on the BGT. For that reason, at least one other screening test for brain dysfunction should be included in the screening battery and it should be one that measures functions other than those tapped by the BGT. Examples to choose from can be found in many neuropsychology texts. Any test chosen should also be one that has shown an ability to discriminate between patients with brain damage and those with schizophrenia or other serious psychiatric diagnoses.

Table 2.1   Neuropsychological Domains and Examples of Measures to Assess Each Domain

Domain or function	Measures or tests
Attention and concentration	Digit Span, Arithmetic Visual Span (Wechsler Memory Scale) Trail Making Test Stroop Color-Word Test
Learning and memory	Digit Span, Digit Symbol Wechsler Memory Scale Rey Auditory Verbal Learning Test Bender Gestalt Test, Recall Benton Visual Retention Test Rey-Osterrieth Complex Figure Test, Delayed Recall
Visual-spatial ability	Bender Gestalt Test Rey-Osterrieth Complex Figure Test Block Design Tactual Performance Test
Abstraction	Boston Naming Test Category Test Raven Progressive Matrices
Motor skills	Finger Tapping
Verbal or language skills	Information, Comprehension Boston Naming Test Aphasia Screening Test
Achievement	Wide Range Achievement Test
Executive functions	Behavioral observations Wisconsin Card Sorting Test
Emotional status	MMPI Beck Depression Inventory Symptom Checklist-90

Webster, Scott, Nunn, McNeer, and Varnell (1984) demonstrated the dangers of using only one screening test for brain impairment. They administered the Cognitive Capacity Screening Exam (CCSE) and the Memory for Designs (MFD) to 43 patients with cortical impairment (of these, 20 had bilateral, 6 had left-hemisphere, and 7 had right-hemisphere damage) and 19 neurologically intact patients referred to a neuropsychological consulting service. Analyses revealed that use of both tests resulted in a higher number of overall diagnostic hits (81%) than use of either measure alone (CCSE overall hit rate = 61%; MFD = 73%). This result appeared to be explained by each test assessing the functions of different parts of the brain: The CCSE was superior in identifying the subset of patients with unilateral, left-hemispheric damage (67% versus 33%); the MFD had more utility in assessing dysfunction from unilateral, right-hemispheric damage (86% versus 29%). The two tests together had a 77% hit rate for identifying the 13 patients with unilateral damage. Further evidence of the bipolar relationship of diagnosis to test score can be found in the correlation between the two tests for the different diagnostic groupings. The correlation for those without brain impairment was .99, and for those with bilateral brain damage was .86. Correlation for those with unilateral damage was .35, showing that they had much more variance of ability on these two tests than did the other patients.

Comprehensive Neuropsychological Assessment

What should happen after a patient has been identified as having brain impairment based upon a screening battery? There are at least three possibilities. One is that further psychological testing will be considered unnecessary and treatment will proceed. Another option is to refer the client for a comprehensive neuropsychology workup. An in-between option is to do some additional neuropsychology testing, using several screening measures of diverse scope to look systematically at the patient's strengths and weaknesses. The tests would be chosen to assess various cognitive and behavioral functions from different areas of the brain, including both hemispheres (see Table 2.1). A number of useful texts describe various brief screening tests from each of these domains. Examples of tests for adults can be found in Gregory (1987) and Berg et al. (1994); for children Franzen and Berg (1989) and Sattler (1992) are helpful.

Finally, if initial screening or additional tests reveal a strong picture of brain damage, a thorough neuropsychology evaluation might be ordered to confirm the diagnosis and provide additional details. This comprehensive assessment, taking 6 or more hours, can pinpoint areas of brain impairment and its causes. It can determine whether the extent of the disability is mild, moderate, or severe and if it is likely to worsen with time. Much has been made in recent years of the need for neuropsychology tests to document the impact of brain impairment on a patient's everyday functioning at different points of recovery. Areas of interest include self-care, independent living, academic achievement, and vocational functioning (Heaton & Pendleton, 1981). For example, Acker and Davis (1989) related results from a battery of neuropsychology tests to the postinjury ($N =$ 6.2 years following injury) functional status of 148 persons with head injuries. Tests were administered an average of 2.4 years postinjury. The number of BGT errors, along with scores on such other neuropsychology tests as the Wechsler Memory Scale and the Stroop Color and Word Test, predicted the degree of independent living. These measures of more specific skills were more associated with patients' later success than were broader-based IQ tests or demographic variables, such as age and education. Such tests are cost effective in the rehabilitation setting because more realistic retraining programs can be planned based on test-identified deficits. Recovery can be tracked over time in a standardized way, and adjustment to community reentry can be periodically monitored.

The distinct advantage of the comprehensive neuropsychology evaluation is that it can aid in planning treatment. Not only can the neuropsychologist recommend a type of remediation, but he or she can discuss the patient's ability to cooperate with the plan. It is true that most psychiatric treatment centers do not have a neuropsychology service. However, Yozawitz (1986) believes that this practice is shortsighted. He also warns of the dangers of simplistically dichotomizing all neuropsychology patients as having brain damage versus not impaired. In a New York State acute care center, he found that when flexible neuropsychology evaluations were provided to referred patients, many with *functional* diagnoses were also found to have impaired brain function. These patients could be divided about equally into those with a developmental language disorder or a visual-spatial disorder. Those in the latter group were amenable to cognitive/academic rehabilitation for improvement of their educational, vocational, communication, and living skills. Yozawitz proposes that psychiatric treatment centers should incorporate routine neuropsychology evaluation and subsequent cognitive rehabilitation into comprehensive mental health care.

WHAT DOES THE BGT MEASURE?

It would be convenient and desirable to have pure psychological tests that only measure one function or ability at a time, that is, that are very *specific* in what they assess. However, in reality, most tests tap multiple and complex functions and abilities. Dodrill (1997) found that generally neuropsychological tests show low levels of *specificity*. For example, successful completion of the seemingly simple BGT appears to require a wide variety of skills using many areas of the brain. A complex series of cognitive and other requirements ensue from the presentation of the BGT's first stimulus card. As described in Chapter 1, the determinants of BGT performance include intact vision, attention and concentration, perception or interpretation of the design, spatial relations, perspective, verbal intelligence, memory, motor skills, perceptual-motor integration, and *executive* skills, such as deliberation, planning, decision making, and drive or motivation.

Because so many disparate abilities are involved in BGT performance, it is obvious that more than one location of the brain is in operation. Lezak (1995) generally attributes the source of executive functions to the frontal lobes; however, they can also be sensitive to damage in other parts of the brain. The perceptual-motor aspects of the BGT are traditionally ascribed to the right parietal lobe (Benton & Tranel, 1993; Black & Bernard, 1984; Joseph, 1996). But Benton and Tranel report negligible differences in visuoconstructive test performance between individuals with left- versus right-hemisphere lesions. They suspect that the visual-perceptual aspects are linked to the right hemisphere. However, the BGT makes demands on other skills, such as deliberation and sustained attention, that may be linked to the left hemisphere. Benson and Barton (1970) examined the effects on constructional ability of lesions localized in four different quadrants of the brain and found impaired performance from lesions in all four quadrants, although more patients with right posterior lesions showed disruption of this function.

Black and Bernard (1984) conducted a study of 52 men who all had brain injury from war-related shrapnel wounds penetrating to one of the four brain quadrants. They were given a neuropsychological battery that included the WAIS and BGT. Although there were no significant differences in Full Scale IQ or in Block Design results among the four groups, there were differences in BGT results. Those patients with right-hemisphere damage did more poorly than those with left-hemisphere impairment; the worst results were for those with *right posterior* damage and the best results were for those in the *left anterior* group. BGTs with more than 2 errors were found for 6% of those with left anterior damage, 25% of right anterior, 20% of left posterior, and 46% of right posterior. Lesion size had only a minor effect on constructional deficits. The researchers concluded that although constructional deficits were more common and severe in those with right posterior lesions, they can occur with a lesion in any quadrant. The latter findings agree with those found by Garb and Schramke (1996) in a meta-analysis of neuropsychological assessment research. They also found that neurological impairment is rarely limited to one small area of the brain. Many patients with structural lesions in one hemisphere may have diffuse brain effects. Head injury, stroke, and tumors can affect the whole brain in addition to causing localized disruptions.

In summary, there is no easy answer to the question of what the BGT measures. Very early attempts to assess brain impairment assumed a unitary concept of *organicity* where damage to any part of the brain would have a single effect upon the brain, varying only in degree, not in type. Later it was thought that any brain damage would interfere with nervous system integration and, therefore, would appear on the radar of any decent neuropsychological test. Psychologists sought single tests or short batteries that could serve to detect all types of brain damage (Gregory, 1987). For some time, however, we have known that each test measures only some of the many brain functions, although rarely only one or two functions. You need a great deal of data, a whole group of tests, to describe the complexity of brain function and dysfunction.

Currently, neuropsychologists choose specific tests to measure certain *domains* of brain function. However, it appears that strict adherence to this specificity theory is overly narrow. As a result of the multiple skills required to reproduce the nine BGT designs, we are probably measuring multiple functions from a number of different parts of the brain. It appears that the BGT casts a rather broad net; that is, it is sensitive to impairment from many areas of the brain. Therefore, it is more of a *marker* of brain dysfunction, not a single test to reveal the complex workings of the brain. The BGT is a good measure of the visual-spatial domain, but it also measures many other functions not confined to this domain or even to the right parietal region of the brain, such as executive functions that are thought to originate in the frontal lobes. Individuals with diffuse brain damage are also likely to do poorly on this test. Examples of this category are alcoholism, aging, and dementia from Alzheimer's disease, HIV infection, parkinsonism, and Huntington's disease. According to Lezak (1995), sensitivity of this test to diffuse brain impairment suggests that "copying tasks require a high level of integrative behavior that is not necessarily specific to visuographic functions but tends to break down with many kinds of cerebral damage" (p. 568).

MYTHS ABOUT THE BGT

Developed in 1938, the BGT is one of the oldest and most used neuropsychological tests. Over time, the situations in which this test is used have gradually changed. At each step of the way, various misconceptions have developed about the BGT. Some of those have reached the status of myth. A few of the most-often expressed myths are briefly examined here.

1. *Many psychologists use the BGT as the only test to measure brain damage.* This bugaboo has persisted for many years. It is one of those statements that are made as absolute fact with no objective evidence as support. In reality, psychologists use the BGT as one instrument in a battery of tests that almost always includes at least the WAIS and an interview. They also generally integrate their test findings with other known patient information, such as history and current symptoms.

2. *You should not use a test like the BGT to differentiate between brain damage and schizophrenia because schizophrenia is a form of brain damage.* No one knows yet what is the exact cause of schizophrenia. We do know, however, that the course, treatment, and outcome for schizophrenia are very different from that of patients with brain damage. The two groups also perform quite differently on the BGT both in number and type of errors, just as the two groups perform differently on many psychological

tests. In a group of 141 patients with psychosis (70% of whom had schizophrenia), the BGT correctly identified 73% of them. The BGT is not used to diagnose schizophrenia but to rule out *traditionally defined* brain damage for the purpose of treatment planning. Diagnoses need to be as precise as possible to apply the most effective treatment. Does it make sense to assert that there is no need to discriminate between brain tumor and epilepsy because both are forms of brain damage? No, because the course, treatment, and outcome for these two disorders are also different.

3. *The BGT has limited use as a screening test because it only measures impairment in the right parietal lobe.* Earlier discussion showed that the BGT also often identifies diffuse damage and frontal lobe dysfunction that affects executive abilities. It seems least able to distinguish unilateral, nonparietal damage to either hemisphere.

4. *You can do a better job with a comprehensive neuropsychological evaluation using tests like the HRB than you can screening with tests like the BGT.* Yes, you can provide much *more* information from a large battery of tests. However, many situations do not warrant such in-depth assessment. Nor do most agencies have the financial or staff resources to give every patient this kind of attention. Furthermore, the typical screening situation is one in which psychologists are asked to *screen* for brain dysfunction in psychiatric clinics or hospitals that have high base rates for schizophrenia (up to 35%). In these typical settings, the elaborate test batteries generally do not show high discriminative ability, especially in comparisons between those with brain dysfunction and those with schizophrenia (Lacks et al., 1970).

5. *If you suspect that a patient has brain impairment, it is best to refer that person to a qualified neuropsychologist.* Most agencies perform a kind of assessment and treatment triage to decide how best to allocate their resources. Just as a family practice physician must limit patient referrals for expensive specialized testing or consultations, clinical psychologists also must carefully consider whether additional specialized assessment is warranted.

6. *With the advent of so many sophisticated neuroradiological measures such as CT, MRI, and PET scans, we no longer need to concern ourselves about psychological diagnostic testing for brain damage.* It is true that sometimes a medical diagnosis of a type and location of brain impairment makes the use of psychological tests unnecessary. However, again, these medical tests are very expensive and not readily available to all neuropsychiatric patients, especially those in publicly funded psychiatric hospitals. In addition, these tests are not infallible. A battery of psychological tests can also provide a great deal of information besides whether the person has brain impairment or not.

Although there are a number of myths about the BGT, there are also some legitimate criticisms. Some psychologists do misuse tests and write reports that are not particularly useful. Too many psychologists persist in using clinical judgment to interpret the BGT and other similar tests rather than relying on an objective scoring system with known diagnostic accuracy. Research has shown this practice to reduce diagnostic accuracy. This same criticism is true of psychologists' interpretation practices with many of our other frequently used tests, such as the Rorschach, MMPI, and WAIS. Although there are extensive norms for the BGT, there are still gaps with not enough known about the performance of various ethnic groups. Some promising research paths have not been cross-validated or investigated further by researchers. Examples are the Pauker scoring system and variations of administration like the Background Interference Procedure and the "perfect" method (McCann & Plunkett, 1984). We still do not have a detailed and exact picture of what brain functions from what location in the brain fully determine BGT performance. These criticisms are more realistic because they refer to common and current practices of many psychologists as well as to unanswered questions that would facilitate use of this test.

In reading the literature on testing for brain dysfunction, there are large differences in opinions and practices between psychologists who work in a primarily *neurological* setting versus those who work in a primarily *psychiatric* setting. It is apparent that the types of patients seen in each of these milieus are different, and this fact may account for some of the contradictory recommendations made in the literature. It would be helpful to extend research on the topic of assessment in various types of settings with various types of patients.

In summary, the BGT serves a number of functions within neuropsychological testing. It has good support as a screening test for brain dysfunction, especially for diffuse impairment or in the right parietal area. It can also be used as a test measuring the visuoconstructive domain when additional assessment is called for. The BGT is an instrument that has been in use for 60 years and applies to all age groups. It can be scored by objective methods and has been the focus of a good deal of research that has provided norms and rates of diagnostic accuracy. The remainder of this book provides many details of administration, scoring, and interpretation of the results of this widely used test.

CHAPTER 3

Clinical Judgment versus Objective Scoring Systems

In the early history of the Bender Gestalt Test (BGT), there were no formal procedures for quantifying test results. In 1946, when Lauretta Bender first published her test stimuli and instructions for their use, she provided only a chart of test responses indicating maturational progression from ages 4 through 11. This chart is reproduced in Chapter 11, which covers use of the BGT with children (Figure 11.1). The first objective scoring system was published in 1951 by Pascal and Suttell. Although the development of this method was the impetus for a great deal of research, it does not seem to have equally influenced clinical practice. Instead, BGT clinical protocols have generally been evaluated by means of *clinical judgment.*

In 1961, only 5% of a sample of experienced clinicians relied exclusively on a scoring system to evaluate BGT protocols; 31% used a combination of objective scoring and subjective impressions; and 56% relied entirely on their subjective clinical judgment (Tolor and Brannigan, 1980). In 1978, Robiner found similar patterns of clinical practice.

Following Meehl's (1954) work on the general disadvantages of clinical prediction and Goldberg's (1959) study demonstrating the particular deficiencies of subjective judgments with the BGT, psychologists became more interested in finding a brief and objective scoring system for this test. Now several scoring systems are available; however, the current rates of clinical usage are unknown.

OBJECTIVE SCORING SYSTEMS What BGT scoring procedures are available to the clinician? The fact that there are numerous possible errors and distortions in drawing these figures has resulted in varying attempts to provide scoring methods that have diagnostic utility. A review of the BGT research for the years 1958 through 1997 indicates that there are at least eight different published scoring systems for the standard administration with adults. At least three additional methods are available for work with children (see Chapter 11). The method developed by Koppitz (1963), called the Developmental Bender Test Scoring System, seems to be the overwhelmingly preferred procedure of scoring for children. For adults, the most popular systems in research reports have been the Pascal-Suttell, the Hain, and the Lacks adaptation of the Hutt-Briskin procedures. Because clinical use of particular psychological tests tends to correlate with research reports on the same tests, it is probable that these are also the three most clinically used scoring procedures.

Interscorer reliabilities are generally acceptable for all these scoring approaches ($r = .79$ to 1.00). Test-retest reliability ranges from .63 to .92, depending upon the degree of pathology of patients and the retest interval (ranging from 24 hours to 18 months). Published overall diagnostic accuracies of these systems range from 55% to 88% (Lacks, 1979).

Pascal-Suttell Method

One of the earliest and most well known evaluation methods was developed by Pascal and Suttell (1951). This is a complex procedure of measuring the degree of psychopathology through 105 possible deviations in reproducing the figures. Each design (excluding figure A) is inspected for from 10 to 13 possible errors (weighted from 2 to 8). For example, figure 1 is assessed for ten possible deviations, such as wavy line of dots, dashes for dots, circles for dots, second attempt, and so on. Then, the overall production is assessed for seven more configuration scores. Raw scores are converted to z scores, based on education, with possible z scores ranging from 32 to 201. The standard z-score cutoff for brain dysfunction is 100.

Although it has been used frequently for evaluation in published research, the Pascal-Suttell approach does not enjoy wide clinical application. It is cumbersome to use (the scoring manual fills 100 pages) and very time consuming (some estimates are as high as 20 minutes per protocol). Also, this method is inapplicable to data obtained from many psychiatric patients because its use is confined to individuals ages 15 to 50 with more than 9 years of education.

Hain Method

Taking a different approach is the Hain system (1964), which consists of 15 signs, each with a weight ranging from 1 to 4 (e.g., omissions = 1 point, partial rotations = 2 points, overlap = 3 points, and perseveration = 4 points). This approach looks at the BGT as a whole rather than scoring each figure separately. Each sign is scored once per record, so total weighted scores can range from 0 to 34, with the standard cutoff score being 9 or greater. This approach takes 3 minutes or less to apply.

Hutt-Briskin Method

Taking an approach similar to Hain's, Hutt and Briskin (1960) suggested the use of 12 "essential discriminators of intracranial damage" (e.g., Closure Difficulty, Simplification, and Fragmentation), a list that has been modified several times in subsequent publications (Hutt, 1985). Evaluations of different versions of this method have been published by Lownsdale et al. (1989). In the original Hutt-Briskin system, each protocol is evaluated for the presence or absence of the 12 signs; the authors suggested that a score of 5 or more classifies a protocol as showing evidence of brain impairment. An error may be scored only once per protocol, so scores can range from 0 to 12. Because Hutt has been more interested in the projective use of the BGT, he has not provided much detail nor empirical validation of these signs. However, Lacks devised a detailed scoring manual of Hutt and Briskin's procedures that was published as the first edition of this book in 1984. This method has the advantage of taking less than 3 minutes per protocol to score. Her adaptation has been used successfully in many studies that are reported throughout this edition. Her methods are referred to here as the *Lacks adaptation* of the Hutt-Briskin scoring system or simply as the *Lacks system*.

Pauker Quick-Scoring Method

Published in 1976, the Pauker Quick-Scoring System takes only about 1 minute per protocol. One reason for its brevity is that no physical measurements are necessary and differential decisions are minimized. Each of the nine figures is rated on a 0-to-4 scale of amount of deviation from the original stimulus. Total scores can range from 0 to 36. Pauker does not suggest a cutoff score nor present any validating data other than a correlation of .88 with scoring by the Koppitz method for a group of handicapped children. Three psychology technicians produced interrater reliabilities of .95 to .98. Only one study has been published on the diagnostic accuracy of this method (Lacks & Newport, 1980). Using an optimal cutoff score of 9 and above for a sample of 50 adult, mixed psychiatric inpatients (cognitive disorder base rate of 34%), three scorers produced diagnostic accuracies of 78%, 78%, and 82%. These results, although promising, still await cross-validation. There are no additional research reports using this method.

This scoring method has been included because it is so simple and brief, and it showed early promise. Unlike the other systems, it has the added advantage of being designed for use with both adults and children.

Marley Differential Diagnostic Method

The most recently developed scoring procedures for adults were published in 1982 by Marley. Her method is based on some of the Hutt and Briskin criteria combined with several of her own. The criteria are also differentially weighted. Hutt (1985) has been very critical of this method for the following reasons: Marley's modification of the stimulus cards, which introduces unknown effects, questionable research practices, resulting in unrealistically positive findings, and insufficient description of the diagnostic criterion for her participants with brain impairment. In addition, her procedures were originally validated on 640 individuals with brain impairment, all of whom were acute stroke victims, making it difficult to generalize to other diagnoses of cognitive impairment. One study has compared the Marley system to the Lacks adaptation and found the latter to be superior in diagnostic accuracy for neurological impairment (Weintraub, 1991). Final evaluation of Marley's procedures await further published research.

POSSIBLE REASONS PSYCHOLOGISTS DON'T UTILIZE SCORING SYSTEMS

In his 1978 study, Robiner suggests that a majority of psychologists still do not rely entirely on an objective scoring system to interpret the BGT. Even when they are familiar with a scoring method, they may not utilize it. With such a proliferation of scoring approaches, why haven't clinicians made more use of them in their day-to-day practice? Possible reasons include the following:

1. Some scoring systems are not readily available or feasible for practitioners. For example, the Hain system is unpublished. The Pascal-Suttell methods are cumbersome and can take up to 20 minutes to score one protocol. It is unlikely that a clinician will use an evaluation technique that takes up to four times longer than is required to administer the test. Pauker's manual is only one page long and does not provide illustrations, making consistent and accurate application somewhat of a problem.
2. Some research reports show considerable overlap between score distributions of brain-impaired and nonimpaired patient groups, making prediction of individual cases hazardous.
3. A confusing array of research findings exists where few direct comparative evaluations of scoring systems have been made.

4. There is some evidence for the superiority of expert judgment over objective scoring.

Given the difficulty of acquiring some manuals, learning other systems, or applying some methods in a reasonable time, it is not surprising that many clinicians rely instead on their own clinical judgment. In the past, child psychologists have more frequently scored BGTs than have adult psychologists. One reason for this pattern may be that the Koppitz (1975) procedures represent the unique and desirable combination of being readily available, easy to apply, and brief to carry out.

Comparative Usefulness of BGT Scoring Methods

It may be that clinicians don't rely on objective scoring systems for the BGT because of the lack of clear evidence regarding which scoring criteria are most effective. Published overall diagnostic accuracies range from 55% to 88% for the diagnosis of brain dysfunction. However, it is difficult to draw conclusions about the relative value of the available scoring systems because the research typically presents data on one system at a time. The different studies vary widely in sample size (30 to 1,003), brain impairment base rate (18% to 67%), composition of the nonimpaired comparison samples, test score cutoffs, and procedures for measuring diagnostic efficiency. There have been few systematic attempts to compare the reliability and diagnostic efficiency of different objective scoring systems.

In an attempt to clarify this issue, Lacks and Newport (1980) compared the usefulness of four brief scoring approaches to the BGT on the same sample of 50 mixed psychiatric inpatients with a brain dysfunction base rate of 34%. With the criteria of relative ease of application, availability, and frequency of recent use in the literature, the following systems were chosen for comparison: the Hain (1964), the Lacks adaptation of Hutt-Briskin (1960), and the Pauker Quick-Scoring (1976). Because rotation of reproductions has been described so frequently as characteristic of the BGTs of those with brain impairment (e.g., Griffith & Taylor, 1960), number of rotations was also used as a very simple diagnostic criterion. Each of these approaches requires less than 3 minutes per protocol to use.

Twelve scorers were used, three for each system. Scorers using the Lacks adaptation of the Hutt-Briskin system, with a standard cutoff score, achieved the highest levels of diagnostic accuracy (84%). Other scoring methods that have been compared to the Lacks system are Pascal-Suttell (Marsico & Wagner, 1990), Koppitz with adolescents (McIntosh, Belter, Saylor, Finch, & Edwards, 1988), and Hutt's Configurational Analysis (Lownsdale et al., 1989). In all three studies the Lacks system was equivalent to the other methods. Additional details of these studies are presented in later chapters.

BGT Evaluation through Clinical Judgment

How do diagnostic accuracies obtained from clinical judgment compare to those from objective scoring systems? Butler et al. (1976) reported diagnostic accuracy of the clinical judgment of an expert at 69% when neither the Pascal-Suttell nor the Hain procedures could discriminate between patients with brain damage and psychiatric patients. Goldberg (1959) found that 22 judges (psychologists, psychology trainees, and secretaries) had an average accuracy of 68%, as opposed to the Pascal-Suttell with 63%, but an expert (taking an average of 40 minutes per protocol) achieved 83% diagnostic accuracy. Kramer and Fenwick (1966) found an expert's judgment to be 80% accurate, compared to

76% accuracy achieved with the Hain. Unfortunately, most of these studies confound the issue of clinical judgment with that of level of experience.

Perhaps the most direct answer to this question can be found in a study by Robiner (1978). Five professional clinical psychologists and five clinical graduate students were asked to evaluate BGT protocols. Although all were familiar with at least one objective scoring system, they chose to use their more subjective clinical judgment. They evaluated 40 of the sample of 50 protocols used by Lacks and Newport (1980), omitting 10 patients with chronic alcoholism. The overall diagnostic accuracy for both groups was 71%, a level almost identical to that found by Butler et al. (1976) and Goldberg (1959). It is also a level considerably below that found with the Hutt-Briskin and the Pauker scoring systems for essentially the same group of patients.

These two studies are the only ones to compare directly a large number of evaluators using various approaches to the BGT on the same sample of patients. Their results suggest that psychologists can achieve high levels of diagnostic accuracy with this test through the use of a brief, easily learned objective scoring system: the Lacks adaptation of the Hutt-Briskin (and, if these findings are cross-validated, the Pauker). Continued reliance on the more subjective clinical judgment will result in less successful diagnostic decisions. One exception to this may be the case of simulators of brain damage or malingerers, where a scoring system may be too sensitive to any distortions but a clinician may be able to detect qualitative differences in the errors made (Bruhn & Reed, 1975).

Level of Experience

Related to the question of scoring approach is the issue of the level of experience and expertise of the scorer. Perhaps some scoring systems require greater amounts of past experience with this test, but others may be more readily learned by anyone, including individuals who function as psychometricians. At least two studies (Goldberg, 1959; Kramer & Fenwick, 1966) show that experts with the BGT have greater success than more typical psychologists in differentiating protocols showing brain-impairment from those showing no impairment. However, Goldberg found no differences among typical psychologists, graduate students, and secretaries. Miller and Hutt (1975) found interscorer reliabilities of .90 between an experienced and an inexperienced scorer. The 12 scorers used by Lacks and Newport (1980) represented three levels of expertise for each of the four scoring systems used: *expert, typical,* and *novice.* There was a maximum of 4% difference in diagnostic accuracy among the three scorers who used each system. High levels of accuracy were achieved with the Hutt-Briskin and Pauker systems after very short training periods, even by individuals with no previous experience with tests for brain dysfunction. Robiner (1978) also found no differences in subjective diagnostic acumen between experienced clinicians and graduate students. In fact, for a range of experience from 1 to 30 years, the correlation between diagnostic accuracy and experience for his ten judges was .07. This means that the scoring of BGT protocols can probably be entrusted in many situations to a capable psychometrician who has been trained to use a proven scoring system.

In summary, it appears that in the past the majority of psychologists did not use an objective scoring system to evaluate the BGTs of adults, probably because there was not a system that was readily available, easy to apply, and required a short amount of time to learn and utilize. Instead, large numbers of psychologists relied on their subjective clinical judgment to arrive at diagnostic decisions with the BGT, a practice that has been repudiated by several research studies. A brief review of the research on this topic indicates that psychologists who now assess BGTs subjectively will increase their diagnostic accuracy considerably (on the average by 10% to 15%) if they use a brief, easily learned objective scoring system such as the Lacks adaptation of the Hutt-Briskin procedures presented in this book. This system has been widely available since 1984 and is brief and easy to learn. No surveys of BGT evaluation practices have been published since 1984. It would be interesting to see if the availability of such a method as well as information about the pitfalls of clinical judgment has led to increased reliance on objective scoring of the BGT.

CHAPTER 4

Administration

Because this test appears so simple, some examiners may believe that the manner of administering it is relatively unimportant. On the contrary, as with all other psychological tests, the Bender Gestalt Test (BGT) has a standardized administration that should be followed meticulously to ensure reliable and valid results. Although a few clinicians advocate some minor changes in the directions, the administration to adults is a relatively standard procedure. Those examiners working with children will find directions for this particular group in Chapter 11 and in Koppitz (1963, 1975).

TEST MATERIALS Materials necessary for administration include a stack of 8½- by 11-inch white unlined paper, several number 2 pencils with erasers (not pens), a smooth writing surface, and the nine stimulus cards. The latter are 4- by 6-inch white cards, printed with geometric designs and numbered A and 1 through 8. The cards may be either the original ones developed by Lauretta Bender (1946), which are presented in Figure 4.1, or the slightly modified ones used by Hutt (1985). Before testing, *always* check to make sure that the cards are face down in a stack where they are in the proper order and orientation. Always give the cards in the correct sequence.

STANDARD ADMINISTRATION As testing begins, without comment, place one sheet of the paper in front of the person in the vertical (usual writing) position and place the extra pencils and remaining paper to the side, near the person. Then give the following instructions (taken from Hutt, 1985, p. 44):

> I am going to show you these cards, one at a time. Each card has a simple drawing on it. I would like you to copy the drawing on the paper, as well as you can. Work in any way that is best for you. This is not a test of artistic ability, but try to copy the drawings as accurately as possible. Work as fast or as slowly as you wish.

> With some individuals, you may want to check to make sure they understood and then repeat all or part of the instructions. There is no need, generally, to explain what you mean as the directions are so simple and straightforward. Most people will be able to proceed with the test. A few may be anxious because they believe they are not artistic or they are afraid they will be required to work quickly. A few reassurances are usually enough to allay their fears.

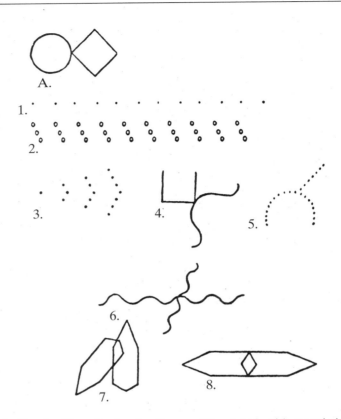

Figure 4.1 Bender Gestalt stimulus figures. (Reprinted, with permission, from *A Visual Motor Gestalt Test and its clinical uses* by Lauretta Bender. Published by the American Orthopsychiatric Association. Copyright © 1938, renewed 1965, by Lauretta Bender and the American Orthopsychiatric Association, Inc.)

Allow the person to adjust the paper (though still maintaining it in the vertical orientation) to suit drawing comfort and then place the first card so that it is aligned with the top of the paper. As the client completes each card, remove it and replace it with the next one. Most people will draw all nine figures on one page of paper. However, there is no limit on the number of sheets that may be used. Golden (1990) discusses the pros and cons of allowing the person only one or two sheets of paper versus an unlimited number. If someone is forced to use only one or two sheets, he or she will be more likely to reveal aspects of planning and organizational ability that may be useful in the evaluation of cognitive skills. However, when a pile of paper is available, this condition may lead to information more useful for personality assessment, such as how many designs the person puts on a page and the size of the drawings. These two approaches have not yet been empirically contrasted; the standard approach is to use the extra pile of paper.

Begin timing when you put out the first card. Split-second times are not necessary. Stopwatches have a tendency to make people believe there is a time limit even though they have been told the opposite. A wall clock or wristwatch will give an accurate enough estimate.

The person being tested may move the card closer or pick it up to get a better look. However, if he or she reorients the stimulus card, you can nonverbally indicate the correct placement by returning the card to its original position. If some-one insists on changing the card's orientation, allow him or her to do so. At the end of the test, immediately indicate the top of the figures with arrows on the protocol itself. The same arrow marks should be used to indicate the top of the paper if the person has placed the page in an unusual position. Don't trust this important step to your memory or you will have difficulty scoring the test later.

The majority of individuals do not ask questions, but there are always some who do. Typical questions are:

Do I have to count the dots?

Does it have to look exactly like this?

May I turn the card?

Should I use more than one sheet of paper?

May I erase?

Do mine have to be the same size as those on the card?

Questions should be answered either by repeating or paraphrasing the instructions or with more indirect replies such as the following:

It's up to you.

Do it the way you think best.

Do the best job you can.

If anyone wants to discuss the reasons for or meaning of the test, you may respond:

Let's wait until we finish this and we can discuss it then.

One occasional question—"May I use a ruler?"—has a very simple answer: "No."

Some people, especially the older adults or those with brain impairment, express insecurity about the competence of their work. They may need steady encouragement and praise throughout the test. For the majority, however, the test proceeds nonverbally until the end, when praise may be given for accomplishment of the task.

A final word needs to be said about sketching. It happens only occasionally that someone tries to reproduce the figures by sketching, that is, by using a series of lighter strokes rather than drawing with one firm line. Examiners should be alert for this practice and stop it as soon as it begins by announcing that sketching is not allowed. A protocol that has been sketched is not scorable by the system presented here.

These directions constitute the basic administration of the *copy* phase and, for many clinicians, the end of the BGT. Others may wish at this point to proceed with some of the variations of administration described later in this chapter, such as the recall or background interference procedures. Occasionally, the BGT will have to be repeated. In such cases, the clinician can be confident that the BGT has little practice effect. Research indicates that practice influences mainly psychological tests that have a large speed component, involve unfamiliar or rarely practiced responses, have a single solution, or involve learning (Lezak, 1995). The standard administration of the BGT has none of these characteristics.

DIAGNOSTIC SIGNIFICANCE OF BEHAVIORAL OBSERVATIONS

The scoring method used in this book consists of 12 errors or *essential discriminators.* In general, the presence of any 5 of these errors is taken to indicate brain impairment or dysfunction. However, all of these errors can also be made by clients or patients who do not put forth their best efforts because of lack of interest in the task, impulsivity, hostility toward the examiner, carelessness, fatigue, malingering, hearing or vision problems, and so on.

Some examiners, lulled into complacency by a deceptively simple test to administer, do not attend to the *process* of the patient's drawing of the figures. Instead, these clinicians believe that all interpretations of the test will be made on the finished product. They may even use an inadequately trained psychometrician to give the test and reserve their own skill strictly for arriving at conclusions. This is not to say that a *well-trained* technician cannot give the BGT. Whoever gives the test, however, must observe the person's behavior during its execution. See Lezak (1995) for additional discussion about the use of technicians in neuropsychological assessment.

At all times, the examiner must try to determine whether an error was made because of true perceptual-motor difficulties or because of other factors. Only in the former case should an error be scored. For example, suppose a person reproduced figure 1 with only four dots. Further, suppose this person showed hostility toward being tested, barely glanced at the stimulus card before copying it, made some comment about there being too many dots to copy, and took only 2 minutes to complete the entire test. It is unlikely that the person is suffering from brain dysfunction, but more likely that he or she is refusing to cooperate. Without having personally observed this performance or been told of it by the actual examiner, the clinician might find 5 errors and erroneously diagnose a cognitive disorder.

At the opposite extreme, a person with brain damage may be able to produce an adequate record (or one with 4 errors) through extreme effort, taking a great deal of time (maybe even 20 to 30 minutes), and making numerous erasures. Again, the behavioral observations would be crucial to making the correct diagnosis.

A list of relevant behavioral observations is presented in Figure 4.2. The list is divided into two parts. First, *general test-taking attitudes,* such as motivation and cooperation, are relevant to the analysis of most psychological tests. The second half of the list contains behaviors more specifically applicable to a visuoconstructive measure like the Bender Gestalt Test. A few items on the second list are even necessary to score some of the errors for the BGT (e.g., repeated unsuccessful attempts to correct errors). For convenience, the examiner may wish to reproduce this sheet for use with each person being tested.

A final point concerns the length of time taken to reproduce the nine BGT figures. Lacks, in a sample of 208 nonpatient adults, found an average copy time of 6 minutes. For 194 consecutive admissions to an urban community mental health center, she found significant differences in copy time between patients with diagnoses of personality disorder and those with cognitive disorders and between patients with psychosis and those with impaired brain function, but not between those with personality disorder and those with psychosis. Table 4.1 presents these figures. Armstrong (1965) found drawing times to average from 3.5 minutes for those with character disorders through 4.5 minutes for those with schizophrenia to 5.8 minutes for those with depression. Adults with brain damage averaged 6.25 minutes. Andert, Hustak, and Dinning (1978) found adults with mental retardation (mean age of 26) to have

General Test-Taking Attitudes

Takes test in serious manner .... Takes test lightly

Cooperative, compliant .... Uncooperative, resistant

Methodical, deliberate .... Careless

Persistent in difficult situations .... Gives up easily

Attentive, concentrating .... Distracted

Motivated to do well .... Unmotivated

Calm, relaxed .... Anxious, agitated

Good rapport with examiner .... Poor rapport

Specific Behavioral Observations

_____Evidence of fatigue

_____Insufficient attention to test designs

_____Drawing difficulty due to physical disability

Trouble understanding instructions due to:
_____Low IQ   _____Language difficulty   _____Hearing

_____Difficulty seeing figures

_____Considerable care and deliberation

_____Expression of dissatisfaction with poorly executed drawings
on figures_____

_____Repeated unsuccessful attempts to correct errors on figures_____

_____Rotation of drawing on figures_____

_____Motor incoordination or hand tremor   _____Mild   _____Moderate   ___Severe

_____Other behaviors_____

Minutes to complete test:_____

Figure 4.2   Behavioral observations for the Bender Gestalt Test.

Table 4.1   Mean Time (in Minutes) to Complete Bender Gestalt Test for Nonpatients and Three Inpatient Psychiatric Groups

Diagnosis	N	Range	M	SD
Nonpatient	208	3.00–20.00	6.01	2.32
Personality disorder	80	2.50–12.50	5.64	3.00
Psychosis	81	2.50–15.50	5.90	2.72
Brain dysfunction	33	2.00–38.50	11.07	8.66

copy times ranging from 7 to 9.75 minutes as degree of retardation increased. For normal children, Koppitz (1975) found average times to range from 5 to 6.5 minutes.

So the average time to copy the nine figures for individuals who are not brain impaired generally falls below 6 minutes. If an individual takes more than 15 minutes to complete the test, it is usually another strong diagnostic sign. Some may wish to count this excessive time as an unofficial additional error when the patient commits 4 errors. For example, someone with brain damage may be able to limit his or her errors to 4 by taking 20 to 30 minutes to complete the test rather than the usual 4 to 8 minutes. If you abide strictly by the 5-error marker to call the BGT performance within the brain-damage range, you will *miss* this case. Adding a point for the excessive time to complete the test allows correct identification of the case. This procedure should be used cautiously after examining all aspects of the BGT performance. It is important to note that taking this liberty has not yet been validated by research.

A final word is in order on the testing of older adults. Because this group is at a higher risk for decline in visual and hearing acuity, it is a good idea to check older persons systematically before testing for possible deficits. Because the BGT is often the first test given in a battery, you may not discover that the person could not see the designs or hear the instructions until after the test is completed. A simple way to check for these sensory deficits ahead of time is to show the person some simple picture and ask them to describe it, or have them read a brief passage from a card. You should also always ask if they ordinarily wear glasses. It is amazing how many older persons arrive for testing without their glasses because of pride, or confusion, or memory problems. For additional details on examining special populations and maximizing performance level, see Lezak (1995, p. 131).

MALINGERING

As psychologists go about the task of psychological assessment, they count on clients or patients to be forthright, to do their best on the task at hand. Even when the evaluation is for a criminal hearing, most people will cooperate and attempt to display their strengths and minimize evidence of their deficits. Many may even view a diagnosis of insanity or incompetence as a very undesirable and esteem-lowering outcome. However, in these highly litigious days, clinicians are increasingly faced with requests to be an expert witness in court actions of all kinds—attempts to diminish criminal responsibility or petitions to receive compensation for personal injury, medical malpractice, or disability. In these situations of potential gain, there is a much higher possibility of the client or patient wishing to look bad. More than ever, psychologists need to be alert to the possibility of deception.

Definition and Prevalence of Malingering

The *Diagnostic and Statistical Manual of Mental Disorders, Fourth Edition* (DSM-IV; American Psychiatric Association, 1994) defines malingering as "the intentional production of false or grossly exaggerated physical or psychological symptoms, motivated by external incentives such as avoiding military duty, avoiding work, obtaining financial compensation, evading criminal prosecution, or obtaining drugs" (p. 683). Malingering is distinguished from factitious disorders that are characterized by intentional physical or psychological symptoms, produced from a psychological incentive to assume a sick role rather than to acquire external gain.

Psychologists are becoming increasingly aware that faking test responses may be more widespread than originally believed and can appear in a wide variety of forms and situations. In an introduction to his book *Clinical Assessment of Malingering and Deception,* Rogers (1997b) reports that forensic psychologists estimate the rates of malingering to be about 16% in overall forensic and 7% in nonforensic settings, 20% of those involved in insanity hearings, and as much as 50% among those in personal injury court actions. Trueblood and Schmidt (1993) examined a sample of 106 consecutive outpatients who completed comprehensive neuropsychological testing and also had external incentives to feign cognitive deficits. They found a 7.5% rate of patients with high scores on a malingering screening test and another 7.5% who had neuropsychological test results of questionable validity. Rates of feigning illness in children are not known. The issue of malingering in children is controversial and relatively unexplored. This topic is covered briefly in Chapter 11.

Markers of Malingering

In the past, when confronted with the possibility of malingering, psychologists have had to rely mostly on their psychological common sense, past experience with such cases, and nonempirical guidelines promulgated by other psychologists. One of the most often suggested markers of malingering has been *inconsistency:* between expected norms and the patient's responses, between test findings and patient symptoms, between reported and observed symptoms, and in performance across successive testings. Other markers are improbable, bizarre, nonsensical (e.g., better performance on difficult than easy items), or rare responses; indiscriminant symptom endorsement; and performance levels *below* the usual range for a given disorder (Franzen, Iverson, & McCracken, 1990; Lezak, 1995; Pankratz & Binder, 1997; Rogers, 1997a; Smith, 1997). Neuropsychologists have also used standardized psychological tests to detect malingering. For example, the MMPI has a number of validity scales designed for this purpose, such as the F − K Index (Franzen et al., 1990).

However, psychologists should exercise healthy skepticism in applying these recommendations, as some tend to be based on clinical folklore. A 1993 study by Trueblood and Schmidt illustrates the need for such caution. They compared two carefully selected samples, one of suspected malingerers and one of patients with test results of questionable validity, with matched patients who had suffered similar injuries and were also pursuing litigation or seeking benefits. They were compared on 14 measures that had been previously suggested as indicators of invalidity on commonly given neuropsychological tests. Many of the suggested signs were rare or absent in their sample. Scores on only three were significantly different between the two suspected groups and their controls. Three more were significant for only one of the suspected groups. The authors caution that relying on such measures could lead to overconfidence in the accuracy of your test results.

Malingering and the BGT   Can a BGT protocol faked by a malingerer be detected by the clinician? That is, can it be distinguished from genuine neuropathology? Early research focused on the clinician's ability to detect simulation of psychosis or faking "disturbed", "bad", or "insane" but looked less frequently at simulation of brain damage. In 1975, Bruhn and Reed did the first formal study of faking on the BGT. Since then, a good deal of research has been done on faking of cognitive deficits, though most does not include the BGT (Schretlen, 1988).

Research on malingering has used a variety of experimental designs: normals simulating brain damage, prisoners acting as simulators, studies of true malingerers, discriminant analyses to construct prediction formulas, and the development and assessment of the effectiveness of specific screening devices. See Nies and Sweet (1994) for a detailed review of this literature. For a clinician to have high confidence in any detection strategy, Rogers (1997a) recommends that it be validated across several of these research designs, using more than one method of assessment with clinically diverse participants.

Generally, psychologists have had little success in separating malingerers from patients with genuine brain damage using standard scoring methods of recognized neuropsychological tests and batteries. For example, Bruhn and Reed (1975) found that neither the Pascal-Suttell scoring (1951) nor Canter Background Interference Procedure (Canter, 1966) could detect simulation on the BGT with high accuracy. However, a board-certified clinical psychologist using clinical judgment could discriminate between college student simulators of brain damage and patients with brain impairment. He achieved 89% accuracy in a pilot study and 100% in the main study. The clinician was able to teach his approach to two other judges who were then able to use these methods to achieve high levels of discrimination with another sample.

Suggested signs for diagnosing the patients with brain damage included simplified drawings, recurring distortions in similar designs, consistence in performance at similar levels of difficulty, and specific types of errors, such as rotations. Specific signs of simulation were not discussed. A criticism of this study is that the diagnostic task was made easier because the patients with brain damage had severe and fairly clear-cut deficits rather than the more usual type of ambiguous cases seen in clinical practice (Trueblood & Binder, 1997). Judges were also told the base rate of malingering for the sample, information not usually known in real clinical situations.

Glasser (1982) reproduced the findings of Bruhn and Reed with three types of participants: nonprofessional hospital employees, psychiatric patients, and patients with brain impairment. All were asked to take the BGT twice, the first time using standard instructions and the second time with instructions to simulate the performance of a person trying to exaggerate an occupational injury in order to gain compensation. All groups were able to significantly distort their BGT results under the malingering condition using both the Hain scoring and the Bruhn and Reed criteria. Several items from each scoring system also differentiated between malingering performance and that of the patients with psychiatric and brain-damage diagnoses under standard instructions.

However, a general criticism of the use of normal simulators in malingering research is that these pseudopatients are often undergraduates who are given little specific instruction on feigning abnormality and little or no financial motivation to do so (Nies & Sweet, 1994). As a consequence, they are inadequate stand-ins for the real thing. They are unlikely to be as motivated to lie nor as skilled or knowledgeable. For example, untrained simulators on the

BGT might make a variety of errors but are unlikely to show the specific types of errors that indicate brain damage on this test, such as rotation, retrogression, and impotence.

Two other researchers of simulation on the BGT have used more plausible simulators to investigate several signs of malingering originally proposed by Lauretta Bender (1938). The signs that are operationally defined by the two researchers are: small and inhibited drawings, inconsistent form quality (at least one drawing with Bender developmental level of 6 years or less and at least one of 9 years or more), figure rotation greater than 45 degrees, figure details that are accurately drawn but are misplaced in relation to one another, addition of complex or bizarre details, and gross simplification (developmental level of 6 years or less). Bash and Alpert (1980) compared diagnosed groups of nonpsychotic inpatients, hallucinating schizophrenics, nonhallucinating schizophrenics, and malingerers who feigned auditory hallucinations. The malingering group had scores on Bender's signs that were over three times as high as the other three groups.

Schretlen and Arkowitz (1990) used individuals who were likely to fake (i.e., prison inmates in a medium security prison), half of whom were told to respond as if they were mentally retarded and the other half who were instructed to fake insanity. Their responses were compared to those of three other groups (psychiatric inpatients, adult nonpatients with mental retardation, and prison inmate controls) who were given standard instructions. Prisoners in the faking condition were offered a $15 incentive if they could fake without being detected by a psychologist.

Three measures of malingering that varied in task demands were used: a specific screening test; the F and F − K scales of the MMPI; and the BGT, using five of Bender's six faking criteria (dropping 45-degree rotation because of intercorrelations with the other signs). Results showed that the BGT distinguished fakers from nonfakers with greater accuracy than the other two tests. On individual signs, fakers produced higher scores on inhibited figure size, inconsistent form quality, gross simplification, and distorted relationship, but not on complex additions. The battery of tests produced higher accuracy than any one test—85% of those who faked insanity with no false positives and 80% of those who faked retardation with 7.5% false positives.

Schretlen, Wilkins, Van Gorp, and Bobholz (1992) replicated this study comparing convicted felons faking insanity, prison controls, and psychiatric inpatients on the same three measures. The BGT alone correctly classified 50% of fakers ($M = 8.8, SD = 5.2$) and 98% of nonfakers ($M = 4.6, SD = 2.9$). A three-variable discriminant function based on the entire battery correctly identified 89% of fakers and 100% of the nonfakers. The optimal discriminant function used predictors from all three measures. Mean MMPI F raw scores were 34.0 ($SD = 8.5$) for the fakers and 12.8 ($SD = 7.3$) for the nonfakers. The F − K index was 23.8 versus −0.9, respectively ($SDs = 9.5$ versus 9.3) A second study cross-validated the discriminant function, using substance abusers asked to fake insanity compared with a sample of inpatient schizophrenics.

A Case of Malingering   A forensic psychologist was asked to review his test files of known malingerers using Bender's faking criteria. He found several that appeared to meet these standards but also many that did not. Figure 4.3 presents one of the BGT protocols that does illustrate Bender's guidelines. This 43-year-old African American man was charged with multiple bank robberies. His early history indicated

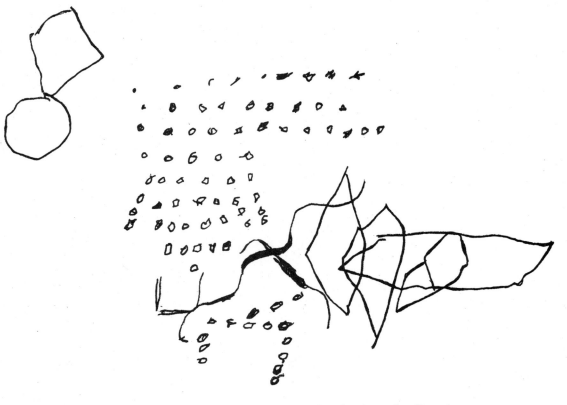

Bender Gestalt scoring		Bender signs of malingering	
Error	Figure	Sign	Figure
Rotation	A, 3	Inhibited size	None
Overlapping Difficulty	6	Rotation >45 degrees	A, 3, 6
Fragmentation	2	Misplaced details	None
Perseveration, Type A	3, 5	Bizarre additions	8
Collision	4, 6, 7, 8	Gross simplification	1, 2, 5, 6, 7
Closure Difficulty	A, 4, 7, 8	Inconsistent form quality	A, 4
Score: 6 errors		Weighted score for 6 signs:	11
		Weighted score for 5 signs:	8

Figure 4.3 A case of malingering.

a conduct-disordered youth, numerous periods of prior incarceration, and long-standing polysubstance dependence with a self-reported history of blackouts. In custody, he showed atypical psychosislike symptoms. Although he had 10 years of education, this man professed to be unable to read or write, a claim that proved false. Psychological assessment was done to evaluate his competency to stand trial.

Test results showed that his WAIS-R IQ was in the mildly retarded range with no differences between verbal and performance scores and minimal variability among subtests. On the MMPI, he had significant elevations on all clinical scales. Also, his F raw score was 45, K raw score was 5, and F − K index was 40. Millon Clinical Multiaxial Inventory (MCMI II) Modifying Indexes were: X (Disclosure Level) = BR 100; Y (Desirability) = BR 43; and Z (Debasement) = BR −1.

Figure 4.3 includes the scoring for both the standard BGT errors and for Bender's malingering criteria. This man made six errors on the BGT, placing him in the brain-impaired range. There may also be evidence of an additional error of motor incoordination (the test-taking behavior was not available for this man though it is generally necessary to score this error). The BGT also meets the informal criterion of looking odd, especially in the way designs 6, 7, and 8 are drawn. Of the faking signs, he did show three rotations of greater than 45 degrees, one added complex or bizarre detail on figure 8, and gross simplification of five figures. In addition, the form quality on figures A and 4 is inconsistently much higher than for the other figures. There were no examples of inhibited size or distorted relationships within figures. When these indicators were weighted for number of occurrences and summed, the total faking score was 11 for all six signs and 8 when rotations were excluded. Both his BGT and MMPI faking indexes were within the range previously found for prison fakers (Schretlen et al., 1992).

Recent Research on Detection of Feigned Cognitive Deficits

More recent research has focused on the development of more effective and proven detection methods. Symptom validity testing, or *forced-choice testing,* is recommended by Rogers (1997a) as the best-validated detection strategy for feigned cognitive deficits (see also Lezak, 1995; Nies & Sweet, 1994). This type of test consists of assessment of a claimed disability by a large number of items in a multiple-choice format. Scores below a chance level of 50% suggest that the patient is deliberately performing below true ability. Application of the forced-choice method to claimed memory problems is seen in two measures: the Digit Memory Test (Hiscock & Hiscock, 1989), and the Portland Digit Recognition Test (Binder, 1993). Another type of measure designed to detect feigned memory problems is Rey's 15-Item Memory Test (described in Lezak, 1995). It is a task that appears difficult but is actually easy to perform even by patients with brain damage or retardation. Schretlen and Arkowitz (1990) developed a Malingering Scale that resembles an IQ test. Reviews of the research on the success of these techniques can be found in Lezak (1995), Nies and Sweet (1994) and Pankratz and Binder (1997).

The literature on detection of faked mental illness and brain damage does not engender high confidence for the practitioner trying to make sense of a battery of psychological tests. Many of the studies used small samples and often inappropriate types of participants. Little has been done that applies to neuropsychological assessment in general nor to the BGT in particular. Bender's (1938) suggested signs of malingering look promising but require more investigation. It does appear that clinicians can improve detection success when they suspect that malingering is a possibility with a particular client or patient. It also appears that multiple measures result in greater success than single tests. Use of specific screening devices to detect faking may also have promise. Psychologists may be doing a better job of detecting malingerers than it appears from the results of research using artificial conditions. Garb and Schramke (1996) call for more research on how well psychologists can identify faking when they receive all the information usually available to them in clinical practice. How much greater accuracy of detection could they then achieve if they made use of the various empirically derived malingering measures?

Possible Actions for Suspected Faking

Sometimes a psychologist has a reason to suspect malingering, such as with a person who has a history of malingering or factitious disorders or a situation where the person may achieve some benefit from a diagnosis of mental illness or brain damage. In this case, there are a number of possible actions to take. Franzen et al. (1990) employ multiple tests in their evaluation battery (with varying response demands), including at least one screening procedure designed to measure deception. Feigning pathology or cognitive deficits on multiple tests will be more difficult than on a few or only one measure. They also suggest that the clinician look thoroughly at the records of the patient or client and interview others who know him or her.

With the BGT, Hutt (1985) recommends that the examiner not reveal any suspicions of simulation. Then, after a few days, the examiner should readminister the copy phase of the BGT. If the original attempt was faked, the person may not be able to recall the previous errors and may either make no errors this time or make different errors. Or the cards may be readministered a second time in the inverse position, again interfering with any memory of previously faked responses. Groth-Marnat (in press) recommends taking a more careful than usual history, obtaining observations on the ward, including personality testing, and paying special attention to symptoms that are inconsistent with neuroanatomical reality.

Some good news is that in studies where psychologists were forewarned of the possibility of malingering of cognitive deficits, they were very accurate in separating malingerers from those with genuine brain injury (e.g., Trueblood & Binder, 1997). After an extensive review of the malingering-detection research, Nies and Sweet (1994) concluded that "malingering of brain dysfunction is not easy to detect, but is *possible* to detect, if looked for deliberately and with forethought. However, given the present state of the art, some malingerers may go undetected despite our best efforts" (p. 540).

VARIATIONS IN ADMINISTRATION

Since the introduction of the BGT in 1938, a number of alterations in the standard procedure have been devised; all show promise of increased testing efficiency or better success in difficult diagnostic decisions. These include group administration, recall condition, tachistoscopic presentation, and the Canter Background Interference Procedure. Because group testing has been used primarily with school children, it is discussed in Chapter 11. However, this method could just as well be adapted for adults.

Recall Method

One BGT variant is the recall phase (Reznikoff & Olin, 1957) for which individuals are asked to reproduce as many of the original designs as they can remember after they have completed the standard copy phase. The score used for this method is generally the number of figures correctly recalled, although sometimes the quality of the designs drawn from memory is also assessed. Apparently, few psychologists use the BGT Recall procedure.

The recall method was developed primarily to increase sensitivity to the effects of brain impairment, especially when trying to differentiate this deficit from that due to schizophrenia. Holland and Wadsworth (1979) found that recall scores differentiated between two groups of male VA inpatients, 20 with brain damage and 20 with schizophrenia, when standard copy scores did not. However, no diagnostic accuracy scores were reported. Armstrong (1965) compared the copy and recall scores of 80 psychiatric inpatients divided into five diagnostic groups. Her results showed that the patients with brain damage copied the designs more poorly, recalled fewer designs, and made more errors in their recalled designs than patients in each of the four other diagnostic groups, including schizophrenia. Those with a diagnosed cognitive disorder recalled an average of 3.85 BGT figures and those in the other four psychiatric groups recalled, on the average, 5.57 to 6.09 figures. The patients with brain damage showed a great deal of variability in copying but were consistently poor in recalling. Using an optimal cutting score, there was little overlap on recall quality scores between the group with brain impairment and the other four patient groups, yielding about 80% accuracy for the correct diagnosis of impaired brain function.

Armstrong (1965) also reported data on frequency and accuracy of recall for each of the nine individual designs. Figure 8 was recalled by the most patients (85%), and figure 4 was recalled by the fewest (31%). Figure 8 was also recalled with the least number of errors (13%), versus figure 4 with the most errors (29%). Rogers and Swenson (1975), using psychiatric patients, found recall scores to correlate .74 with the Wechsler Memory Scale but only .40 with a Freedom from Distractibility Scale. Their results led them to conclude that BGT recall is a good measure of memory function and is not just tapping deficit from distractibility.

Figure 4.4 shows the recall portion of the BGT for a 45 year-old male with a tenth-grade education. He sustained a severe, diffuse head injury in a car accident 3 years before this testing. He was only able to recall three of the designs and made errors in each of them. The copy phase of his BGT is presented as Case H (Figure 13.9) in the selected clinical cases of Chapter 13.

Other studies report success in differentiating groups of adult patients with brain injury from nonimpaired groups. However, with the exception of Armstrong (1965), they do not indicate the diagnostic efficacy of such a practice (although it has been well documented for the standard copy format). Also, it is not clear how accurate the drawing must be for it to be considered correctly recalled or how long an interval should pass after the copy phase before recall is requested. Until these important matters are dealt with, clinicians cannot use the recall method with much confidence. However, the research does suggest potential usefulness warranting further study.

Tachistoscopic Presentation Another variation in administration of the BGT is to present the stimuli one at a time for a limited exposure, usually a 5-second interval, and then require the person to draw the figure from memory rather than copy it. Hutt (1985) suggests the following instructions:

> I'm going to show you some cards, one at a time, that have some designs on them. I shall let you look at the card for only a few seconds. Then I'll

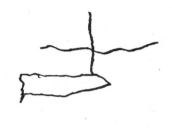

Figure 4.4   Bender Gestalt Recall.

take the card away and ask you to draw the design from memory. Do you
understand? Remember, I'll show you the card for only a few seconds.
Study it carefully so that you can draw it from memory when I take the
card away (p. 56).

Sometimes the examiner needs to caution the person not to start drawing until
the card is removed. The copy method and even the recall method may be
added after the tachistoscopic presentation.

With psychiatric patients and nonpatient adults in South Africa, McCann and
Plunkett (1984) administered the BGT using four different variations: standard,
tachistoscopic, nonpreferred hand, and redrawing to eliminate errors. Using
ideal cutting scores, they found that their three diagnostic groups (brain
impaired, schizophrenic, and nonpatient) differed from each other on all four
formats. However, no method had a clear predictive advantage.

Clearly, there is not enough evidence on the usefulness of the tachistoscopic
presentation of the BGT for clinicians to rely on it in their diagnostic work. At
this point, more research on this variation is also called for.

Background Interference
Procedure
Perhaps the most promising of the BGT variants and, certainly, the one that
has attracted the most attention is Canter's (1966) Background Interference
Procedure (BIP). This method uses an individual's own performance on the
standard administration as a baseline for comparison with a second performance drawn on paper previously marked with wavy lines. Both the copy and
BIP phases are scored with a modified Pascal-Suttell (1951) method. The BIP
is a procedure developed in part to reduce diagnostic inaccuracy caused by
psychiatric patients' defective performance on the BGT. Canter (1971) found
that 94% of a group of patients with brain damage did *worse* on the BIP phase

compared to 24% of the long-term hospitalized ($M = 12.1$ years) patients with schizophrenia, 13% of the short-term hospitalized ($M = 1.5$ years) patients with schizophrenia, and 13% of the patients with neither schizophrenia nor brain damage. In terms of *improved* BIP performance, 53% of short-term hospitalized schizophrenics, 29% of long-term hospitalized schizophrenics, and 38% of patients without schizophrenia did better on the BIP phase. No patient with brain injury showed improved performance on the BIP. The additional demands of the BIP appear to disrupt the cognitive integration of patients with brain dysfunction.

This variation has received a good deal of research attention, and normative data and reliability figures have been published. Summarizing the literature (94 studies) on neuropsychological tests with psychiatric patients, Heaton et al. (1978) compared the diagnostic hit rates for cognitive disorders of the five most used tests. For eight classification attempts of patients with deficits in cognitive functioning compared to those with other than process or chronic schizophrenia, the BGT standard copy administration had a median diagnostic accuracy of 76% (range = 62% to 86%). The BIP had a median hit rate of 84% in 11 studies (range = 52% to 95%). Based on these studies with their multiple experimental differences and deficiencies, Heaton et al. concluded that there was no strong and consistent evidence to use the BIP instead of the standard copy phase as a screening test. They believe that the BIP modification may be somewhat more effective than the standard procedure, but this conclusion awaits the results of research that makes such a direct comparison. Not only should such research as the direct comparison of the standard BGT and the BIP be done, but also it would seem worthwhile to try the BIP using scoring methods other than the Pascal-Suttell system.

Boake and Adams (1982) are critical of the research methodology of earlier BIP validity studies that generally did not control for group differences on such variables as age and IQ. They claim that high hit rates for the BIP have not emerged consistently in studies that controlled for these variables, making hit-rate summaries such as that of Heaton et al. (1978) suspect. In their study, Boake and Adams found only a 61% overall hit rate for the BIP.

Although the Canter BIP has generated a good deal of research, it does not seem to be widely used clinically. This may be due to inconsistent research findings or increased time demands from having to administer the test twice and use the time-consuming Pascal-Suttell scoring method.

In summary, although the BGT appears very simple, examiners must still exercise caution in following the standardized administration procedures meticulously. Behavioral observations are particularly important in the implementation of a scoring system and in the final diagnosis. Psychologists who utilize psychometricians to administer the BGT but who evaluate the results themselves should emphasize to the examiner the importance of these observations. Recently, because of a large increase in forensic cases, neuropsychologists have begun to stress the need to be alert for feigned cognitive deficits. A number of signs of malingering have been proposed for the BGT.

A number of variants of BGT administration were also presented in this chapter. Although group administration has a sound research basis, the recall and tachistoscopic methods do not at this time. The usefulness of the BIP seems more controversial. Although early research with this modification reported very promising diagnostic hit rates, more recent and more controlled studies have produced less consistent success.

CHAPTER 5

Description of the Scoring System

The scoring system advocated in this book originated with a list of 12 "essential discriminators of intracranial damage" first described in the work of Hutt and Briskin in 1960. The authors stated that this diagnostic configuration was validated through their years of clinical experience, by experiments where they attempted blind diagnosis, and by a number of unpublished experimental studies. They recommended that this type of configurational analysis be augmented with a more thorough inferential analysis by the testing of a logical series of hypotheses about the client.

Hutt and Briskin's (1960) original list of 12 *essential discriminators* or errors for the Bender Gestalt Test (BGT) is reproduced in Table 5.1. These 12 errors are subsumed under five factors. The five factors and the errors that were included are: (1) Organization, which included the error of Collision; (2) Size (Cohesion); (3) Changes in Form of the Gestalt (Closure Difficulty and Angulation Difficulty); (4) Distortion of the Gestalt (Rotation, Retrogression, Simplification, Fragmentation, Overlapping Difficulty, and Perseveration); and (5) a Movement and Drawing factor (Motor Incoordination). The error called Impotence is not included in the five factors.

Table 5.1 Hutt and Briskin's 12 Essential Discriminators of Brain Dysfunction

1. Rotation: severe
2. Overlapping Difficulty
3. Simplification
4. Fragmentation
5. Retrogression
6. Perseveration
7. Collision or Collision Tendency
8. Impotence
9. Closure Difficulty
10. Motor Incoordination
11. Angulation Difficulty
12. Cohesion

Source: Hutt and Briskin (1960).

In this same book, Hutt and Briskin briefly describe each of the errors, as follows:

1. Rotation: severe.   This error is scored when there is a change in the orientation of the major axis of the design of from 80 to 180 degrees. Rotation is not to be confused with turning of the stimulus card or of the drawing paper. Examples of Rotation can be seen on designs 3 and 4 of Figure 5.1.* Design 2 of Figure 5.2 illustrates a mirror image, another form of Rotation.

2. Overlapping Difficulty.   This error consists of difficulty in drawing those parts of figures that overlap (only designs 6 and 7). Such difficulty can take the form of failing to draw those portions of the figure that are supposed to overlap, simplifying the drawing of either figure at the point where they overlap, sketching or redrawing the overlapping portions of the figures, or distorting the figures where they overlap. See Figures 5.1 (design 6) and 5.2 (design 7) for examples.

3. Simplification.   Part or all of the design is replaced with a different and more simplified form that is not more primitive in terms of maturation. If it were more maturationally primitive, it would be Retrogression. Examples are figure 7 drawn as two nonoverlapping hexagons and figure A drawn as an adjacent rather than touching circle and square (see designs A, 6, and 7 of Figure 5.3). Designs 5 and 6 of Figure 5.2 shows another form of a very simplified drawing.

4. Fragmentation.   This error refers to destruction of the gestalt of a figure by reproducing it incompletely or by breaking it up in such a way as to destroy the gestalt. Extreme examples of this error can be seen in Figures 5.1 (design 8), and 5.3 (designs 2, 3, and 5).

5. Retrogression.   This error requires an individual to substitute a maturationally more primitive figure for the design on the stimulus card (e.g., loops for circles, persistent dashes for dots, a triangle for a diamond or hexagon). There must be evidence that the person is capable of drawing the more mature forms. Figures 5.1 (design A), 5.2 (design 7), and 5.3 (designs 7 and 8) are all examples of Retrogression.

6. Perseveration.   *Type A* consists of the persistent and inappropriate substitution of the elements of a previous figure such as continuing to use the dots of design 1 in design 2 or the circles of design 2 in designs 3 or 5 (see the latter on design 3 of Figure 5.4).

Type B refers to the inappropriate continuation of the elements of a figure beyond the limits called for by that stimulus. In design 1 (see Figure 5.4), this would mean drawing 14 or more dots (instead of 12), and in design 2 (see Figures 5.1 and 5.3), drawing 13 or more rows of circles (instead of 11). A less common example is to draw an additional row of circles on design 2 or dots on design 3 (see Figure 5.5). The person continues to draw the stimulus sometimes

---

* Complete scoring for the case illustrations in this chapter can be found in the appendix. Design numbers for the BGT can be seen in Figure 4.1, on page 42.

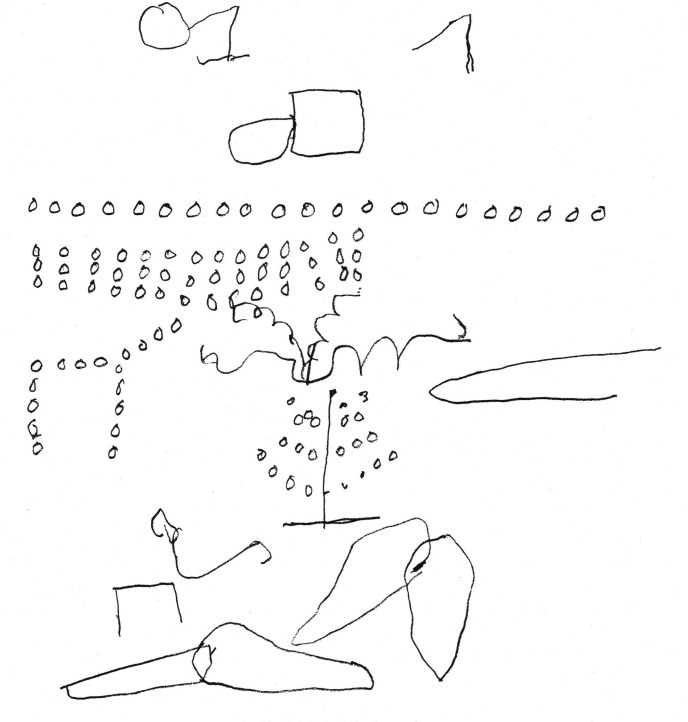

Figure 5.1 Vascular Dementia.

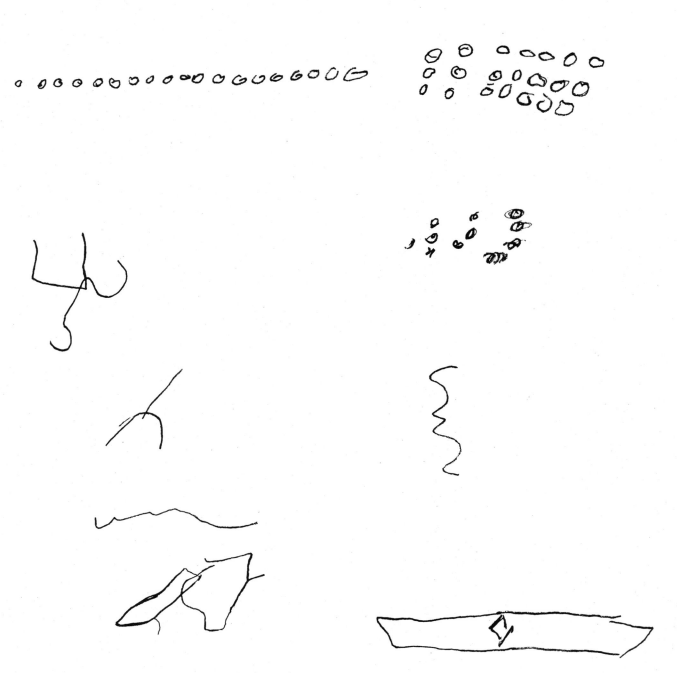

Figure 5.2 Inpatient adolescent with "positive evidence of neurological impairment."

Figure 5.3 Delirium associated with toxic metabolic disturbance.

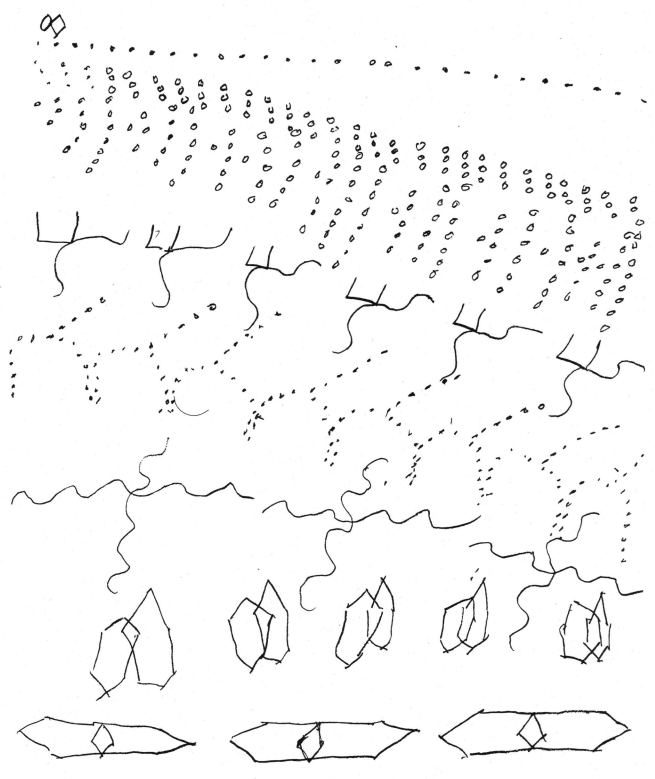

Figure 5.4 Nonhospitalized older adult.

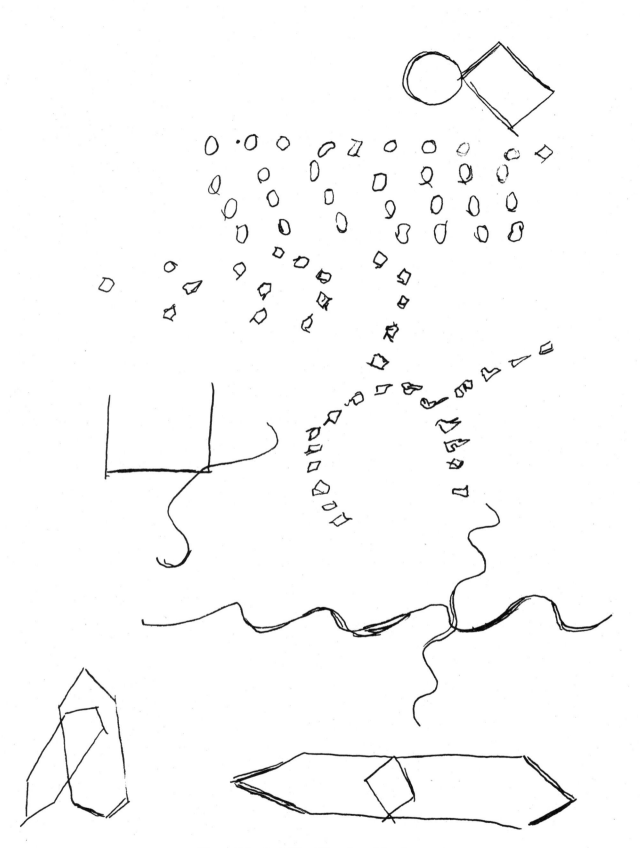

Figure 5.5 Cognitive Disorder with seizures.

until he or she reaches the edge of the page (and, in one instance the author observed, continuing right on across the top of a white table with no apparent awareness). In rare instances, this may even include the repeated drawing of a whole figure, but usually it is confined to reproducing elements within figures 1 and 2. Figure 5.4 is an extreme example drawn by a nonhospitalized older adult.

7. Collision or Collision Tendency.   The error of Collision occurs when figures are drawn so close that they actually overlap or collide. Examples are designs 3 and 6 of Figure 5.1 and designs 2 and 3 of Figure 5.4. Collision Tendency is when a figure is drawn too close to another figure (within ¼ inch). See designs 1 and 2, 2 and 3, and 3 and 4 in Figure 5.5.

8. Impotence.   A person draws a figure incorrectly, seems to recognize this fact, but is unable to correct the error or makes repeated but unsuccessful attempts to improve the reproduction. These attempts usually take the form of successive incorrect drawings of the figure, many erasures with repetitions of the errors (see A and 8 in Figure 5.1), or expressions of frustration and inability to correct the errors.

9. Closure Difficulty.   This error is scored when the person shows repeated difficulty in getting parts of figures to join that should join, for instance, closing circles and hexagons, or joining the circle and square of design A (see Figure 5.2, designs 4 and 8; Figure 5.5, designs A and 8). The difficulty may manifest itself in gaps, erasures, increased pressure, and overworking the lines at the points where figures join.

10. Motor Incoordination.   Lines of figures are irregular rather than smooth-flowing, indicating tremulousness. Examples of Motor Incoordination will be seen on a number of protocols later in the book.

11. Angulation Difficulty.   Difficulty in producing the angles of the figures is shown through either increasing or decreasing the required angulation or showing variability of angulation (see design 2 in Figure 5.1).

12. Cohesion.   This term refers to an isolated increase or decrease in the size of a figure in relation to the other figures in the protocol (e.g., design A versus 1 in Figure 5.3 or design A in relation to many of the others in Figure 5.4). The increase or decrease in size may also be to only part of a figure in relation to the other parts of the same figure. Examples of the latter are the two hexagons of design 7 on Figure 5.2 and the relatively smaller circle versus the diamond of design A on Figures 5.3 and 5.5. The size must be decreased by more than one third of the dimensions used in the rest of the figure or by more than one third of the dimensions of some other figure in the protocol.

As the reader can see, the description given by Hutt and Briskin (1960) for each of the 12 errors is very brief; each includes only one or two examples to aid in scoring. The major part of their book consists of the clinical significance of personality interpretations of each test factor. For example, Closure Difficulty is described as "correlated specifically with fearfulness in interpersonal relationships" or "an inability to maintain constant cathexes with appropriate objects in the environment" (p. 59).

Although this approach may be helpful in understanding the personality dynamics of the client, it does not serve as a major aid to the clinician in his or her most frequent use of the BGT—as a screening instrument for brain dysfunction or as a separate measure of visuoconstructive ability. For the latter uses of the test, a *psychometric* rather than a projective stance is necessary—an objective scoring system to assess brain impairment or disruption of visuoconstructive function.

In 1961, there was a need in BGT research for a brief, objective scoring method for the BGT. The method most frequently used in research at the time, developed by Pascal and Suttell (1951), is cumbersome to use and is not applicable to many patients, such as those over age 50 (see Chapter 3). Hutt and Briskin's (1960) 12 essential discriminators seemed promising. However, their list and very brief definitions were not adequate to score protocols consistently. Lacks developed an informal scoring manual to clarify the 12 errors. This manual was used effectively in several subsequent experiments (Brilliant & Gynther, 1963; Johnson, et al., 1971; Lacks et al., 1970; Lacks & Newport, 1980; Lacks & Storandt, 1982). This Lacks adaptation of the Hutt-Briskin system proved to have consistently high interscorer reliability and diagnostic accuracy (see Chapters 7 and 8).

In his later work, Hutt (1985) provided more illustrations of these errors, but he continued to revise his list of signs while publishing diagnostic accuracies for the new groupings. Furthermore, Hutt continued to place most of his emphasis on the projective use of the BGT rather than on its psychometric utility.

Therefore, because research has consistently supported the utility of Hutt and Briskin's original 12 signs, because attempts at revision have served only to lower diagnostic accuracy, and because Hutt has deemphasized the objective scoring of the BGT for brain impairment, it was deemed desirable to publish a detailed scoring manual of the 12 original signs suggested by Hutt and Briskin. The author published this manual and supporting data in the first edition of this book in 1984. Chapter 6 in this revised edition presents this detailed scoring manual or the Lacks adaptation of Hutt and Briskin's scoring system. Many examples are provided to make it clear when to score an error as well as when not to score an error. Chapter 13 presents scored examples of 12 clinical cases with a detailed discussion of the scoring. The reader is also provided with ten practice scoring cases that are followed by a detailed explanation of the correct scoring. The aim of these two chapters is to enable the reader to become rapidly proficient in the use of this objective scoring method for the BGT. In addition, Chapter 7 presents in more detail the results of research confirming the validity of this approach so that the clinician may have confidence in it. The first edition of this book stressed heavily the acquisition of proficiency in scoring the BGT. It continues to be a primary mission of this new edition. However, this book also includes new material on the *interpretation* of the test results, including computer-assisted report writing (see Chapter 9). Furthermore, the reader will also find new material on the use of the BGT with older adults (Chapter 10), children (Chapter 11), and adolescents (Chapter 12).

CHAPTER 6

Detailed Scoring Instructions and Examples

The 12 signs of brain impairment described in the following pages are Hutt and Briskin's "essential discriminators of intracranial damage" (1960). Descriptions have been expanded and multiple examples provided to aid the clinician to make decisions about which errors to score. In general, the presence of any 5 of these errors is taken to indicate organic brain impairment.

However, all of these errors can also be made by individuals who do not put forth their best efforts because of such factors as lack of interest in the task, hostility toward the examiner, impulsivity, or carelessness. At all times, the examiner must try to determine whether the final score is due to factors such as these or to true perceptual-motor difficulties. The behavioral observations section in Chapter 4 and the sample Scoring Summary Sheet in Figure 6.1 can help you make this judgment. Other factors that may produce distortions that are not true errors are a rough drawing surface or improperly presented stimulus card, a debilitating physical handicap, or an inadequate drawing instrument.

Furthermore, at times an individual with brain dysfunction may, through extraordinary effort, make fewer than 5 errors but take considerable time to draw the figures. The average time for psychiatric patients without cortical damage to complete the Bender Gestalt is 6 minutes. Some may wish to count it as an unofficial extra error if the client takes more than 15 minutes to complete the task (see Chapter 4).

There are numerous types of errors or distortions possible in drawing these figures. Beginning scorers often want to account for every distortion of the original stimulus figures. However, with this scoring system you should focus *only* on the 12 specific distortions described here. All others are irrelevant to this scoring system. For example, bizarre or symbolic behavior, such as drawing stars or figure eights for circles, is usually indicative of psychosis rather than a cognitive disorder.

Finally, in this system, errors should be scored rather conservatively or only when clear-cut deviations are observed. Frequently, an error must be *severe* or *persistent* if it is to be scored. If in doubt, it is best *not* to score an error. Beginning scorers always err in the direction of *overscoring*. This overly stringent practice lowers diagnostic accuracy considerably. Also note that some of the errors can occur only on certain figures (e.g., Angulation Difficulty only on figures 2 and 3) but others may occur on any figure (e.g., Rotation). Consult Chapter 13 for further examples and practice exercises.

The most efficient way to proceed is to utilize a sign-by-sign approach. For example, take the first sign, which is Rotation, and examine the entire protocol for any instances of rotation of 80 to 180 degrees. Then move on to the second sign and examine the whole protocol for its presence and so on.

Be careful not to put the individual in double jeopardy by scoring the same distortion as two different errors. Any figure may contain more than one distortion (e.g., the figure may be rotated and also demonstrate poor motor coordination), but each *distortion* may only be scored as 1 error. For example, on figure 2, a person may draw all the columns of circles tilted to the right, instead of to the left as presented on the stimulus figure. This reversal of angulation is an example of mirror imaging, a type of Rotation error. If you scored both Rotation and Angulation Difficulty errors, you would have penalized the person twice for the same mistake. But if the person also drew 13 or more of these columns of circles, you can also score Perseveration, Type B, because it is a second type of distortion of the figure. In the former example, two separate errors were not committed; in the latter example, two *different* errors are evident. Remember, you are looking for the presence or absence of each of 12 signs. If the sign appears once or five times, it is still scored as only 1 error. The maximum number of errors is 12 (or 13 if you choose to add a time penalty).

Figure 6.2 shows the BGT protocol of a psychotic inpatient in an acute psychiatric treatment center. It is an error-free protocol, using this scoring system, and as such it may serve as a model against which to compare the scoring criteria in this chapter and the practice scoring examples in Chapter 13.

Bender Gestalt Test Scoring Summary

Name _____ Age _____ Education_____

Gender_____ Ethnicity_____ Date of Testing _____

General Test-Taking Attitudes

Takes test in serious manner . . . . Takes test lightly

Cooperative, compliant . . . . Uncooperative, resistant

Methodical, deliberate . . . . Careless

Persistent in difficult situations . . . . Gives up easily

Attentive, concentrating . . . . Distracted

Motivated to do well . . . . Unmotivated

Calm, relaxed . . . . Anxious, agitated

Good rapport with examiner . . . . Poor rapport

Specific Behavioral Observations

____Evidence of fatigue

____Insufficient attention to test designs

____Drawing difficulty due to physical disability

Trouble understanding instructions due to:
____Low IQ   ____Language difficulty   ____Hearing

____Difficulty seeing figures

____Considerable care and deliberation

____Expression of dissatisfaction with poorly executed drawings on figures_____

____Repeated unsuccessful attempts to correct errors on figures_____

____Rotation of drawing on figures_____

____Motor incoordination or hand tremor: ____Mild   ____Moderate   ____Severe

____Other behaviors_____

Minutes to complete test:_____

Figure 6.1 Bender Gestalt Test Scoring Summary. (Developed by Patricia Lacks; adapted and reproduced by special permission of the publisher, Psychological Assessment Resources, Inc., Odessa, FL 33556, from the *Bender Gestalt screening software for Windows* (*V. 1*), Copyright © 1996.)

Scoring Checklist

____ 1. Rotation   ____ 7. Collision or Collision Tendency

____ 2. Overlapping Difficulty   ____ 8. Impotence

____ 3. Simplification   ____ 9. Closure Difficulty

____ 4. Fragmentation   ____ 10. Motor Incoordination

____ 5. Retrogression   ____ 11. Angulation Difficulty

____ 6. Perseveration   ____ 12. Cohesion

____Time to complete greater than 15 minutes

Total score_____Test diagnosis_____

Comments

Figure 6.1 (Continued)

70

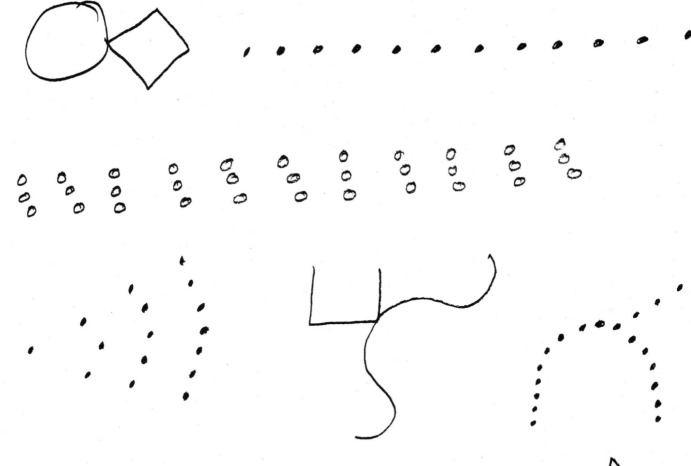

Figure 6.2 Model of error-free Bender Gestalt Test protocol.

1. ROTATION   *Definition.*   Score if there is a rotation of 80 to 180 degrees (including mirror-imaging) of the major axis of the whole figure (not a part of the figure). Do not score if the individual shifts the position of the card or the paper and then draws the figure accurately.

Figures. Score for all figures.

90-degree rotations

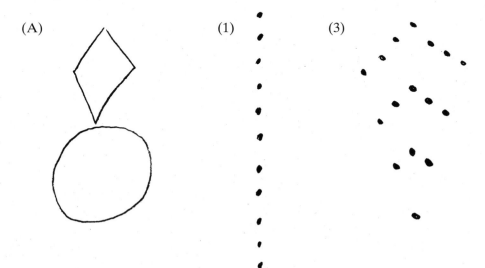

180-degree rotations

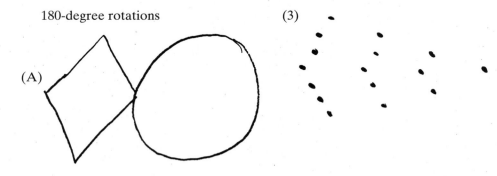

mirror-imaging

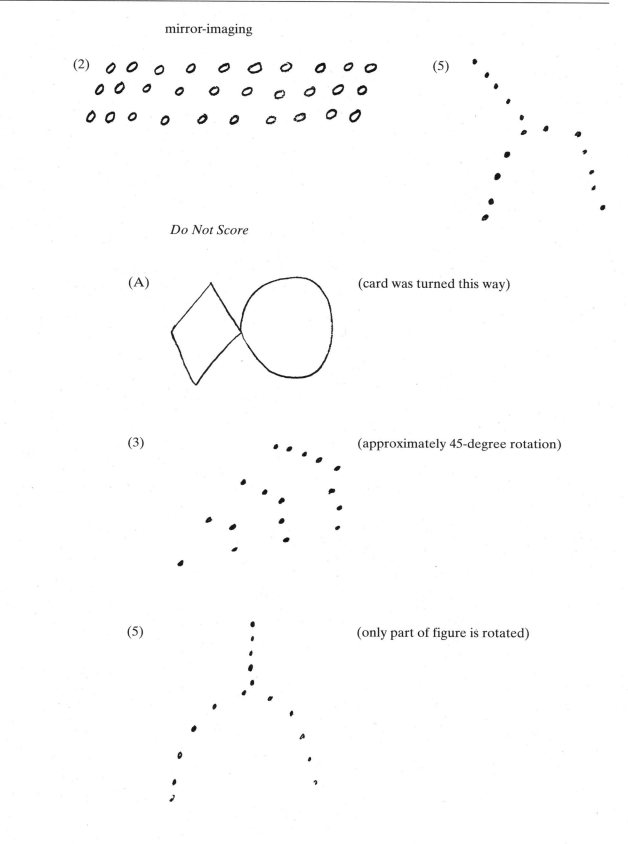

(2)

(5)

Do Not Score

(A)   (card was turned this way)

(3)   (approximately 45-degree rotation)

(5)   (only part of figure is rotated)

2. OVERLAPPING DIFFICULTY

Definition. Difficulty in reproducing the portions of the figures that should overlap.

Figures. Score only for figures 6 and 7.

(7) 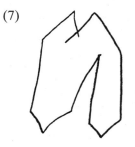   Omission of the portions of the figure that overlap

(7) 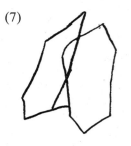   Simplification of figures only at the point of overlap

Marked sketching or reworking only at the point of overlap

(6)    (7)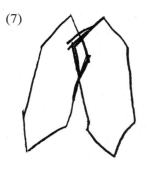

Distortion of the figure at the point of overlap

(7) 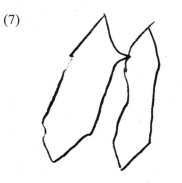   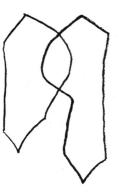

Figures overlap at the wrong place

(6)

(7)

Failure of figures to overlap

(6)

(7)

Do Not Score

(6)

(7)

(parts of figures
more than ⅛ inch
apart, score
Simplification)

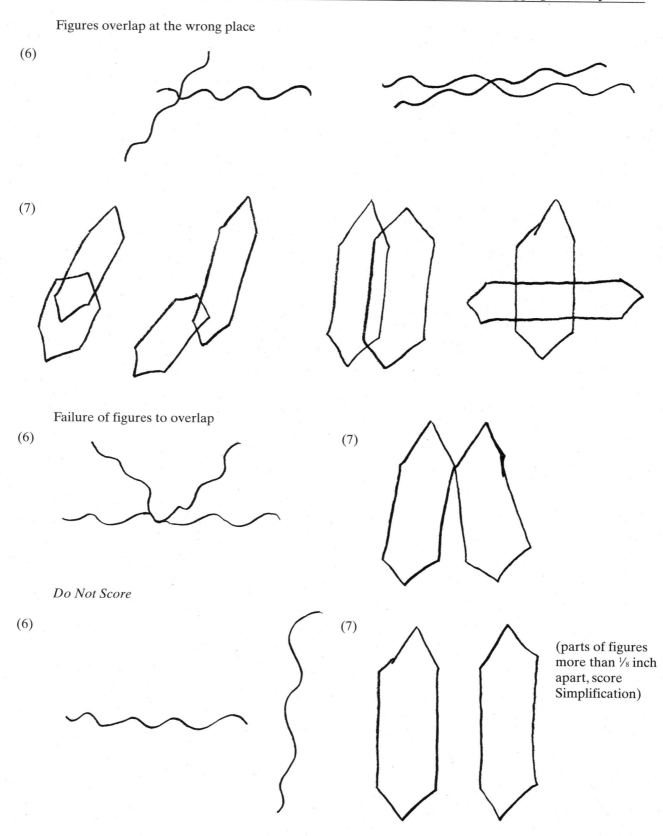

3. SIMPLIFICATION   ***Definition.*** Score if the figure is drawn in a simplified or easier form that is not more primitive, from a maturational point of view, from the stimulus. If a more primitive form is drawn, score Retrogression.

Figures. Score for all figures.

Circles for dots on figure 1

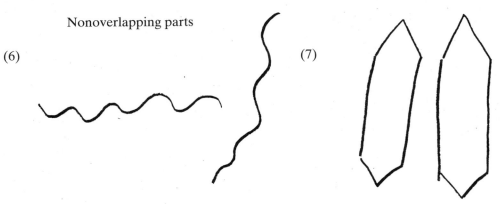

Nonoverlapping parts

(6)   (7)

Joining parts of figures are more than ⅛ inch apart

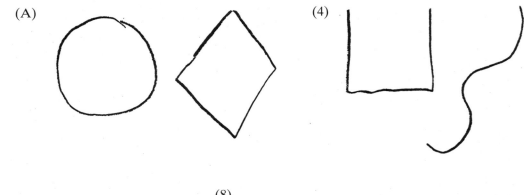

(A)   (4)

(5)   (8)

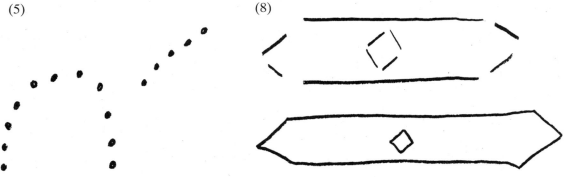

Very simplified drawing

(A)   (3)   (4)

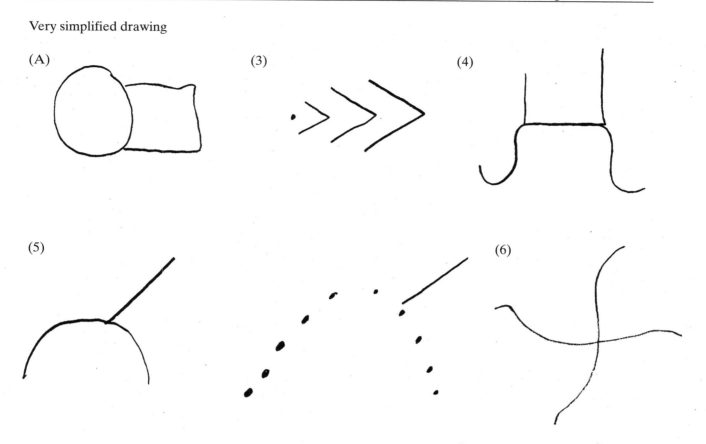

(5)   (6)

Do Not Score

(A)   (figures are less than ⅛ inch
                                         apart, score Closure Difficulty)

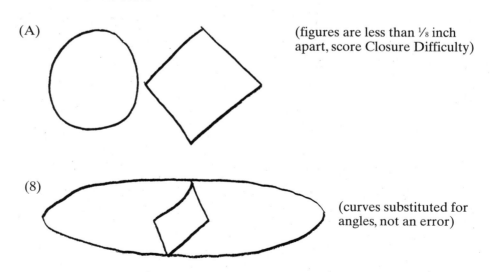

(8)   (curves substituted for
                                         angles, not an error)

4. FRAGMENTATION   *Definition.*   Score if the figure is broken up into parts destroying the gestalt or if the figure is incomplete (unless the individual refuses to draw the entire figure).

Figures. Score for all figures.

Figure broken into parts resulting in destruction of the gestalt

(1)   • • • • • • • •• •
         • • • • •

(2)

(one long row of 33 circles)

(2)   ○ ○ ○ ○ ○ ○ ○ ○ ○ ○

(2) 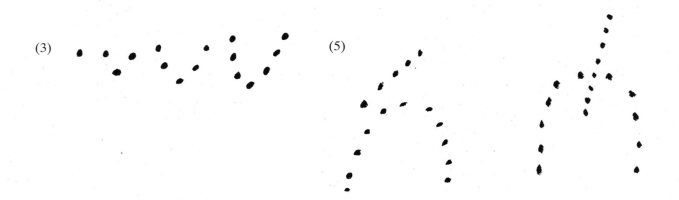   (random drawing of 33 circles with no recognition of the stimulus pattern)

(3)   (5)

(8)

Incomplete figure

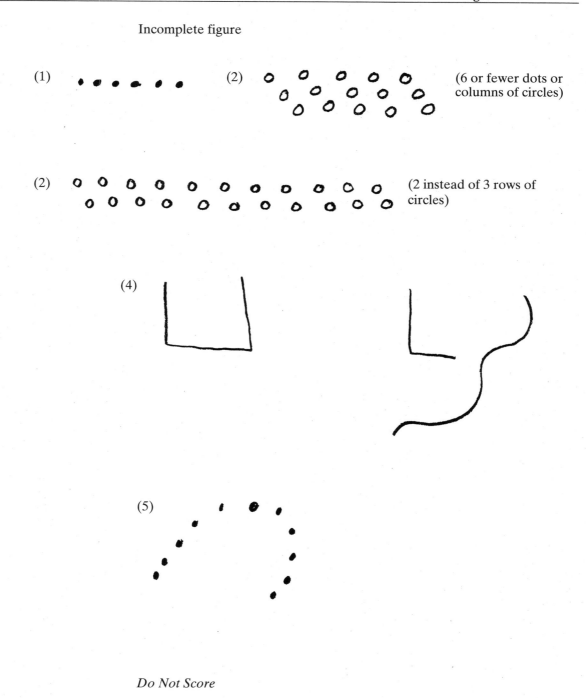

(1) . . . . . .   (2) (6 or fewer dots or columns of circles)

(2) (2 instead of 3 rows of circles)

(4)

(5)

Do Not Score

(2) (statement was made that the individual did not want to draw the other circles)

5.   RETROGRESSION   *Definition.*   Substitution of a more primitive gestalt form than the stimulus.

Figures. Score for all figures except 4 and 6.

Loops for circles (if persistent)

(2)

Dashes for dots (if extreme and persistent)

(1)   (5)

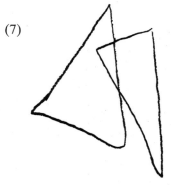

Triangle for diamond or hexagon

(A)   (7)

Square for diamond

(A)   (8)

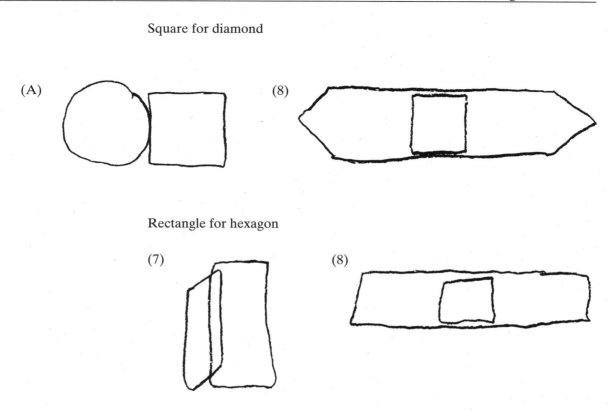

Rectangle for hexagon

(7)   (8)

Do Not Score

Do not score if curves are substituted for angles or if angulation of bottom of hexagon on figure 7 is omitted.

(7)   (8)   (7)

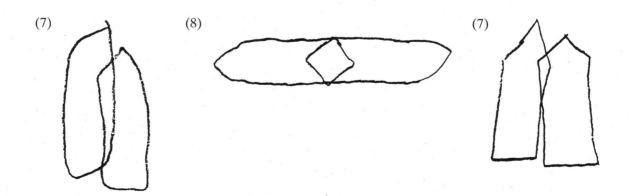

6.   PERSEVERATION   There are two kinds of Perseveration errors. If both occur, this error is still only scored once.

Type A   *Definition.*   Inappropriate substitution of the features of a preceding stimulus, such as replacing the circles of figure 2 with the dots of figure 1 (must have made dots, not circles on figure 1); replacing the dots of figures 3 and 5 with the circles of figure 2 (must have made circles on figure 2 and dots on 1).

Figures. Score only for figures 2, 3, and 5.

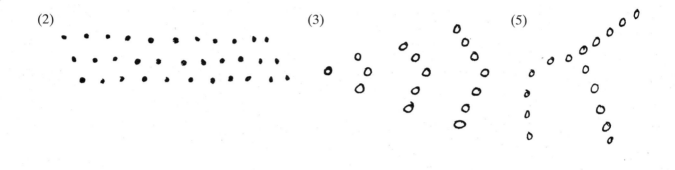

Type B   *Definition.*   Intradesign perseveration or continuing to draw a figure beyond the limits called for by the stimulus. For figure 1, 14 or more dots must be present; for figure 2, 13 or more columns of circles; for figure 3, 5 or more lines of dots (instead of the 4 lines on the stimulus figure).

Figures. Score only for figures 1, 2, and 3.

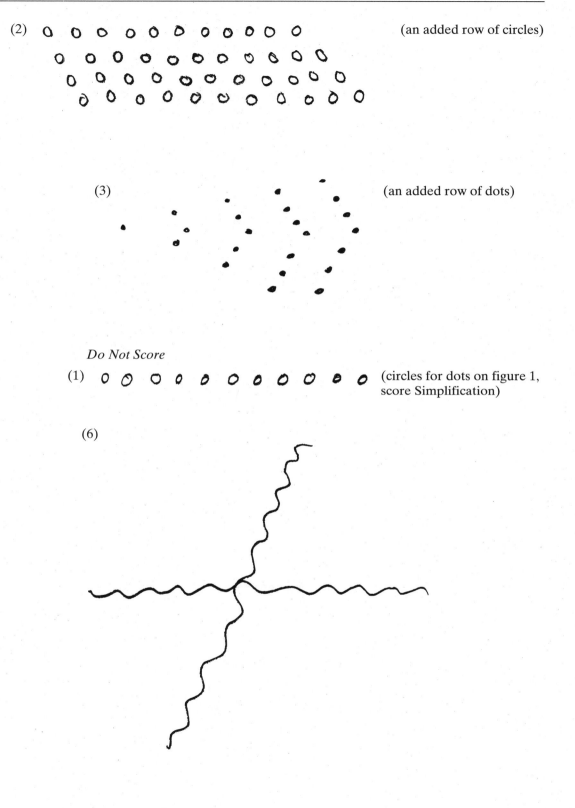

(2)   (an added row of circles)

(3)   (an added row of dots)

Do Not Score

(1)   (circles for dots on figure 1, score Simplification)

(6)

7. COLLISION OR COLLISION TENDENCY   *Definition.*   One figure is drawn as touching or overlapping another figure (collision) or is drawn within ¼ inch or less of another figure but does not touch (collision tendency).

Figures. Score for all figures.

(5,6)

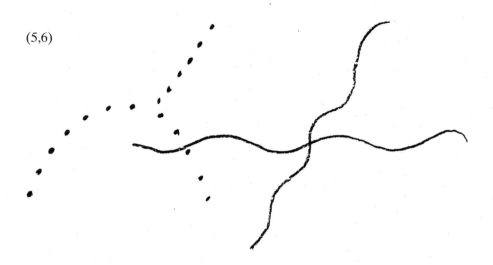

(4,5)

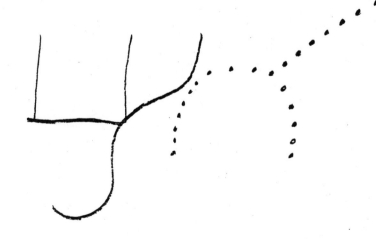

Do Not Score

(5,6)

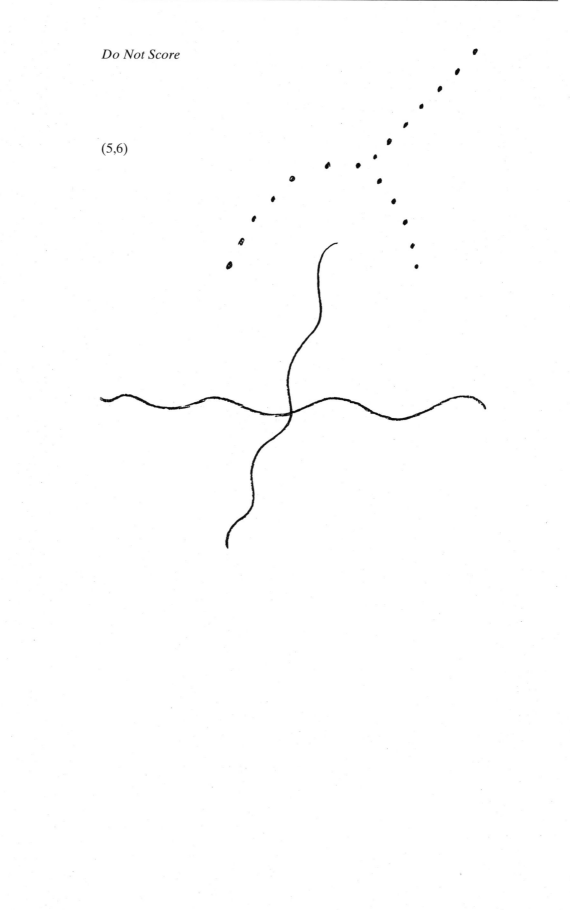

8. IMPOTENCE   ***Definition.***   Behavioral or verbal expressions of inability to draw a figure correctly (often accompanied by statements such as "I know this drawing is not right but I just can't make it right").

Figures. Score for all figures.

Repetitious drawings or numerous erasures of figures with similar inaccuracies

(A)

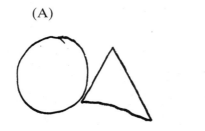

(4)

The individual realizes that an error has been made and tries to correct it unsuccessfully or expresses inability to correct it

(4)

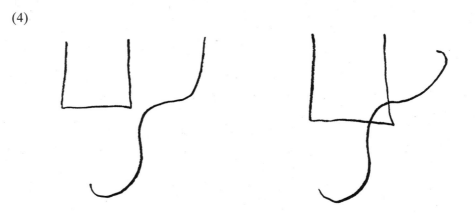

Do Not Score

(4)

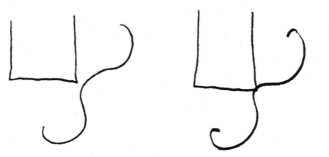

(second attempt corrects the error)

9. CLOSURE DIFFICULTY

Definition.   Difficulty in getting the joining parts of figures together or getting adjacent parts of a figure to touch. If figures are more than ⅛ inch apart at joining point, score Simplification.

Figures.   Score only for figures A, 4, 7, and 8.

Consistent but not significant joining problems on 2 out of these 3 figures

(A)

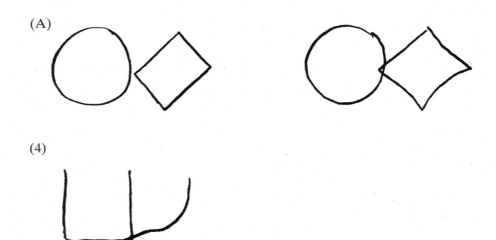

(4)

(8)

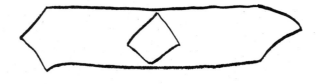

One *significant* problem with closing circles or figures or joining adjacent parts of a figure

(A)

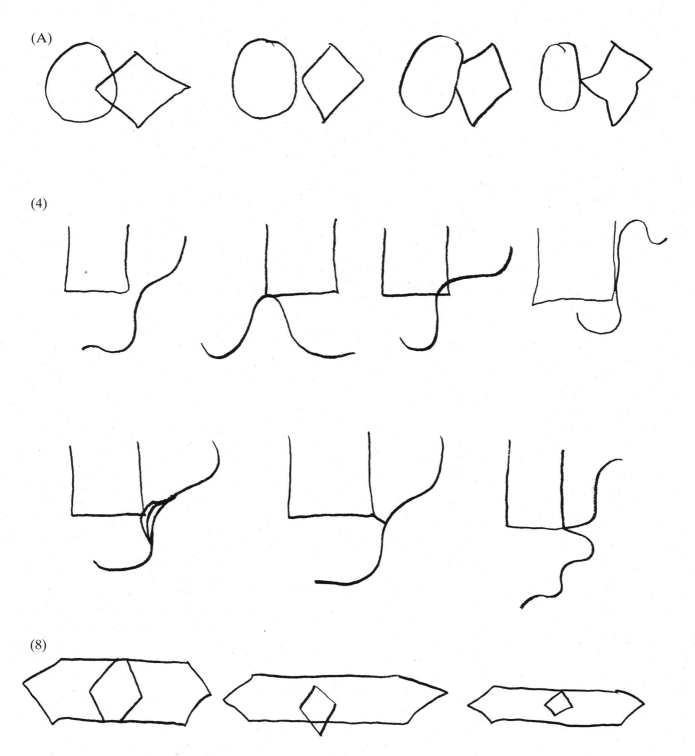

(4)

(8)

Marked and persistent gaps, overlap, redrawing, sketching, erasures, increased pressure at points where parts of the design join one another

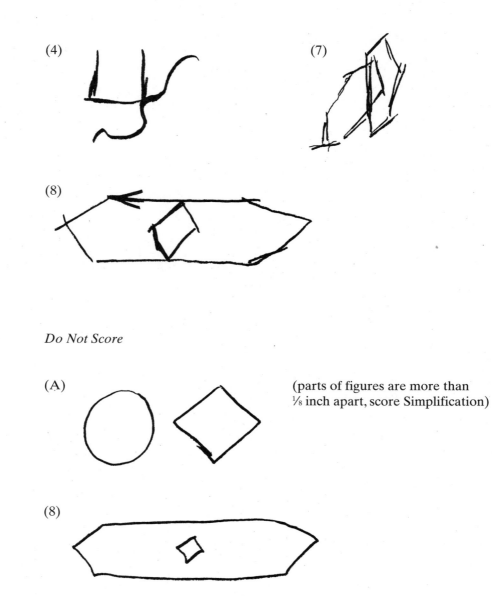

(4)

(7)

(8)

Do Not Score

(A)

(parts of figures are more than ⅛ inch apart, score Simplification)

(8)

10. MOTOR INCOORDINATION

Definition. Irregular (tremorlike) lines, especially with heavy pressure. Behavioral observations are important for scoring this error. Be sure the individual is drawing on a smooth surface.

Figures. Score for all figures.

(1)

(8)

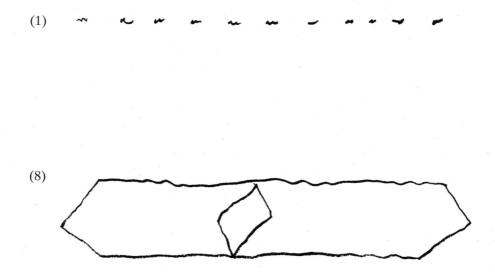

11. ANGULATION DIFFICULTY

Definition.   Severe difficulty in reproducing the angulation of figures.

Figures. Score only for figures 2 and 3, but especially figure 2.

Failure to reproduce angulation of a figure

(2)

(3)

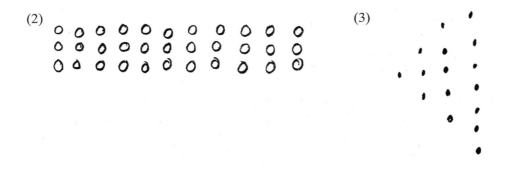

Angulation of the whole figure 45 to 80 degrees rather than parts of a figure (but not by greater than 80 degrees, which would be Rotation)

(2)

(3)

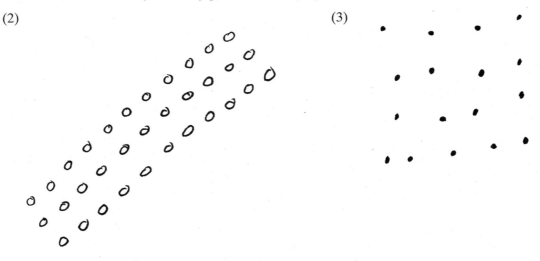

Variability of the angulation of more than half the rows of circles of figure 2

(2)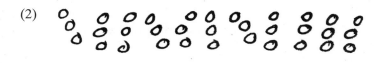

Do Not Score

(3) 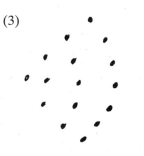   (figure 3 should be scored
leniently because its angulation
is especially hard to reproduce)

(2)   (reversal of
angulation on
figure 2,
score Rotation)

12. COHESION   *Definition.*   Isolated decrease or increase in size of figures. Score very conservatively. This error is most frequently overscored.

Figures. Score for all figures.

Decrease in the size of *part* of a figure by more than ⅓ of the dimensions used in the rest of the figure (i.e., the *smaller* figure is less than ⅔ the size of the larger figure in height or width).

(A)

(4)

(7)

(8)

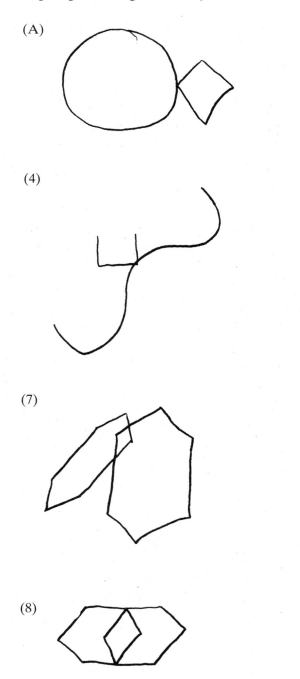

Increase or decrease in the size of a figure by ⅓ of the dimensions used in the *other drawings* (*not* compared to the size of the stimulus cards). Exclude parts of drawing that are larger due to Perseveration.

(5,6)

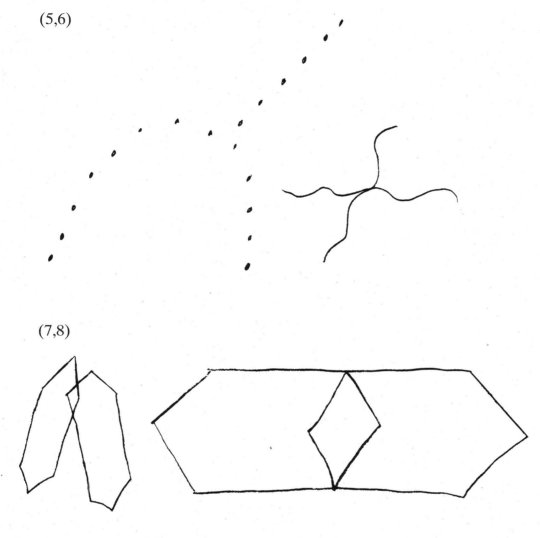

(7,8)

CHAPTER 7

Validity

The validity of a test refers to the degree that it measures what it purports to measure. In the case of the Bender Gestalt Test (BGT), used with adults, the most agreed-upon goal is the identification of brain dysfunction, especially as discriminated from psychiatric disorders not usually associated with brain impairment. There is no one indicator of the validity of a test. Rather, it is a judgment that the clinician makes after surveying and weighing all the information available. This information may take a number of forms, all of which have value.

First are the norms of a test. For this type of instrument the norms should show clear differences between those individuals for whom there is no reason to suspect brain dysfunction (i.e., community nonpatients) and those for whom there is evidence of some cognitive disorder. In addition, the latter group should be clearly different from psychiatric patients without cortical dysfunction. Second, because there is a well-known relationship between age and perceptual-motor ability, the norms for such a test should reveal some orderly progression of scores with increasing age.

Another method of evaluation is criterion-related validity, both concurrent and predictive. Performance is checked against some criterion or an independent measure of what the test is supposed to assess. *Concurrent validity* refers to the test's ability to estimate a current criterion or the diagnosis of existing status. In the case of the BGT this means comparison to some criterion of brain impairment, most often a psychiatric diagnosis but sometimes scores on another psychological or neurological test or a battery of tests. Usually we want to know if the test being evaluated will provide a simpler, more effective, or less expensive alternative to the criterion. Findings should be reproducible on cross-validation to assure that results were not statistically maximized. *Predictive validity* shows a test's ability to predict some future criterion or outcome. For example, can the BGT predict the development at a future date of a cognitive disorder such as Huntington's disease?

All of the contributors to validity mentioned so far are applicable to the BGT. There are two other general means of assessing validity: content validity and construct validity. *Content validity* involves the determination of whether the content of the test is representative of the behavioral domain being measured. This type of validation procedure is used most frequently to evaluate achievement tests and has received little or no attention for the BGT, probably because it is inappropriate. *Construct validity* has also been virtually ignored with the BGT (with the possible exception of Arbit & Zager, 1978; Field,

Bolton, & Dana, 1982; Nemec, 1978), but not because it is inappropriate. This more abstract type of validation refers to the extent to which the test assesses a theoretical construct or trait, such as anxiety or ego strength. It is most applicable when a single criterion is either unavailable or difficult to obtain. Research on the BGT has generally had no difficulty obtaining a criterion for comparison with test scores; the problem has been more with the adequacy of the criterion.

So it can be seen that there are a number of ways to answer the question, "How valid is this test?" (For more detailed discussion of validity refer to Anastasi, 1996 and the American Psychological Association's *Standards for Educational and Psychological Tests,* 1985.) The focus in this chapter is on norms and on the most commonly assessed criterion-related validity. In addition, the effects of demographic variables and influences, such as drugs and ECT, are discussed. Before we turn to this exploration, however, a number of issues relating to validity need to be examined briefly. Chapter 9, on *interpretation* of BGT results, indicates how the various validity data can be used for *clinical* prediction.

ISSUES OF VALIDITY

The primary issue of importance in criterion-related evaluation is the adequacy of the criterion. Validity can only be as adequate as the criterion permits. Failures of the test to predict the criterion may be due more to the inadequacy of the criterion itself than to deficiencies in the measuring instrument.

Diagnosis as a Criterion

In research on the BGT, the criterion most frequently employed is psychiatric diagnosis, a standard notorious for its lack of reliability. However, alternative approaches to the criterion problem (e.g., autopsy, CT scan, or neurological tests) are usually impractical, prohibitively expensive, and vulnerable to the same reliability criticism.

A number of suggestions have been made (Heaton et al., 1978; Parsons & Prigatano, 1978) for improving psychiatric diagnosis as a criterion in studies of neuropsychological tests. Diagnoses should be made in a standard way, using clearly specified criteria, by experienced clinicians. Final or discharge diagnoses that are based upon more information, including some laboratory test data, are preferable to admitting diagnoses.

Although it is usually the inadequacy of the diagnosis of brain damage that is criticized, researchers must also exercise caution with the psychiatric diagnoses that do not involve brain impairment. Particular care should be exercised in the diagnosis of schizophrenia because a number of studies show that individuals with chronic or process schizophrenia perform much as individuals with brain impairment do on neuropsychological tests (Heaton et al., 1978). Using a largely heterogeneous sample of patients with schizophrenia for comparison with patients with brain impairment will generally produce unsatisfactory hit rates.

Reporting Diagnostic Accuracy

Diagnostic accuracy is another issue of concern in evaluating test validity. Early studies of the BGT reported only findings of statistically significant group differences in test scores. These results were not helpful to clinicians in assessing a test's clinical *utility*. What is necessary is an index of the brain-impaired and nonimpaired cases correctly classified by the test. This measure of diagnostic accuracy is called the *hit rate*. It can be calculated separately for cases of brain impairment and nonimpairment as well as for the combined groups. Clinicians evaluating the usefulness of a test for their particular setting need to know all three of these figures.

Standard versus Optimal Cutoff Scores

Of importance also is what type of *cutoff score* was used to determine the diagnostic accuracy. The *standard cutoff* score is the one suggested by the manual or used across many settings. The *optimal cutoff* score is the one that was set in a specific study to provide the best results for that particular set of data. Accuracies achieved with optimal cutoffs usually experience shrinkage on cross-validation. Any optimal cutoff results should be utilized very conservatively or not at all. Heaton et al. (1978), in a review of 94 studies of neuropsychological tests, found that optimal cutoffs had a median hit rate 14 percentage points above the median for standard cutoffs. All the results reported in this chapter on the Lacks system are based on the standard cutoff of 5 or more errors. However, in each of these studies, the optimal cutoff score was always identical to the standard cutoff of 5 or more errors.

Base Rates

Another issue that influences diagnostic validity is that of *base rate* or the prevalence of a condition in the setting being studied. Meehl and Rosen (1955) demonstrated how the correct classification of patients is influenced not only by the true and false positive rates of a test but also by the base rate of the diagnostic categories in the particular setting. For the BGT, the most important base rates would be those for brain dysfunction and for schizophrenia. In a neurological clinic, a general hospital ward, and a mental health center, the base rates of these two diagnostic categories would differ considerably. Base rates for both diagnostic categories average about 20% to 30% in typical inpatient psychiatric settings.

To be truly effective, a test must be able to predict at higher rates than could be achieved by the use of base-rate prediction alone. For example, if the base rate for cognitive disorders is 10% in an institution, then one could achieve a 90% rate of diagnostic accuracy using the base rate alone, that is by classifying everyone as not having brain damage. This success rate would surpass that of any currently known psychological or neurological measure. If the cognitive disorder base rate is the more typical 30%, then a test would need a hit rate of 70% or more to have diagnostic utility. Several authors (Garb & Schramke, 1996; Heaton et al., 1978; Satz, Fennell, & Reilly, 1970) discuss at length the contributions of base rates to the predictive validity of neuropsychological tests. Besides the overall diagnostic base rates, related factors that must be considered are: (1) the relative rate of false positive and false negative calls, (2) the risk-benefit ratio of misclassification errors, and (3) the costs and medical risks of the diagnostic procedure.

The predictive validity of the BGT has frequently been investigated under artificial base rate settings (i.e., 50% cognitive disorders) that are optimal for maximizing validity. This means that the published hit rates may overestimate the diagnostic success that this test would produce in real clinical settings. Given this fact, clinicians may want to improve their success by altering cutoff scores to make the test more conservative in the labeling of cognitive disorders. Alteration of cutoffs would vary depending on base rates in the setting in question. Heaton et al. (1978) suggest that a 30% base rate of brain dysfunction would justify the use of most popular neuropsychological tests. Much of the validity data collected by Lacks consisted of consecutive admissions to several psychiatric hospitals. This approach was taken in an attempt to collect data that reproduced the agencies' diagnostic base rates.

Some suggest setting test cutoff scores to minimize false negative errors, even if it means increasing false positive errors and, consequently, lowering overall diagnostic accuracy. Whether it is more serious to miss a case of brain dysfunction or to mistakenly diagnose an individual's symptoms as evidence of brain damage is a subject of controversy. Factors important to the decision strategy would be the expected course of the pathology and the availability, cost, and potential efficacy of treatments for the conditions.

NORMATIVE DATA

Essential to the decision-making process with any psychological test is information about how various groups typically perform on that test. For the BGT, most of the available normative data are from neuropsychiatric patients. This group is the most important one for comparison purposes because the majority of decisions are made in this context. Normative data from 349 adult psychiatric inpatients are presented in this chapter. This chapter also provides a summary of BGT findings, using the adapted Hutt-Briskin procedures, for nonpatient adults, both a college ($N = 40$) and a noncollege ($N = 495$) sample. In keeping with the growing need for information about older adults, this book also includes BGT norms for those over the age of 60 ($N = 334$). That information is located in Chapter 10, which covers the use of the BGT with an older population. In 1988, McIntosh et al. showed that this scoring system has merit in the evaluation of adolescents, ages 12 through 16. Their results ($N = 337$) are presented in Chapter 12, which covers the use of the BGT with adolescents. As previously stated, this scoring system is not used to evaluate children's protocols. The reader with this interest is referred to Koppitz (1975) and to Chapter 11 of this book, which reviews many of the issues related to use of the BGT with children.

College Students

A sample of 40 students from a large, midwestern private university volunteered to take the BGT for normative purposes. The students were divided almost equally among males and females and among the four college classes. Ages ranged from 17 to 22 years with a mean of 19.5 years ($SD = 1.28$). Two individuals were Asian American; all others were white.

The BGT protocols for this group were randomly mixed with those of nonpatient adults of all ages and psychiatric patients of varying diagnoses, and then all were scored blind as to age and group by the author. For the college group, Lacks method scores ranged from 0 ($N = 22$) through 1 ($N = 13$) to a high of 2 ($N = 5$). The mean score for the group was 0.53 ($SD = 0.72$). Copying time ranged from 2 to 18 minutes with a mean of 6.21 ($SD = 3.60$). Two types of errors accounted for 75% of the total errors: Collision Tendency and Cohesion.

Therefore, anyone working with college students can expect them to do very well on this task. They work quickly, and the modal number of errors is 0. Not one student from this group came even close to making 5 errors, the criterion for brain dysfunction.

Nonpatient Adults

Presented here is a sample of *nonpatient* adults who are broadly representative of the gender, ethnicity, age, and education of the population of the United States. One hesitates to use the word *normal* to define this group, although some attempt was made to screen out those with brain impairment or psychiatric pathology before they were tested. Potential participants were asked to not volunteer for testing if they had any known previous history of brain damage, head injury, seizures, substance or alcohol abuse, or psychiatric hospitalization.

The tables that follow present normative data for this sample of 495 nonpatients ages 17 through 59. Older adult nonpatient norms can be found in Chapter 10. A large part (66%) of the sample ($N = 325$) was collected in St. Louis by three research assistants working for the author. All were extensively trained in administering the BGT and recording appropriate behavioral observations. In St. Louis, participants came from university night-school classes ($N = 29$), a secretarial school ($N = 22$), and from a wide array of settings: the airport, the bus station, bowling alleys, beauty parlors, shopping centers, hospital waiting rooms, cafeterias, laundromats, and public libraries.

In addition to the BGTs collected by the three research assistants, a sample of 112 middle-aged males was used from a study by Patricia West, Robin Hill, and Lee Robins (1977) at the Washington University Medical School. The participants were patients at a public hospital and individuals from the roster of a prepaid medical facility operated by the Teamsters Union.

Another 171 nonpatient BGT protocols were obtained from a variety of settings in other locations: Lawrence, Kansas; Long Island, New York; West Haven, Connecticut; and Toronto, Canada (from Jerome Pauker of the Clarke Institute of Psychiatry and the University of Toronto). Another group of 49 female rehabilitation clients with medical disabilities was provided by Brian Bolton and Richard Dana. The protocols were selected from their personality assessment research project, sponsored by the Arkansas Rehabilitation Research and Training Center and the Department of Psychology, University of Arkansas at Fayetteville. The data were retrieved from the files by Karin Hampton, a graduate assistant on the project.

All protocols were scored by the author. The majority were randomly mixed in a larger group of psychiatric and brain-damage protocols and then scored blind as to patient characteristics, including diagnosis.

Of the total 495 nonpatients, 356 were white (191 males and 165 females) and 139 were African American (82 males and 57 females). African Americans constituted 28% of the sample but other ethnic groups were barely represented. Education ranged from 3 to 20 years. Overall, the cell frequencies for the five age categories ranged from 67 to 139; for the five education categories they ranged from 75 to 143. Table 7.1 presents the percentages of the entire nonpatient normative sample by the categories of ethnicity, age, and education. The particular age and education ranges were chosen to match those frequently used by the U.S. Census Bureau. These individuals also encompass a wide range of socioeconomic levels and occupations. Although some geographical diversity was attained in the sample, it is not entirely representative. The Midwest is overrepresented and the western part of the country is not represented at all. Furthermore, the participants are almost entirely urban residents; approximately 15% could be described as living in a small town or rural setting. Comparison of the age and education characteristics of this sample with the 1980 U.S. Census figures indicates that the sample is broadly representative of the population on these two variables.

Initially, the BGT scores were analyzed to determine whether there were any differences in performance attributable to ethnicity or gender. Statistical analyses revealed a main effect for both ethnicity and gender; error scores for African Americans were significantly higher than those for whites, and males

Table 7.1   Composition of Nonpatient Adult Sample by Ethnicity, Age, and Education

Age	Years of Education					Total
	<9	9–11	12	13–15	>15	
White						
17–24	0.3	2.0	7.0	4.8	3.1	17.2
25–34	0.8	3.9	4.2	7.3	5.1	23.3
35–44	2.3	2.3	5.6	5.1	3.4	18.7
45–54	6.5	1.4	7.3	4.5	8.7	28.4
55–59	3.9	3.9	3.4	0.3	3.1	14.6
Total	13.8	13.5	27.5	22.0	23.4	
African American						
17–24	0.7	2.2	9.4	7.2	2.3	21.7
25–34	0.0	2.2	12.2	5.8	3.6	23.8
35–44	1.4	4.3	4.3	3.6	1.4	15.0
45–54	10.1	9.4	4.3	0.0	3.6	27.4
55–59	7.1	3.6	2.2	0.0	0.0	12.9
Total	19.0	21.7	32.4	16.6	10.8	

Note: Cell entries represent the percentage of the sample by ethnicity (i.e., 356 white and 139 African American participants).

had significantly higher scores than females. Table 7.2 indicates these mean BGT error scores. Large numbers of participants rendered relatively small differences statistically significant. However, the differences presented here in general have no *clinical* significance. Therefore, in Table 7.3, the reader will find BGT scores arranged by age and education for all participants; data are not displayed separately by ethnicity and gender. Two cells were eliminated from the table because they contained fewer than three individuals.

Examination of this table reveals the age and education effect. Data in Chapters 10 and 11 will show that during childhood and adolescence, there is a gradual improvement in perceptual-motor skill. Once adulthood is reached, there begins a slow decline in these abilities with growing age; that is, individuals' mean BGT scores increase from a low of 1.47 errors for ages 17 to 24 to a high of 2.62 errors for ages 55 to 59. Similarly, as individuals' education advances from less than 9 years to graduation from college, the mean BGT scores decrease from 3.20 errors to 1.02 errors. The same age trend can be seen within each education category and the same education trend within each age category.

Only 23, or 5% of the entire sample of 495 nonpatients, earned scores in the brain-damaged range (5 or more errors). Of these, 70% were made by individuals aged 45 or over and 70% by those with less than 9 years of education. Only four types of errors were committed by more than 10% of the sample: Perseveration (18%); Collision, which almost always consisted of the lesser error of Collision Tendency (45%); Closure Difficulty (33%); and Cohesion (31%). Impotence was found for only two nonpatients.

Therefore, nonpatient adults ages 17 to 59, with no history of impaired brain function or psychiatric problems, consistently execute the BGT drawings

Table 7.2 Mean BGT Scores by Gender and Ethnicity for Nonpatient Adults

	White			African American			Total		
	N	M	% > 4 errors	N	M	% > 4 errors	N	M	% > 4 errors
Male	191	1.88	4	82	2.50	10	273	2.07	6
Female	165	1.22	1	57	1.79	9	222	1.37	3
Total	356	1.58	3	139	2.21	9	495	1.75	5

Table 7.3 Mean BGT Scores by Age and Education for Nonpatient Adults

	Years of education																	
	<9			9–11			12			13–15			>15			Total		
Age	N	M	SD	N	M	SD	N	M	SD	N	M	SD	N	M	SD	N	M	SD
17–24	2	—	—	10	2.20	0.99	38	1.71	1.43	27	0.93	1.00	14	0.86	1.03	91	1.47	1.37
25–34	3	2.00	1.00	17	1.94	1.56	32	1.44	1.27	34	1.06	0.92	23	0.52	0.67	109	1.22	1.18
35–44	10	2.70	2.16	14	2.00	1.36	26	1.23	0.91	23	1.30	1.33	14	0.71	0.91	87	1.46	1.39
45–54	37	3.08	1.38	18	2.72	1.27	32	1.81	1.18	16	1.69	1.25	36	1.25	1.02	39	2.11	1.41
55–59	23	3.61	1.62	19	2.37	1.01	15	2.07	1.28	1	—	—	11	1.91	1.58	69	2.62	1.53
Total	75	3.20	1.51	78	2.27	1.25	143	1.62	1.23	101	1.18	1.08	98	1.02	1.00	495	1.75	1.45

Note: Empty cells contain fewer than three cases each.

within the unimpaired diagnostic range. The younger and more educated they are, the better they perform on this instrument. In a later section of this chapter the effects of age and education are examined in more detail.

Neuropsychiatric Patients   The data presented here for neuropsychiatric patients are from three research samples collected by the author. The first is a sample of 109 inpatients who were consecutive, testable admissions to a large urban acute psychiatric treatment center located in the Midwest (Brilliant & Gynther, 1963). The BGT was administered within 3 days of admission to minimize differences in length of hospitalization and degree of medication. Because the average length of stay in such an institution is 3 to 4 weeks, this testing in the first few days of admission also matches the time frame in which inpatients would typically be tested for diagnostic purposes. Consecutive admissions were tested to ensure that patients were representative of the clinical population and would match the hospital diagnostic base rates (30% brain dysfunction, 35% psychosis, and 17% personality disorder). Admissions with other diagnoses were not included. Table 7.4 presents demographic information on the sample. Nearly all could be described as falling in the lower socioeconomic class, with occupational classifications of unskilled or semiskilled workers.

Participants were assigned to the three broad diagnostic groups based on the final hospital discharge diagnosis. Diagnostic decisions were made by senior staff training psychiatrists from the faculty of a large affiliated medical school, usually after at least several weeks of observation, interviews, assessment of response to treatment, interdisciplinary staff conferences, and physical and neurological exams and tests. Almost all participants were given an EEG. No patient was included whose diagnosis was based in any part upon psychological tests. Tests were scored by the author without knowledge of the diagnosis.

The second sample consisted of 194 patients selected in the same way from the same hospital. Table 7.4 also presents demographic data for this group. The

Table 7.4   Demographic Variables for Three Samples of Neuropsychiatric Inpatients

Sample source	Diagnostic category	N	Male	Female	African American	White	Mean age	Mean education	Mean IQ[a]
Acute psychiatric inpatient	Personality disorder	43	28	15	8	35	37.70	10.30	97.80
	Psychosis	33	12	21	19	14	39.67	9.42	92.49
	Brain dysfunction	33	23	10	10	23	45.79	8.09	89.80
	Total	109	63	46	37	72	40.75	9.38	93.76
Acute psychiatric inpatient	Personality disorder	80	61	19	24	56	33.49	9.94	101.48
	Psychosis	81	31	50	22	59	37.75	10.50	96.93
	Brain dysfunction	33	23	10	14	19	45.67	8.94	88.85
	Total	194	115	79	60	134	37.34	10.01	97.43
VA inpatient	Psychosis	27	27	0	0	27	39.07	11.67	109.90
	Brain dysfunction	19	19	0	0	19	44.89	10.58	101.42
	Total	46	46	0	0	46	41.50	11.22	106.39
	Grand total	349	224	125	97	252	38.95	9.97	97.46

[a]IQ is estimated from the WAIS Vocabulary subtest.

third sample is a group of 46 psychiatric and neurological inpatients, primarily from a large eastern general VA hospital (Lacks et al., 1970). Many of these patients were undergoing long-term hospitalization. Only patients with a diagnosis of brain impairment ($N = 19$) made by a neurologist were selected. Only patients with a clear-cut primary diagnosis of schizophrenia ($N = 27$) and no background of cognitive disorder (particularly alcoholism) were included. The patients in this third sample were tested at varying times during their hospitalization, on the average between 2 and 3 years after admission. The demographic information for this group can also be found in Table 7.4.

In the tables that follow, these three samples were combined, for a total of 349 patients. To maximize diagnostic reliability, data were collapsed into three diagnostic groups: personality disorder ($N = 123$), psychosis ($N = 141$), and brain dysfunction ($N = 85$). Patients with a diagnosis of chronic alcoholism ($N = 83$, or 74% of personality disorders) were included in the personality disorder category because they had been carefully screened for impairment of brain function and because the BGT scores of these two groups were not different from each other. Approximately 30% of the psychotic patients had diagnoses of Bipolar Disorder, and the remainder had schizophrenia. Patients with brain impairment represented a diverse spectrum of etiologies, such as head trauma, chronic substance abuse, encephalitis, and dementias (e.g., Alzheimer's, vascular, and Huntington's).

Table 7.5 presents BGT scores by diagnosis for the three samples as well as the combined group. The mean scores for the two groups of nonimpaired patients in each sample ($M = 3.59$ and 3.38 errors) are significantly lower than those for the patients with brain damage ($M = 5.87$). The scores for the groups with personality disorder and psychosis are not significantly different from

Table 7.5　Mean BGT Scores for Three Psychiatric Diagnostic Groups

Sample source		Personality disorder	Psychosis	Brain dysfunction
Acute psychiatric inpatient	N	43	33	33
	M	3.07	3.15	5.61
	SD	1.37	1.79	1.50
	% > 4 errors	14	30	85
Acute psychiatric inpatient	N	80	81	33
	M	3.86	3.83	6.48
	SD	1.92	1.99	2.39
	% > 4 errors	29	35	85
VA inpatient	N	—	27	19
	M	—	2.89	5.26
	SD	—	1.48	1.48
	% > 4 errors	—	7	74
Total	N	123	141	85
	M	3.59	3.38	5.87
	SD	1.78	1.97	1.94
	% > 4 errors	24	27	82

Note: All comparisons between patients with brain damage and without brain damage reached statistical significance, while none of the comparisons between the two groups without brain damage did.

each other. The average score for the patients with brain impairment falls in the range indicating brain dysfunction, but those for the other two patient groups do not.

Another useful bit of information is the percentage of each group that had scores of 5 errors or more, that is, those that would lead to a test diagnosis of brain dysfunction. For patients with a diagnosis of personality disorder, the percentage with scores of 5 or more averaged 24%; for those with a diagnosis of psychosis, the average was 27%; for those with a diagnosis of brain dysfunction, the range across three samples was 74% to 85% and the overall average was 82%. It is interesting that fewer individuals in the VA sample, both with psychosis and with brain impairment, earned BGT scores of 5 or more. This result may be due to the fact that these patients were generally tested some time after admission and were not in states of acute disturbance, as were patients in the other two samples. The VA patients also had somewhat higher levels of education and IQ.

In Table 7.6, the reader will find a list of all 12 of the possible scoring errors with corresponding percentages of each diagnostic group that committed each error. For example, for the error of Rotation, 9% of patients diagnosed as having personality disorders committed this error, but 13% of those with psychosis and 26% of those with brain dysfunction did so. Again, across all errors there were no significant differences between those two groups of patients with nonimpaired diagnoses: personality disorder and schizophrenia. They make similar numbers and kinds of errors. With the exception of Collision or Collision Tendency between patients with psychosis and patients with brain impairment ($p < .08$), all comparisons between nonimpaired patients and patients with brain impairment reached statistical significance. Only three of the errors were found in the records of 40% or more of the nonimpaired

Table 7.6   BGT Error Percentages for Three Psychiatric Diagnostic Groups

Error	Personality disorder ($N = 123$)	Psychosis ($N = 141$)	Brain dysfunction ($N = 85$)
1. Rotation	9	13	26
2. Overlapping Difficulty	26	26	45
3. Simplification	17	20	49
4. Fragmentation	6	10	27
5. Retrogression	21	18	42
6. Perseveration	31	32	56
7. Collision or Collision Tendency	50	52	65
8. Impotence	2	4	24
9. Closure Difficulty	55	53	79
10. Motor Incoordination	24	13	55
11. Angulation Difficulty	15	18	41
12. Cohesion	50	47	68

Note: All comparisons between brain dysfunction and the other two groups except Collision ($p < .08$) were significantly different between psychosis and brain dysfunction. All comparisons between personality disorder and psychosis were nonsignificant.

patients: Collision or Collision Tendency, Closure Difficulty, and Cohesion. In contrast, nine errors were committed by 40% or more of the patients with brain impairment. The three least frequent errors for all three diagnostic groups were Rotation, Fragmentation, and Impotence. Essentially, these same error distributions were found for the sample of 495 nonpatient adults, and a group of 334 nonpatient older adults (Lacks & Storandt, 1982; see Chapter 10), a group with schizophrenia compared to a group with brain damage (Hutt, 1985), and 112 male forensic patients classified as having schizophrenia, brain damage, or personality disorder (Friedt & Gouvier, 1989).

Patients with schizophrenia, on the other hand, sometimes also make specific kinds of errors, though they tend to be ones that are not scored in the Lacks system. Examples of these errors are drawing symbols, such as stars for dots (for an example, see Figure 13.3 in Chapter 13), or making figure 3 into a Christmas tree; and making elaborations, embellishments, or doodles on the paper (Hutt, 1985).

Table 7.7 presents the percentile distributions of total number of errors for several comparison groups. Examination of this table reveals that 74% to 96% of the three groups without brain dysfunction had BGT scores in the nonimpaired range (4 or fewer errors) but only 18% of the group with brain impairment did.

DIAGNOSTIC ACCURACY

The normative data for psychiatric patients show clear group differences between patients with brain dysfunction and those with no known cognitive disorders. However, this information alone is insufficient to assess the discrim-

Table 7.7 Percentile Distributions of BGT Total Scores for Various Comparison Groups

Number of errors	Nonpatient adults ($N = 495$)	Nonpatient older adults ($N = 334$)	Nonimpaired psychiatric inpatients ($N = 264$)	Psychiatric inpatients with brain damage ($N = 85$)
0	20	5	3	0
1	51	17	10	0
2	75	35	31	4
3	87	52	55	9
4	96	74	74	18
5	98	85	85	51
6	99	92	93	71
7	100	96	96	80
8		99	99	87
9		99	100	95
10		100		99
11				100
12				

Note: The cutoff score for brain dysfunction is 5 or more errors.

inative power of the BGT. A number of studies have investigated the diagnostic accuracy of the Lacks scoring method with neuropsychiatric patients. All are described in Chapter 1. Before 1984, Lacks published three studies to establish norms and diagnostic accuracy of the BGT. The first study by Brilliant (now Lacks) and Gynther (1963) assessed 109 consecutive admissions to a large urban acute psychiatric treatment center. The research methodology has already been described in the section on norms for psychiatric patients and so will not be repeated here (see Table 7.4 for a description of the patients). As has already been shown in Table 7.5, patients with brain damage made significantly higher error scores than those without brain damage even when initial differences in age and education were controlled by analysis of covariance.

In 1970, Lacks et al. administered the BGT to 63 white male inpatients, the majority from a VA hospital in Connecticut. The patients were divided into three diagnostic groups: 19 with brain impairment, 27 with schizophrenia, and 17 general medical patients. All diagnoses of brain dysfunction were made by a neurologist and of schizophrenia by a psychiatrist. Cases of borderline schizophrenia were excluded. Every effort was made to eliminate from the nonimpaired patients anyone having a background of brain impairment of any type, particularly alcoholism. Mean age, education, and WAIS Vocabulary IQ did not vary significantly among the three diagnostic groups. However, the patients with schizophrenia had been hospitalized significantly longer than those in the general medical group (36.7 versus 17.6 months). The sample is more fully described in Table 7.4.

In Table 7.5, the reader can see the mean scores of the two psychiatric groups. The 17 general medical patients had a mean BGT score of 2.88 ($SD = 1.41$), with 12% earning scores of 5 or more. Again, the patients with brain damage earned significantly higher error scores than those in the two groups without neurological impairment.

Using the same methodology and population as Brilliant and Gynther (1963), Lacks and Newport (1980) selected 50 patients from a larger sample of 194 consecutive admissions to a large urban acute psychiatric treatment center. The subsample was chosen to match hospital base rates and to match groups on ethnicity, gender, age, education, and IQ. Three scorers of varying levels of experience and blind as to diagnosis independently scored the test protocols. Mean BGT scores for all three judges combined for the 17 patients with brain damage was 5.80 ($SD = 2.37$), with 71% earning scores of 5 and above. The 33 nonimpaired individuals had mean error scores of 2.58 ($SD = 1.55$) and 10% with scores of 5 and above. The BGT scores of these two groups were significantly different.

After the publication in 1984 of the Lacks scoring method, four more studies examined BGT accuracy using this method with diverse populations (see Chapter 1 for research details). In these seven published studies evaluating the validity of the BGT, scores were consistently found to be significantly higher for individuals with brain dysfunction when compared to psychiatric patients with no known cognitive disorders. The latter groups include both severely disturbed psychiatric patients and nonpatient older adults. Although encouraging, these findings do not indicate whether the BGT has discriminative power as a neuropsychological screening test. To answer this question, the diagnostic accuracies presented in Table 7.8 must be examined. For correct diagnosis of all cases, the BGT hit rate for all seven studies ranges from 70% to 86% when comparing neuropsychiatric inpatients with brain-impairment to those with-

Table 7.8 BGT Diagnostic Accuracy (Percent Correctly Diagnosed)

Study	N	No brain damage	Brain damage diagnosis	Total
Brilliant & Gynther (1963)	109	92	67	82
Lacks, Colbert, Harrow, & Levine (1970)	64	89	78	86
Lacks & Newport (1980)	50	80	87	84
McCann & Plunkett (1984)	60	63	77	70
Friedt & Gouvier (1989)	112	85	55	74
Lownsdale, Rogers, & McCall (1989)	45	85	77	82
Marsico & Wagner (1990)	80	88	65	79

Note: The first three and the last study used the standard cutoff score of 5 or more errors to determine brain damage; the other three studies used an optimal cutoff score.

out such impairment. The mean accuracy overall was 80%; the median was 82%. These hit rates compare very favorably to prediction from base rates alone (about 65% to 70%) and to the median hit rates reported by Heaton et al. (1978) for five of the most used neuropsychological tests: 68% to 84% across all tests; 76% for eight studies of the standard BGT (see Table 1.1).

This accuracy also matches the results of a meta-analysis of 11 studies using the Halstead-Reitan Battery (HRB) combined with the WAIS-R reported by Garb and Schramke (1996). All of these studies used neuropsychologists as judges. In terms of detection of brain impairment, for 2,383 ratings, these researchers found an overall hit rate of 84% (compared to an average brain-damage base rate of 65%, going as high as 80% in one setting). Accuracy varied considerably across the 11 studies. For 1,682 ratings, the correct prediction of no impairment was 79%; the correct prediction of presence of impairment was 86%. These figures are comparable to those achieved with the BGT (see Table 7.8). Accuracy rates from the 11 neuropsychological studies that were achieved for the impaired/nonimpaired dichotomy gradually declined as more specific diagnoses were made: 89% for left versus right hemisphere impairment; 65% for no brain damage, versus diffuse left or right hemisphere impairment; and 29% for the more specific brain region (e.g., left frontal, right temporal, etc.).

The results of the BGT studies described in this chapter are especially impressive when compared to the 11 HRB/WAIS studies reported by Garb and Schramke (1996), because the latter collected a very large amount of neuropsychological data. Also, none of the latter attempted the very difficult task of discriminating between patients with brain damage and those with diagnoses of severe psychiatric disorders, such as Bipolar Disorder or Schizophrenia. In fact, some of these comparisons were made between neurological patients and nonpatient controls recruited for research. Diagnostic accuracy varies greatly depending upon the comparison you are attempting to make.

The results of the BGT studies also are particularly strong because four of the seven used the standard rather than an optimal cutoff score and the diagnostic accuracies are very consistent across different scorers and across different patient populations (even though the brain dysfunction base rate was approximately the same, 30% to 35%, for all but one of the neuropsychiatric samples). It appears that the BGT can be a useful screening tool to aid discrimination of neuropsychiatric and neurological patients with and without neurological impairment.

It is also important to remember than these rates of diagnostic accuracy represent *minimal* success rates because they are based upon the artificial situation of blind prediction based on a *single* test. In real practice, the psychologist would be arriving at diagnostic conclusions based on a *battery* of tests combined with at least demographic information, clinical observations, and a history.

COMPARISON WITH OTHER SCORING SYSTEMS

It has been very difficult to evaluate the relative value of the available BGT scoring systems because the research typically reports on only one method at a time. Furthermore, the different studies vary widely in sample size (30 to 1,003), base rate of brain dysfunction (18% to 67%), composition of the non-brain-impaired comparison samples, test score cutoffs, and procedures for measuring diagnostic efficiency. Marsico and Wagner (1990) compared the Pascal-Suttell method of scoring the BGT with the Lacks procedures. Initially, they used data on 52 outpatients with brain damage and 52 without brain damage (taken from files of patients referred for testing). Results of the two scoring systems correlated highly. Using optimal cutoffs, overall hit rate for the Lacks procedures was 68%, versus 74% for the Pascal-Suttell method. When the sample was revised to 80 patients who met the clinic base rates and the standard cutoff score was used, the Lacks procedures had an overall hit rate of 79%, versus 81% for the Pascal-Suttell. Hit rates for both systems were higher for diagnosing the absence of brain damage rather than its presence, leading to a high rate of missed cases. The brain-damage hit rate for the Pascal-Suttell system was well below that for the Lacks method. Because the two systems were highly correlated ($r = .83$), the researchers suggested using the Lacks method for its relative ease of scoring and broader scope and application.

Another study was done to compare the interscorer reliability and diagnostic accuracy of the Lacks method with several other BGT evaluation methods. Using criteria of relative ease of application, availability, and frequency of recent use in the literature, Lacks and Newport (1980) chose the following methods for comparison with the Lacks method: the Hain (1964), the Pauker Quick-Scoring (1976), and the number of rotations. The latter very simple diagnostic criterion was chosen because rotation of reproductions has been described so frequently as being characteristic of the protocols of those with brain impairment (e.g., Griffith & Taylor, 1960). Each of these approaches generally requires less than 3 minutes per protocol to score.

The BGT protocols for this study were from a sample of 50 mixed psychiatric inpatients. Methods of testing and arriving at the diagnosis were similar to those already described for Brilliant and Gynther (1983).

Cases were chosen randomly from a larger group of consecutive admissions until the base rates had been achieved for a group of 50. Minor changes in group composition were then made so that diagnostic groups were also statistically matched for ethnicity, gender, age, education, and WAIS Vocabulary scores. Among the patients, a wide variety of diagnoses was represented; they were assigned to the two broad diagnostic groups of brain damage (34%) and no brain damage (66%) based on the final discharge diagnosis.

Twelve different scorers were selected to represent three levels of Bender Gestalt expertise: *expert, typical,* and *novice.* All 50 BGT protocols were scored by all scorers, who were blind as to any patient characteristics. Although the four experts all used scoring systems with which they were very familiar, the remaining eight scorers were asked to learn a system.

In terms of interscorer reliability, those scoring with the Hain system achieved the lowest levels of agreement (Pearson product-moment correlation coefficients among scorers on total test scores averaged .79). All scorers using the three other approaches were able to achieve acceptable levels of agreement: Lacks method, .87 to .90; Pauker, .92 to .96; and rotations, .93 to .97.

Table 7.9 presents these diagnostic accuracies for the four scoring strategies. Because no a priori or standard score had been established for the Pauker system, results were reported using the optimal cutoff scores for this sample. The optimal cutoff score for the Hain system was 14 or greater and for the Pauker system was 11 or greater. However, the standard and the optimal cutoffs were identical in the present study for the Lacks method (5 or greater) and number of rotations (1 or greater).

For correct diagnosis of all cases, the Lacks method was most successful, with a mean of 84% correctly classified, and the Pauker system was next with 79% correct. Both the Hain system and the number of rotations demonstrate lower overall diagnostic accuracy (71% and 63%, respectively). Essentially the same relative results emerge when the hits for presence or absence of brain damage are viewed separately. When the standard cutoff score was used for the Hain system, diagnostic accuracy was considerably reduced, to a mean of 42% for diagnosis of brain damage, 73% for absence of brain damage, and 61% for total diagnosis.

The results of this study do not encourage continued use of the Hain system. Although Hain's original validation findings (Hain, 1964) of an 86% overall hit rate were promising, his own cross-validation and subsequent studies (e.g., Kramer & Fenwick, 1966) indicate much less successful discrimination.

Table 7.9 Diagnostic Accuracy (Percent Correctly Diagnosed) for Four Scoring Approaches to the BGT[a]

Scoring approach	No brain damage	Brain damage diagnosis	Total
Hutt-Briskin	80	87	84
Pauker	79	80	79
Hain	75	72	71
Rotations	45	70	63

Note: Because a standard cutoff is not available for the Pauker system, optimal cutoffs for all approaches were used: Hain, 14 and above; Hutt-Briskin, 5 and above; Pauker, 9 and above; and rotations, 1 and above. Optimal and standard cutoffs were identical in this study for the Hutt-Briskin and rotations.

[a]Three different scorers scored a sample of 50 neuropsychiatric inpatients for each approach (Lacks & Newport, 1980).

No previous studies report diagnostic accuracy for number of rotations alone, although in clinical practice many psychologists rely heavily on this classical sign and most scoring systems include it. The present findings show that strong reliance on this sign alone is not a sound clinical procedure.

The results clearly indicate that the Lacks procedures can be used with good diagnostic efficiency to discriminate psychiatric patients with and without brain impairment. The findings also suggest that the Pauker system might be used effectively if these findings were cross-validated. The 84% accuracy of the Lacks procedures also meets the criterion of a substantial increase in accuracy over prediction from base rates alone (66%).

COMPARISON WITH OTHER TESTS FOR BRAIN DYSFUNCTION

In their 1978 review of studies of neuropsychological tests, Heaton et al. found the median diagnostic accuracy in 36 studies of the five most frequently used tests to range from 68% for the Graham-Kendall Memory for Designs Test to 84% for the BGT given with the Background Interference Procedure (see Table 1.1). However, most of these studies investigated only one single test; there were few attempts to compare the efficacy of more than one test within the same study. Moreover, only two of eight BGT studies utilized the Hutt-Briskin scoring procedure. In this section, three studies are presented that used the Lacks adaptation of this scoring system and that also evaluated concurrently more than one neuropsychological test.

Earlier in this chapter, the participants and research methodology of a study by Brilliant and Gynther (1963) are described in detail. They gave the BGT to 109 neuropsychiatric inpatients who were classified as having brain damage or not, based on the hospital discharge diagnosis by experienced psychiatrists (see Table 7.4 for a description of the participants). All participants were also administered in counterbalanced order the Benton Visual Retention (BVRT) and the Graham-Kendall Memory for Designs (MFD) tests. All tests were scored without knowledge of the patients' diagnoses. The BGT was scored using the Lacks scoring method with the standard cutoff of 5 or more errors. The optimum cutoff score was also 5 errors. The other two tests were scored using the standard procedures and cutoffs included in the manuals. Two scores were obtained for the BVRT, number correct and number of errors.

On all three tests, the patients with brain impairment performed significantly more poorly than those who were nonimpaired. These results held true even when the effects of age and education were held constant through analysis of covariance. Intercorrelations between the BGT and the other two tests were: .46 with the BVRT correct score, .57 with the BVRT error score, .34 with the MFD raw score, and .07 with the MFD difference score.

Table 7.10 indicates the differential diagnostic accuracy of the three tests. For correct diagnosis of all cases, the BGT appears to be the best single measure, with 82% accuracy overall. The BVRT error score was least adequate, with only 66% of the total number of cases correctly classified. When only the number of correctly identified patients without brain damage was considered, the combination of the two Benton scores classified 98% accurately. When only those cases correctly diagnosed as brain impaired were considered, the Bender was the best measure with a 67% hit rate. The most unsatisfactory result was the number of individuals with brain dysfunction correctly diagnosed by the Benton error score; only 47% were correctly classified.

Table 7.10   Diagnostic Accuracy (Percent Correctly Diagnosed) of the Bender Gestalt (BGT), Benton Visual Retention (BVRT), and Graham-Kendall Memory for Designs (MFD) Tests for Brain Dysfunction

	No brain damage	Brain damage diagnosis	Total
BGT	92	67	82
BVRT (correct)	85	62	76
BVRT (error)	95	47	66
BVRT (combined)	98	62	81
MFD	88	63	78

Source: Brilliant, P. and Gynther, M. D. (1963) "Relationships between performance on three tests for organicity and selected patient variables." *Journal of Consulting Psychology, 27,* 474–479. Copyright 1963 by the American Psychological Association. Reprinted by permission.

For proper evaluation of the predictive powers of tests, the brain dysfunction base rate of a hospital population must also be considered. In this study, the base rate was 30%; therefore, a diagnosis of no brain dysfunction would be correct in 70% of the cases. Using the Bender, however, one would expect to be correct 82% of the time, resulting in a 12% increase in hits over what would be obtained by using the base-rate strategy. The Benton error score, on the other hand, correctly diagnosed only 66% of the patients, demonstrating that use of a "good" diagnostic instrument may lead to a decrease in diagnostic accuracy.

Owen (1971) also used the BGT and the BVRT in a study of the effects of chlorpromazine upon the test performance of inpatients with schizophrenia. She administered these two tests to 45 inpatients with mixed schizophrenia (omitting 15 patients receiving acute drug therapy) in a large urban acute psychiatric treatment center. Patients were classified as having schizophrenia by senior supervising psychiatrists. Using the Lacks procedures with standard cutoff, the BGT correctly classified 73% of the patients as not brain damaged. With BVRT correct score, diagnostic accuracy was 64%; for the error score it was 53%.

The discriminative power of the BGT exceeded that of the BVRT in both of these studies and in one study exceeded that of the MFD. In the second study the diagnostic accuracies were lower for both tests than in the first study. This finding is most likely due to the fact that participants in the Owen (1971) study were exclusively diagnosed with schizophrenia, the most difficult diagnostic comparison group. Only 34% of Brilliant and Gynther's (1963) unimpaired participants had schizophrenia. In their review of research on neuropsychological tests, Heaton et al. (1978) found a median hit rate of 77% in discriminations between patients with reactive schizophrenia and patients with brain dysfunction but a median hit rate of only 54% when the discrimination involved chronic or process schizophrenia. It is not known how many patients with process schizophrenia were in Owen's sample of mixed schizophrenic disorders; however, their presence is likely to have lowered the discriminative power of the test over the more typical diagnostic task studied by Brilliant and Gynther.

The third study to compare the BGT with Lacks scoring to another neuropsychological measure was done by Lacks et al. (1970). The BGT and five of the eight tests from the Halstead-Reitan Battery (HRB; Category, Tactual Performance, Seashore Rhythm, Speech Perception, and Tapping) were given to 63 white, male VA patients (19 with brain damage, 27 with schizophrenia, and 17 general medical patients). This sample was described earlier in this chapter (see Table 7.4). The total number of HRB tests on which each participant scored within the brain impairment range was multiplied by 0.143 to correct for the omission of three tests from the original battery and to obtain the composite Impairment Index. The BGT correlated with the Impairment Index ($r = .66, p < .01$). Using Reitan's cutting scores, the percentage of patients with brain damage who were correctly diagnosed ranged from 44% for the Memory score of Tactual Performance to 84% for the composite Impairment Index. The percentage of unimpaired patients correctly diagnosed ranged from 44% for the Category test to 86% for the Memory score of Tactual Performance. The composite Impairment Index correctly diagnosed 64% of the unimpaired patients. These findings contrast with the BGT's ability to identify correctly those patients with (74%) and without brain dysfunction (91%).

Lacks et al.'s (1970) findings suggest that use of the HRB will lead to a high percentage of correct classifications of those patients with some cognitive disorder. However, use of this battery in a setting with large numbers of patients with schizophrenia will also lead to very frequent misclassification of this category of patient. Because this battery of tests requires 3 to 4 hours to administer, the results are especially disappointing when compared to the diagnostic accuracy of the 6-minute BGT. Of course, the multiple tests of the HRB provide much more extensive information about abilities in various domains.

OTHER CLINICAL APPLICATIONS OF THE BGT

The major part of this book focuses on usage of the BGT as a screening instrument in the typical inpatient psychiatric setting and as a measure of visuoconstructive abilities within a comprehensive neuropsychological evaluation. With children, the BGT has also been used widely as a measure of maturation and school readiness (see Chapter 11). However, within the scientific literature there are reports of other applications of this test, such as to investigate the relationship of perceptual-motor impairment to more sophisticated neurological criteria. For example, one innovative use of the BGT was as a gauge of the effectiveness of different surgical techniques in curtailing postoperative neurological impairment. Landis, Baxter, Patterson, and Tauber (1974) conducted this study on 28 patients who received open-heart surgery at a university medical center. During surgery, the patient's blood was circulated and oxygenated outside the body through cardiopulmonary bypass equipment. The oxygenation of blood in the heart-lung machine caused microemboli to form. These fragments of protein and damaged red blood cells were believed to travel in the returned blood and settle in small blood vessels, blocking blood flow and resulting in brain tissue destruction.

In this study, the BGT (administered 1 to 2 days before and 5 to 8 days after surgery) was used to assess the relative efficacy of two types of heart-lung machines (a bubble oxygenator and a membrane oxygenator) in reducing central nervous system damage. In addition, each machine was used with and without a special screen filter that was devised to remove microemboli from the blood before returning it to the patient's body. Results showed that central nervous system damage was most extensive in those patients who received the bubble oxygenator without the filter and was least extensive with the use of the membrane oxygenator with filter. The BGT was an especially suitable choice of assessment instrument in these circumstances because a more complex or time-consuming tool would not have been feasible with postsurgery patients. Future research may find the BGT equally helpful in evaluating neurological sequelae associated with techniques used in other types of surgery or medical procedures, such as hemodialysis.

In the 1950s, 156 offspring of victims of Huntington's disease took part in psychometric testing and were retested 15 to 20 years later (Lyle & Quast, 1976). At the time of retesting, 60 participants were still free of Huntington's disease and 28 had developed the disease (premorbid group) during the followup period. For comparison purposes, 25 individuals who were already affected with the disease were also tested during the initial research.

The BGT was analyzed through clinical judgment and through recall scores. Comparing the recall scores at the original testing with current disease status, the researchers found that still-normal participants recalled 5.7 designs; late-onset premorbid participants (6 to 18 years after testing), 4.8 designs; early-onset premorbid participants (within 2 years of the first testing), 3.7 designs; and those already affected when tested, 4.5 designs. These results showed erosion of perceptual-motor abilities long before the clinical choreic movements were apparent (2 to 18 years), indicating that the process of brain degeneration had been set in motion many years before the clinical manifestations of the disease appeared.

Other clinical applications of the BGT will be described in later chapters covering older adults, children, and adolescents.

COMPARISON OF LEVEL OF EXPERTISE OF SCORER

Another issue concerning tests for brain dysfunction concerns the level of expertise or experience of the scorer. It is important to know for any psychological test whether the accuracy of the test's evaluation will depend on special skills or years of experience. A second goal of the Lacks and Newport (1980) study was to compare the accuracy of scorers of varying levels of experience with the Bender Gestalt on four scoring systems. For each scoring system three scorers were chosen, one each to represent expert, typical, and novice levels of experience with this test.

The clinical experience of the *expert* scorers ranged from 12 to 25 years, and each had previously scored approximately 800 to 1,000 Bender Gestalt protocols. In addition, all four had published research on tests for brain dysfunction. The *typical* clinical psychologists had clinical experience ranging from 4 to 16 years, and they had scored an average of 20 to 40 protocols per year. All eight of these two groups of scorers had doctoral degrees in clinical psychology and represented diverse academic, institutional, and private-practice work settings. The *novice* scorers had just completed a bachelor's degree in psychology and had no previous knowledge of any tests for cognitive impairment. They were representative of the degree of experience of many psychometricians.

Table 7.11 compares the diagnostic accuracy for the Lacks method only of scorers with differing amounts of experience. For correct diagnoses of all cases, there was only a maximum of 4% difference in accuracy among the three scorers who used each system. In fact, for the Lacks system, the highest level of diagnostic accuracy was achieved by the least experienced scorer. In addition,

Table 7.11   BGT Diagnostic Accuracy (Percent Correctly Diagnosed) for Different Levels of Scorer Experience[a]

Level of scorer expertise	No brain damage	Brain damage diagnosis	Total
Expert scorer	85	84	84
Typical scorer	70	90	82
Novice scorer	86	86	86
Mean	80	87	84

[a]For a sample of 50 neuropsychiatric inpatients (Lacks & Newport, 1980).

within each of the four scoring systems the level of agreement or interscorer reliability was consistent among scorers of widely differing levels of experience with the BGT.

From the results of this study, we can see that psychologists, regardless of their level of experience, can achieve high levels of diagnostic accuracy with the Bender Gestalt through the use of this brief, easily learned, objective scoring system. Similar results were found in Garb and Schramke's (1996) meta-analysis of 11 studies using the HRB and WAIS-R for neuropsychological assessment. They also found scant evidence of the influence of experience upon the neuropsychologists' diagnostic accuracy. Also, the correlation between accuracy and clinicians' confidence in their judgments was only .29. However, Garb and Schramke suggest that the artificial diagnostic situation of a research study may not allow experts the opportunity to apply their expertise fully.

RELATIONSHIP OF BGT SCORES TO DEMOGRAPHIC VARIABLES

The task with neuropsychological tests is to determine if the test performance falls within the *nonpatient range* and whether the test score represents a drop in performance from a previous level, that is, whether any *impairment* in ability has taken place (Heaton, Ryan, Grant, & Matthews, 1996). Norms provide us with the means to make such judgments. However, to be useful, norms must be unbiased and representative of the general population and of the group from which the patient comes. Norms must also account for demographic variables that may influence test performance. In many instances clinicians are unaware of relationships between psychological test performance and relevant demographic variables, leading to inappropriate uses of tests and the drawing of inaccurate conclusions. Relevant demographic variables include gender, ethnicity, age, education, and IQ. Unfortunately, many neuropsychological tests do not have norms that are adjusted for such variables. Information is presented here for children and adults, both psychiatric patients and nonpatients. In general, the effect of these variables upon neuropsychological test scores is greater for those individuals without impairment than it is for those with brain impairment (Heaton et al., 1996). The assessment dilemma is to determine if the test score of an individual falls within normal limits. This section will help you to make that judgment for the BGT, adjusting for these important demographic variables.

Gender

Most research findings suggest that clinicians can confidently apply the BGT impartially to males and females, whether adults or children. For example, Pascal and Suttell (1951) found no differences in BGT performance between 87 nonpatient adult males and 87 females matched for age (15 to 50) and education (high school or college). This result allowed them also to combine normative data for the two genders.

However, Lacks, in her much broader and more extensive sample of 495 nonpatient adults, did find a small but statistically significant gender effect ($r = .24, p < .01$). This effect persisted even when analysis of covariance was used to control for differences in age and education. The mean for females was 1.37 errors and for males was 2.07 errors, indicating a slight advantage for females.

As for psychiatric patients, Parsons and Prigatano (1978) reported that possible differences in performance between males and females on neurological tests have received little attention. Many studies have used only male patients. Others do not report the composition of their sample in terms of gender. The remaining studies have generally not measured gender differences. There are, however, three studies relating to the Hutt-Briskin scoring method that examine the gender variable.

Hutt and Miller (1976) gave the BGT to 40 hospitalized patients with schizophrenia and 100 outpatient therapy patients. The tests were scored for Hutt's Psychopathology scale, which contains 9 of the 12 signs of the Hutt-Briskin scoring for cognitive deficits. No gender differences were found for this scale in either the schizophrenia or the outpatient group. Using the Lacks adaptation of the Hutt-Briskin scoring procedures, Brilliant and Gynther (1963) and Fjeld, Small, Small, and Hayden (1966) found negligible relationships between gender and BGT scores for psychiatric inpatients. It may be that psychiatric disorders and brain dysfunction introduce enough variance to override the gender difference found with nonpatients.

Ethnicity   A number of researchers found that ethnicity is related to BGT scores for adults and for children (see Chapter 11). In terms of adult nonpatients, Pascal and Suttell (1951) included only whites in their normative sample. However, West et al. (1977) found that for nonpatient males ages 45 to 65, more African Americans than whites were classified as neurologically impaired on the BGT-BIP, although primarily those older participants with less than 8 years' education and a rural Southern background. The normative group in this book does include the BGTs of 139 African Americans. When the BGT scores of the broad and extensive sample of 495 nonpatient adults were analyzed, a significant ethnic difference emerged ($r = .20, p < .01$). African American individuals had a slightly greater mean error score of 2.21, compared to 1.58 for whites. The difference persisted even when analysis of covariance was utilized to control for differences in age and education.

As for psychiatric patients, Adams, Boake, and Crain (1982) demonstrated ethnic bias on the BGT-BIP. They studied a sample of male psychiatric inpatients, 97 with brain damage and 62 nonimpaired, of whom 100 were white, 46 were Mexican American, and 13 were African American. They found distinct ethnicity differences that led to higher misclassification rates for ethnic groups other than whites.

In contrast to the findings of these two studies, another carefully done study did not find ethnic differences on the BGT. In the most thorough comparison of African American and white BGT performance, Butler et al. (1976) studied 72 African American and white male psychiatric inpatients diagnosed as having either brain damage or psychiatric disorders and individually matched for diagnosis, age, education, and IQ. BGT protocols were scored with both the Pascal-Suttell (1951) and Hain (1964) systems. They found no ethnicity effect for the Hain system with and without epilepsy or the Pascal-Suttell system with epilepsy. A significant ethnicity effect did appear for the Pascal-Suttell scoring with nonepileptic patients, with African American patients performing better than whites. Butler et al. (1976) suggest that previous findings of ethnic differences may be due to IQ and other differences between African American and white individuals rather than to ethnicity per se. In terms of the Lacks scoring method, Brilliant and Gynther (1963) found no differences between the BGTs of white and African American patients when the effects of age were controlled. Fjeld et al. (1966) found no differences attributable to ethnicity for psychiatric inpatients.

As with females, there appears to be a slight advantage for white individuals on the BGT. This is likely due to cultural rather than inherent differences. For example, African Americans may have received less early emphasis on activities requiring perceptual-motor coordination. Vega and Powell (1973) did find that allowing African American children to practice with graphic materials enabled them to improve their repeat BGT performances significantly over those of children not given this opportunity. Furthermore, it appears that the variance introduced by any kind of psychopathology may override the effects of ethnic differences, causing them no longer to be apparent in psychiatric groups. The reader is referred to Heaton et al. (1996) for a discussion of additional issues related to ethnicity and test performance. They recommend caution when testing anyone from an ethnic group other than white Anglo American.

Age   Many psychological tests, such as those measuring memory, cognition, and perceptual-motor coordination, are influenced by the age of the person being tested. For example, Price, Fein, and Feinberg (1980) found that 56% of retired, healthy school teachers (mean age = 72) scored in the brain-impairment range using the standard norms of the HRB. The age-related deficits were more dramatic on some subtests in the battery than on others (the range of participants misclassified on different subtests was 18% to 90%). Heaton et al. (1996), in assessing demographic effects on the WAIS-R and the HRB, found substantial age and education effects. In general, the WAIS was more related to education and the HRB to age; that is, performance declined with advancing age and less education. A second issue was the *sensitivity* of the battery of tests, that is, the ability to correctly classify individuals into categories of impairment versus no impairment. In terms of sensitivity, the effects of age and education differed for nonpatients as compared to those with neurological impairment. For the nonpatients, diagnostic accuracy decreased with advancing age but increased with more education. The *opposite* pattern was true for the group with brain damage; accuracy increased with greater age and decreased with more education. Therefore, the HRB had relatively more difficulty identifying younger and more educated individuals with brain damage. The hit rate was 55% for those under age 40 and 94% for those over 60; for education, accuracy was 87% when education was less than 12 years and 60% when over 16 years. As a result, the norms were most accurate, overall, at the middle range of age and education and were unacceptably low at either extreme. This type of information is a strong indication of the need to take into account such demographic variables when evaluating neuropsychological test performance.

The BGT is no exception. Developmental studies of children (e.g., Bender, 1938; Koppitz, 1975) show a maturational process up to the age of 12, at which time all of the designs can be successfully executed. McIntosh et al. (1988) found continued BGT improvement from ages 12 through 16. Tolor and Brannigan (1980) concluded that, for nonpatients, age is significantly related to BGT performance only before full maturation is reached and after impairment due to aging begins. Pascal and Suttell (1951) found no significant correlation between BGT scores and age in the range of 15 to 50 years.

The BGT normative data presented earlier for nonpatient adults do show a trend for error scores to increase gradually with age. The correlation between age and BGT score was .30 ($p < .01$). Differences in results between this sample and Pascal and Suttell's are probably due to the very restricted age range of the latter. However, in spite of this trend, even individuals well into their 70s and 80s do not generally exhibit scores in the impaired diagnostic range. Only 7% of nonpatients age 45 to 59 had scores of 5 or more errors. This increases to 22% of those age 60 to 74 and 39% of those over age 80. So for individuals who are not psychiatric patients, the significant relationship of age to BGT scores does not appear to constitute any hazard to diagnostic accuracy.

Many studies (e.g., Hain, 1964) also report significant correlations between age and BGT errors for psychiatric adults. Brilliant and Gynther (1963) even found such relationships ($r = .26$ to $.40$) with the Benton Visual Retention Test and the Graham-Kendall Memory for Designs, both of which contain age corrections in their scoring.

Hutt and Miller (1976) did not find significant correlations ($r = -.08$ to $.20$) between the Psychopathology scale and age when the age range studied was 16 to 62 years for patients with schizophrenia and outpatients. Brilliant and Gynther (1963), who studied psychiatric inpatients from a broader age range (17 to 84 years) with the 12 Hutt-Briskin signs, did find a significant correlation with age ($r = .40, p < .01$).

Table 7.12 presents BGT results, across six age ranges, for the three diagnostic groups previously described. For all three diagnoses, there is a trend for error scores to increase with age. However, even in the oldest nonimpaired groups the mean scores are well within the unimpaired range and the mean scores for the younger patients with brain dysfunction are still well within the impaired range. Table 7.13 shows also that, for the same patients, age has little

Table 7.12   BGT Scores by Age and Diagnosis for Three Psychiatric Diagnostic Groups

Age	Personality disorder				Psychosis				Brain dysfunction			
	N	M	SD	% > 4 errors	N	M	SD	% > 4 errors	N	M	SD	% > 4 errors
18–24	28	3.32	1.76	14	17	2.47	1.81	18	—	—	—	—
25–34	32	3.03	1.67	16	43	3.26	1.73	30	14	5.00	1.41	79
35–44	33	4.33	1.95	45	41	3.78	2.04	32	23	5.26	1.81	70
45–54	27	3.33	1.24	11	25	3.92	1.87	28	22	5.64	1.89	77
55–64	—	—	—	—	13	3.92	1.75	31	12	6.67	1.78	100
65+	—	—	—	—	—	—	—	—	9	8.11	1.62	100

Table 7.13   Percentage of Correct Diagnoses for Patients with Brain Damage and Psychiatric Patients without Brain Damage, Grouped by Age and IQ Range

Diagnosis	N	Age range					
		18–24	25–34	35–44	45–54	55–64	65+
Brain damage	82	—	79	70	77	100	100
Psychiatric disorder	264	84	76	62	80	72	—
		IQ range					
	N	60–69	70–79	80–89	90–99	100–109	110+
Brain damage	82	86	93	84	100	57	82
Psychiatric disorder	264	35	50	64	78	79	95

effect upon diagnostic accuracy. Clinicians should be well aware of the relationship of age to BGT performance in psychiatric patients, particularly at the extreme ends of the age continuum. Interpretation of neuropsychological test data should be adjusted for persons who fall in this category.

IQ and Education   Similarly, there seems to be fairly consistent evidence of IQ and education effects upon BGT scores. For nonpatient adults, Pascal and Suttell (1951) found no effect for education as long as the individual had at least 9 years of schooling. In the Lacks method normative data presented earlier in this chapter, both education ($r = -.51, p < .01$) and IQ ($r = -.13, p < .05$) were significantly related to BGT scores. Error scores increase with *decreasing* education and IQ. However, this effect appears to be clinically significant only in those with very low education (i.e., less than eighth grade) or IQ. Even then, only 16 of the 75 or 21% of individuals with 8 or fewer years of education had scores in the impaired diagnostic range. It is entirely possible that at older ages or with low education or IQ there are some persons who are more likely to have some type of previously undetected brain dysfunction. Golden (1990) gives the example of brain damage that "occurs early in a child's life or results in generalized destruction of the brain" (p. 251). Table 7.13 dramatically demonstrates the relationship between age, IQ, and diagnostic accuracy. As with age, it appears that the relationship between education or IQ and the BGT is not sufficient to jeopardize the diagnostic accuracy of this instrument with nonpatients.

For psychiatric patients, Tolor and Brannigan (1980) report that in the absence of severe ego impairment there does not seem to be much correlation between IQ and BGT performance. Hutt and Miller (1976) did not find education to be related to the Psychopathology scale in a sample of 546 patients. However, a number of researchers found small but significant correlations between education or IQ and BGT performance. Adams et al. (1982) also found such a relationship with the BGT-BIP. Brilliant and Gynther (1963) found that IQ and education correlated −.33 and −.41 with BGT scores. Johnson et al. (1971) found an even greater correlation ($r = -.53$ to $-.59$) between BGT scores and IQ with 240 inpatients. They found high diagnostic accuracies only for patients with brain damage with less than average IQs and for unimpaired patients with average or greater IQs.

Contrary to the findings of Johnson et al. (1971), the author has found no decrease in percentages of correct identification of patients with brain impairment with higher levels of IQ (see Table 7.13). This discrepancy in patients with brain dysfunction is probably due to the fact that Johnson et al. used a history of epilepsy or seizures as one of the criteria for inclusion in the brain dysfunction group. Bender (1965) has stated that "epilepsy has no specific organic cortical pathology that would interfere with the perceptual motor or gestalt function demonstrable in this test" (p. 189). A number of researchers confirm this statement (e.g., Delaney, 1982; Hauer & Armentrout, 1978). Johnson et al.'s overall reported diagnostic accuracy of 64% is also considerably lower than that of other published results on this system. In one other study that also found remarkably low BGT accuracy (Butler et al., 1976), almost half of the patients with brain damage had epilepsy. However, the author found that considerably lower percentages of unimpaired patients were correctly identified in the IQ range of 60 to 89 (see Table 7.13). Part of the problem may be that individuals with lower IQs are indeed more likely to have brain impairment undetected by psychiatrists or ascribed simply to low IQ. In any event, clinicians should exercise additional caution in the differential diagnosis of individuals in the lower IQ or education ranges.

In summary, clinicians can use the BGT with males and females, African Americans and whites with confidence that the variables of gender and ethnicity will not generally jeopardize the test results. However, there should be more concern for the variables of age, IQ, and education because significant correlations do exist between them and BGT scores. When individuals are examined who fall into the extreme ends of the distributions of age, education, and IQ, clinicians should interpret test results with more caution, taking these factors into account.

EFFECTS OF MEDICATION AND ELECTROCONVULSIVE TREATMENT UPON BGT PERFORMANCE

One dilemma that daily confronts clinicians, especially those working in inpatient settings, is the degree of interference with psychological test results from psychotropic medications and electroconvulsive treatments. The question warrants even more concern when the tests are neuropsychological in nature. Because both these types of treatments are in widespread usage in many psychiatric settings, psychologists must be aware of any effects that may influence the conclusions drawn from these tests.

Medication and the BGT

The question of the effects upon BGT performance of psychotropic medications arises because of the routine use of these drugs to treat the majority of seriously disturbed psychiatric patients. These drugs are also well known for producing a wide variety of side effects. Is it possible for drugs to alter performance on psychological tests, in particular the BGT? Would the alteration take the form of making test results look worse, that is, raising the likelihood of a diagnosis of brain damage?

A number of reviews on the effects of psychotropic medication on psychological test performance are available (e.g., Baker, 1968; Essman, 1973). Yozawitz (1986), in a study of 90 psychiatric patients, found that those who were taking psychotropic medication did not do more poorly on neuropsychological tests than those not taking these medications. In fact, there was some evidence of improved test performance while on medication. One study has examined this question for the BGT. Owen (1971) gave the BGT to a sample of 60 inpatients with schizophrenia and no known brain damage who had not received drugs or ECT at least 2 months prior to hospitalization. Patients were randomly assigned to one of four groups ($N = 15$ each): a pretreatment group tested within 48 hours of admission and prior to medication; a group tested after 4 to 6 days of standard chlorpromazine treatment; a group tested after 7 to 9 days of the antipsychotic treatment; and a group tested after 15 to 20 days of the drug treatment. Groups were found not to be different in terms of gender, ethnicity, age, or IQ.

The BGT was scored by the Lacks method. No significant drug effects were found on the BGT for any of the three intervals studied. This study specific to the BGT and reviews of research on the effects on other tests appear to eliminate the need for concern about major effects on the BGT after a few weeks of acute administration. Heaton et al. (1978) warn, however, that there probably is a significant correlation between *chronic* antipsychotic drug usage and impairment on neuropsychological tests.

Electroconvulsive Treatment and the BGT

A second type of psychiatric therapy that may affect psychological test results is electroconvulsive treatment (ECT). Lezak (1995) reviews this topic and concludes that memory complaints are common for patients who have undergone ECT. Memory deficits occur most often during the course of treatment and briefly afterward. Deficits most often affect recent memories and are most severe and lasting for those patients where ECT is applied bilaterally rather than unilaterally. Some studies show more memory problems and greater likelihood of irreversible deficits when the number of treatments exceeds 20. Pettinati and Bonner (1984) even found better Trail Making Test, Form B results for older adult patients with depression who had never been given ECT versus a similar group who had undergone ECT when younger.

Only two studies directly tested the relationship between ECT and BGT performance. Erwin and Hampe (1966) gave the BGT to 20 psychiatric patients before and on every day after ECT. Patients received from 3 to 16 treatments, with a mean of 7. BGT protocols were scored by the Pascal-Suttell (1951) method. Of the 20 patients, 18 showed slight improvement over trials, one showed slight deterioration, and a 53-year-old patient with depression was unable to draw the designs at all after three shock treatments. Although BGT performance of the majority of patients did not worsen, it was highly variable during ECT.

The second study compared pre- and post-ECT test scores with repeated measures from control patients who had not received ECT. Garron and Cheifetz (1968) tested 19 psychiatric patients who received between 3 and 10 ECT, with a mean of 6. The retesting interval ranged from 11 to 43 days, with a mean of 24. Retesting was done on the average of 2 days after the last ECT was administered (range = 0 to 6 days). The control group consisted of 19 psychiatric patients individually matched to those receiving ECT on the variables of age, ethnicity, gender, education, and retest interval. The results, using the Hain (1964) scoring system, showed no impairment on the BGT following ECT. In fact, on the average those receiving ECT showed slight improvement of BGT performance.

Although none of these studies utilized the Hutt-Briskin scoring system, it seems probable, based on two studies and two different scoring systems, that the clinician may use the BGT with confidence after short (3 ECT) to moderate (15 ECT) courses of this type of therapy. Testing should probably wait until the day after ECT is given. At present there is no definitive knowledge about the effects of longer courses of ECT; caution should be utilized in interpreting test scores collected under these conditions.

SUMMARY There is considerable evidence that attests to the validity of the Lacks version of the Hutt-Briskin scoring system when it is used as a screening test for brain dysfunction. Individuals across a wide range of ages and years of education who are not psychiatric patients exhibit test scores that are considerably different from the scores of those with diagnosed brain pathology. In addition, as a group, psychiatric patients with psychogenic disorders are demonstrably different on the BGT from those with neuropathology. Not only can these groups be discriminated from each other, but individual cases can be predicted with high accuracy, on the average between 80% and 85%. These results were cross-validated using the standard cutoff score across several samples as well as across scorers.

The BGT has also been found to correlate significantly with several other neuropsychological tests: the Benton Visual Retention, the Graham-Kendall Memory for Designs, and the Halstead-Reitan Battery. However, when diagnostic accuracies are compared, the BGT is consistently superior to the others when used in a neuropsychiatric setting. When the Lacks scoring method is compared to several others for the BGT, it also is consistently superior to them. The high accuracy rates are achieved with BGT experts, typical users, and novices.

Although statistical differences are apparent for ethnicity and gender in the BGT scores of nonpatients, they do not appear to be large enough to be of clinical significance. However, little data are available on the BGT performance of adults by ethnic groups other than African American. For psychiatric patients, ethnicity and gender differences are not apparent, perhaps overridden by the onset of psychopathology. As with other cognitive or information-processing tests, there are significant age, education, and IQ effects for both patients and nonpatients. However, these relationships appear to warrant interpretive caution only in the extreme ranges of these variables.

CHAPTER 8

Reliability

Relatively little attention has been paid to the topic of the reliability of the Bender Gestalt Test (BGT). Instead, the primary focus has been on validity issues. One reason for this neglect may be some confusion about what type of reliability is appropriate for the BGT. First, reliability can be looked at in terms of either the consistency of the measuring instrument itself or the consistency with which individuals use that instrument. There is high agreement on the importance of the latter type of reliability for the BGT. Any scoring system for a test must enable different scorers to produce comparable results and enable the same scorer to be consistent over time. It is the area of test reliability, not scorer reliability, that raises more difficult issues and differences of opinion. The American Psychological Association, in its *Standards for Educational and Psychological Tests* (1985), recommends comparison of parallel forms of a test if possible and, if not, then some kind of matched-half comparison (e.g., split-half or odd-even). However, neither method is appropriate for this particular test. There is no alternate set of BGT stimulus designs; nor can the test be divided up in any way to form matched halves, because the nine designs vary considerably in difficulty, in complexity, and in which of the 12 errors of this scoring system apply (i.e., Overlapping Difficulty can be scored only for figures 6 and 7).

The one kind of test reliability that does seem suitable for this test is that of *temporal stability.* An important facet of any test is the consistency of results when it is repeated over time. Temporal stability is particularly important with a neuropsychological test that may often be repeated either to assess degree of deterioration or as a check against equivocal findings. Also, patients frequently may have been tested before in a different setting or in a previous hospitalization, making practice effects an issue.

For the clinician to be confident of judgments about changes in a patient's functioning over time, there must be stability of test results in the absence of any real changes in the person being tested. But temporal stability of a test can only be demonstrated if the characteristic being assessed does not fluctuate over time. In other words, the test-retest reliability of a psychological measure may be attenuated by true changes in the individual who is the subject of the assessment. Because brain functioning, the focus of the BGT, can fluctuate over time with deterioration, drugs, health changes, or aging, any test-retest comparisons should probably be considered as the lower bounds of the estimate of temporal stability of this instrument. Naturally, the longer the time that passes before the second testing, the more time for real changes to take place, thus lowering reliability.

In the following sections, the temporal stability of the BGT and, in particular, of the Hutt-Briskin method are reported. In addition, the interscorer reliability of the test is explored.

TEST-RETEST RELIABILITY   For the psychometric theorist, the index of a test's temporal stability is the correlation coefficient between first and second testing. However, this index often may not provide the most useful information about reliability for the clinician. For a neuropsychological test, the practitioner is more often concerned about *diagnostic* reliability, or the ability of the test to produce consistent conclusions or classifications rather than just consistent scores. Using the Hutt-Briskin scoring method as an example, scores can range from 0 to 4 and result in a test diagnosis of no brain dysfunction or range from 5 to 12 and qualify for a test diagnosis of brain dysfunction. For the BGT, scored with this system and used in its most common screening role, the most important information to the clinician is this dichotomous classification: brain dysfunction or no brain dysfunction. Whether the score is 4 errors at first testing and 2 on retesting or 7 errors at first and 9 at a later assessment has less relevance to the clinician. Whether the patient makes exactly the same errors is of even less importance.

Matarazzo and his colleagues refer to this distinction as one between psychometric and clinical reliability (Matarazzo, Matarazzo, Wiens, Gallo, & Klonoff, 1976). Neither type of reliability is necessarily more "correct," but each has value for certain purposes. A test could be both reliable and unreliable, looking at it from these two different perspectives. In the discussion that follows, whenever possible, reliability will be presented in three ways to reflect both the psychometric and the clinical perspective: (1) the traditional Pearson product-moment correlation coefficients between one set of total scores and another; (2) the correspondence between the *exact* kind of errors scored at different times; and (3) a more clinically useful index of the agreement over time on diagnosis as derived from the cutoff point of 5 or more errors (i.e., brain impairment versus nonimpairment).

In their review of the literature, Tolor and Brannigan (1980) conclude that research has demonstrated satisfactory BGT test-retest reliabilities using a variety of objective scoring systems and scorers with varying amounts of clinical experience. For example, test-retest reliability using the Pascal and Suttell procedures ranges from .63 to .76, depending upon degree of psychopathology and length of time between testings (24 hours to 18 months). Koppitz (1975) found similar results using her scoring system with children. Both Koppitz and Tolor and Brannigan do caution clinicians, however, to rely on total scores for their classifications rather than on specific individual errors that show lower reliabilities.

In a study on Hutt's 17-item Psychopathology scale (which includes 9 of the 12 Hutt-Briskin errors suggestive of cognitive impairment), Miller and Hutt (1975) retested 40 psychiatric inpatients over a 2-week period. Test-retest reliability of Psychopathology scores was .87 for males and .83 for females. These levels were found for both low-scoring and high-scoring patients.

The author has calculated test-retest reliability for the Lacks adaptation with 40 psychiatric patients: 22 VA inpatients, 13 private psychiatric inpatients, and 5 outpatients from a university psychology clinic. The sample included 30 males and 10 females, of whom 33 were white and 7 were African American. Age ranged from 18 to 60, with a mean of 36 years ($SD = 12.83$); education ranged from 7 to 18 years, with a mean of 12.03 ($SD = 2.21$). Diagnoses ranged widely, including schizophrenia, alcoholism, depression, and cognitive disorders.

Patients were given the BGT twice after an interval that ranged from 5 to 21 days, with a mean of 9.56 days. In 32 of the 40 cases, both test administrations were given by the same person, an undergraduate honors student who had been extensively trained in the standard procedure. In the remaining cases, the second testing was done by one of two other examiners, either a hospital psychometrician or an experienced clinical psychologist.

All BGT protocols were scored by the author using the Lacks scoring method (18 years experience, over 2,000 protocols). Before scoring, all the protocols were arranged in random order, within a larger pool of participants that included nonpatients, allowing scoring to be done blind as to patient status and time of testing.

The mean BGT score at initial testing was 2.30 ($SD = 1.40$) and at retesting was 2.05 ($SD = 1.65$), a nonsignificant difference. For agreement of the total scores, the test-retest correlation coefficient was a satisfactory .79. Concurrence on the exact signs from first to second testing was 86%. Agreement of diagnosis (either brain impairment or absence of impairment) was 93% between the two times of testing.

Test-retest reliability of the Lacks scoring method was also examined in a sample of dementia patients.* This sample consisted of 25 individuals with well-documented, mild senile dementia of the Alzheimer's type. Age ranged from 64 to 81, with a mean of 72.2 years. The retesting interval was 12 months. For the patients with Alzheimer's disease, mean BGT scores at the two times of testing were 4.52 ($SD = 2.14$) and 5.67 ($SD = 1.97$), a nonsignificant difference. Test-retest reliability of total scores was .66 and correspondence of exact scoring was 63%. When clinical reliability is considered, there was 72% agreement for diagnosis between the two times of testing for this sample.

Table 8.1 summarizes the results of these two temporal stability studies, one with patients with mixed neuropsychiatric disorders and one with patients with

---

* I would like to thank Drs. Leonard Berg and Charles Hughes, former codirectors of the Memory in Aging project, for making these data available, and Dr. Warren Danziger, research coordinator of the project, for cooperation in the data analysis.

Table 8.1   Test-Retest Consistency on the BGT

Subjects	Time interval	Test M	Test SD	Retest M	Retest SD	Reliability	Agreement on exact signs	Agreement on diagnosis
40 neuropsychiatric patients	5–21 days	2.30	1.40	2.05	1.65	.79	86%	93%
25 patients with mild Alzheimer's	12 months	4.52	2.14	5.67	1.97	.66	63%	72%
57 nonpatient older adults	12 months	2.26	1.11	2.55	1.25	.58	81%	93%
186 nonpatient older adults	3 months	3.56	2.19	3.57	2.09	.57	76%	75%
175 nonpatient older adults	12 months	3.55	2.19	3.67	1.95	.63	78%	73%

Note: All reliability coefficients are significant at $p < .001$. None of the test-retest changes in scores is significantly different.

Alzheimer's disease, using the Lacks scoring system. Also included are data from several samples of nonpatient older adults. The first sample consisted of 57 healthy matched controls for the patients with Alzheimer's disease. All were extensively interviewed, examined neurologically, and found to be free of brain dysfunction. The other sample is from a study (Lacks & Storandt, 1982) on the BGT performance of a large sample of healthy, self-sufficient older adults who were retested after 3 months ($N = 186$) and again after 12 months ($N = 175$).

Examination of this table reveals that the Lacks scoring method demonstrates psychometric test-retest reliability ($r = .57$ to $.79$) that is adequate and is comparable to that shown for other BGT scoring systems, such as those of Pascal and Suttell and Koppitz. This method is also comparable to the levels of reliability shown by even more extensive batteries of neuropsychological tests. For example, Golden, Berg, and Graber (1982) found test-retest reliability of .88 on the Luria-Nebraska battery for a very stable group of 27 patients with chronic, unchanging brain conditions over an average interval of 167 days. For the Halstead-Reitan battery, Matarazzo et al. (1976) found reliability coefficient ranges of .63 to .83 for groups with various psychiatric and cognitive impairment diagnoses. Retest intervals were from 12 to 52 weeks.

When one looks at reliability of the Hutt-Briskin scoring criteria from a clinical perspective, the results are very encouraging. For neuropsychiatric patients retested after a short interval and for nonpatient older adults carefully screened for any neurological deficits, the diagnostic agreement in both cases was 93%, a highly consistent finding. In other words, in two groups where the actual behaviors measured by the BGT were probably relatively stable, either due to a short passage of time or the absence of a condition leading to deterioration of cognitive function, the BGT led to very consistent diagnostic conclusions, even after as long as a full year. In the group with Alzheimer's disease, where diffuse deterioration was known to be taking place due to the degenerative nature of this disease, the diagnostic agreement dropped to 72%. All 7 cases of a different diagnosis after 1 year involved a change from a diagnosis of nonimpairment to cognitive-impairment. Therefore, the reduced agreement is highly likely to be the result of real changes rather than test instability. A similar level of diagnostic agreement (73% to 75%) was found for two groups of nonpatient older adults who were healthy and self-sufficient but who were not carefully screened for neurological disorders. It may be that consistency over time for this group was also attenuated by real changes because the participants' ages ranged from 60 to 87 years. In summary, the available evidence points to high diagnostic stability over time in the absence of actual changes in patient behavior. This means that the clinician can be confident that changes in diagnosis over time, based on the Hutt-Briskin scores, reflect true changes in the individual being tested.

INTERSCORER RELIABILITY

Garb and Schramke (1996) recently reviewed judgment research for neuropsychological instruments. They looked at interrater agreement in three decision-making situations: impairment versus no impairment; location of impairment; and identification of strengths and deficits, including visual perceptual-motor skills. They found good to excellent interrater agreement in all three areas; however, often the examined diagnostic task was not as difficult as the one facing psychologists in many settings—to distinguish between psychiatric inpatients with cognitive disorders versus those who do not have cognitive impairment.

In general, most scoring systems for the BGT have enjoyed satisfactory agreement among scorers; the Hutt-Briskin method is no exception. Most of the published work focuses on Hutt's 17-item Psychopathology scale, which includes 9 of the 12 errors related to a diagnosis of brain dysfunction. For example, two experienced clinicians who scored 100 schizophrenic protocols obtained a correlation between them of .96. Only 3 of the 17 individual items on this scale yielded a reliability coefficient of less than .81 (Rotation, Simplification, and Overlapping Difficulty) with a total range for individual errors from .76 to 1.00. Interscorer reliability dipped slightly to .90 when a relatively inexperienced and an experienced scorer were compared (Miller & Hutt, 1975). In a study comparing pre- and posttests of 120 male delinquents (Hutt & Dates, 1977), three judges produced a Kendall's coefficient of concordance of .91 (pretest) and .95 (posttest).

As for consistency among scorers using the 12 signs of the Hutt-Briskin system, one study (Lacks & Newport, 1980) had three scorers evaluate 50 neuropsychiatric inpatient BGT protocols using the Lacks method. One very experienced scorer (the author of this book) was an *expert,* with 18 years of experience and 2,000 BGTs. Another scorer was a more *typical* psychologist, with 6 years of clinical experience and an average of 50 BGT protocols scored per year. The third scorer was a *novice* who had an undergraduate degree in psychology and no previous knowledge of the BGT or any other neuropsychology test.

Interscorer reliability of the three scorers using the Lacks method was measured by Pearson product-moment correlation coefficients among scorers on total test scores. The three scorers were able to achieve acceptable levels of agreement, with reliability coefficients that ranged from .87 to .90.

In terms of *exact* agreement of scoring, there were 600 scoring opportunities (50 protocols multiplied by the presence or absence of 12 signs). Percent exact agreement for these 600 opportunities ranged from 77% to 86% for any two scorers and was 72% when agreement was measured for all three scorers at the same time. The agreement on diagnosis ranged from 86% to 94% for any two scorers, with 84% agreement among all three scorers.

Essentially the same results were found when three scorers of varying experience all scored the BGTs for a sample of 30 inpatients with mixed psychiatric disorders. Again, one scorer was a relative expert, with about 5 years of clinical experience and about 500 previously scored protocols using the Lacks system. Another scorer represented a more typical clinician, with 5 years of experience but far fewer protocols scored. The third scorer was a psychometrician with an undergraduate degree and only 1 year of experience.

Interscorer reliability ranged from .89 to .95 among these three scorers. Concurrence on the exact signs for any two scorers ranged from 85% to 88%, with 81% achieved when all three scorers agreed. Agreement on a diagnosis of cognitive impairment versus no impairment (based only on the BGT score) ranged from 87% to 97%. All three scorers taken together agreed on diagnosis 87% of the time. In another study (Friedt & Gouvier, 1989), researchers found similar results between two examiners scoring 30 BGTs from a neuropsychiatric forensic population. They found 94% agreement on Lacks system total scores and 97% concurrence for classification into brain impairment versus no impairment categories. They found that the reliability of overall scoring (i.e., whether a score is present or not present) ranged from 77% to 97% across the 12 types of errors; the average was 88%.

A similar issue is one of intrascorer reliability, that is, the consistency over time of the same clinician's efforts. Several years after the data for the Lacks and Newport (1980) study were collected, the expert scorer for the Lacks method was asked to rescore the 50 BGT protocols. The correlation for total scores between these two times of evaluation was .93, with 82% agreement on the exact signs and 94% on diagnosis.

These studies indicate high levels of agreement among scorers using the Lacks adaptation of the Hutt-Briskin method for the BGT, even when those scorers differ radically in level of general experience and specific background with this particular method. Also, for at least one psychologist, high consistency over time with the same scorer has been demonstrated. However, it should be noted that the novice scorers did receive about 2 hours of training where they studied a scoring manual, scored 10 practice protocols, and received feedback on their practice scoring. Less training than this has resulted in increased scoring inconsistency. To facilitate maximum scoring consistency, this book provides case examples and practice scoring exercises. This feature should allow clinicians to accomplish satisfactory training independently. It must be stressed, however, that achievement of adequate consistency in scoring will require at least a 3- or 4-hour commitment of time on the part of the clinician.

CHAPTER 9

Interpretation of Bender Gestalt Test Results

EIGHT STEPS FOR INTERPRETATION

After you have carefully administered the test, noted relevant behavioral observations, and diligently scored the drawings for errors, you are ready to interpret the results. Remember, this interpretation is based solely on the Bender Gestalt Test (BGT). However, the BGT results are meaningless until integrated with patient history and your findings from other tests given to the patient. Use the test conservatively; always require multiple confirmation of conclusions.

Responsible interpretation of the BGT results requires at least eight steps, ranging from estimating the validity of the test score to applying scientific decision-making rules (see Table 9.1). Remember to refer back to previous chapters for more detail on topics relevant to interpretation, such as behavioral observations (Chapter 4), validity and reliability (Chapters 7 and 8), and norms (Chapter 7). Also, Chapters 10 and 12 contain norms for older adults and adolescents.

1. Determine the validity and reliability of the patient's effort. The initial step in test analysis requires the psychologist to determine if the person being assessed took the BGT in a manner that inspires confidence in the results. Some items from Figure 4.2, listing general test-taking attitudes and specific behavioral observations, will help you make this decision. You are trying to decide if test errors are the result of true constructional difficulties or are due to other factors, such as insufficient attention, trouble understanding instructions, vision problems, malingering, or extreme anxiety. For example, if the person was careful, serious, and motivated to do well, if he or she took 4 to 10 minutes to complete the test, and if he or she showed no specific behavioral observations, such as fatigue or hearing problems, then it is likely that the results of the person's efforts are valid and reliable. On the other hand, if the patient displayed poor test-taking attitudes and behaviors, they should raise questions about the validity and reliability of the BGT results. If the latter is true, proceed with caution.

Another behavior that relates to validity and reliability is the amount of time the patient takes to complete the test. Lacks found that the average time to take the standard BGT was 5 to 6 minutes ($SDs = 2$ to 3 minutes) for nonpatients and inpatients without brain damage (see Table 4.1). Two situations regarding time to complete the test are especially relevant to validity and reliability. In the first situation, the patient takes a very short time, say 2 or 3 minutes, and makes 5 or

Table 9.1   Interpretation Strategies for the Bender Gestalt Test

1. Determine the validity and reliability of the patient's effort.
2. Compare the number of errors to the appropriate norms.
3. Classify the patient's score.
4. Take an actuarial approach to prediction.
5. Analyze the patient's specific errors.
6. Note other variables that can affect the test interpretation.
7. Familiarize yourself with the recent research on the most common diagnostic categories.
8. Apply scientific decision-making rules.

more errors. In this instance, the number of errors probably represents an *overestimation* of the true number of errors. Generally, this person will also demonstrate test behaviors that indicate low motivation, carelessness, and poor rapport with the examiner. The second situation occurs when the patient takes a much longer time than most people, say, over 10 minutes, but is only able to do an adequate job, that is, makes 3 or 4 errors. In this case, the number of errors probably *underestimates* the true score. Often this person's test behaviors show considerable amounts of care and deliberation.

2. Compare the number of errors to the norms.   The second step in the interpretative process is to compare the number of errors made to the appropriate norms. Normative data have been provided for the following groups:

Group	Table number	Page numbers
Nonpatient adults	7.2, 7.3	103
Psychiatric inpatients	7.5, 7.12	105, 119
Nonpatient older adults	10.1	143
Older adults with dementia	10.2	147
Adolescents	12.2	175

Unfortunately, except for nonpatients, there are no separate norms for other ethnic groups or for outpatients (except for the group with dementia).

By using these tables, you can describe the average number of errors and the standard deviation for someone of the same age and diagnostic group as the person you tested. For example, suppose you tested a 30-year-old inpatient who made 3 errors. From Table 7.12, you have the information by age for patients diagnosed with personality disorder, psychosis, and brain damage. Table 9.2 provides the same information collapsing the two groups with no brain damage into one. The average number of errors for a 30-year-old adult with a previous psychiatric history is 3.16 ($SD = 1.70$). You could then contrast this number with the number of errors made by an inpatient with brain impairment. For this same age, the average number of errors made by an inpatient with known brain impairment is 5.00 ($SD = 1.41$). You can also indicate what percentage of these groups made a score of 5 or more and 4 or less. About 21% of 30-year-old inpatients with a diagnosis of brain damage made a score of less than 5 errors, compared to 76% of those without brain damage. Table 9.2 allows you to arrive at these normative figures for psychiatric inpatients ages 18 through 64.

Table 9.2 BGT Scores for Psychiatric Inpatients without Brain Damage and with Brain Damage (N = 339)

Age	No brain damage				Brain damage			
	N	M	SD	% > 4 errors	N	M	SD	% > 4 errors
18–24	45	3.00	1.78	16	—	—	—	—
25–34	75	3.16	1.70	24	14	5.00	1.41	79
35–44	74	4.03	2.00	38	23	5.26	1.81	70
45–54	52	3.62	1.54	20	22	5.64	1.89	77
55–64	13	3.92	1.87	28	12	6.67	1.78	100
65+	—	—	—	—	9	8.11	1.62	100

Note: This table was formed by combining data from Table 7.12. Personality disorder and psychosis diagnoses were combined to form the group with no brain damage.

3. Classify the patient's score. Groth-Marnat (1997) notes that the two most used strategies to classify neuropsychological test scores are a "qualitative pathognomic sign approach and the use of quantitative cutoff scores" (p. 536). BGT analysis uses both approaches. For the Lacks adaptation of the Hutt-Briskin scoring system, research has consistently verified that the quantitative cutoff score that best identifies persons with brain damage is 5 or more errors. Five errors is now considered to be the *standard cutoff score.* Therefore, a score of 0 to 4 errors is classified as an absence of brain impairment *on this test,* and a score of 5 to 12 errors is classified as indicative of brain damage on this test. You may want to use the following evidence descriptors of different ranges of scores.

Number of errors	Evidence of brain impairment
0–3	Absence of brain impairment
4	Borderline
5–6	Some evidence
7–8	Strong evidence
9–12	Very strong evidence

4. Take an actuarial approach to prediction. It is useful to determine, for each case, your confidence in the accuracy of the diagnostic classification. What are the chances that a person with a score of less than 5 errors is really a missed case or that a person with 5 or more errors has a false positive diagnosis? The lower the score, the less chance of a missed case; the higher the score (e.g., 8 or more errors), the less chance of a false positive outcome. We can use the percentile distributions of BGT scores (see Table 7.7) to estimate the chances that either of these mistaken diagnoses has been made. For a missed case, look at the column labeled "Psychiatric inpatients with brain damage." Note that no inpatient from this sample of 85 patients with known neurological disorders made as few as 0 or 1 errors, meaning that none with these low scores were misjudged by being labeled nonimpaired. Therefore, in this sample, the chance of a missed case for these very low scores is 0%. For this same group, 4% with a score of 2 errors were misclassified; 9% with a score of 3; and 18% with a score of 4. In a similar manner, we can estimate the chances of a false positive error by examining the column labeled "Nonimpaired psychiatric inpatients." Note that 74% were correctly classified by earning a BGT score of 4 or less. However, 26% earned scores of 5 or more, resulting in a false positive diagnosis. Table 9.3 spells out the risks of incorrect diagnoses based on the data from Table 7.7. Note also that adolescents perform similarly, but exact hit rates for this age group are unknown. You may want to use adult hit rates as an estimate until further data are available.

It is important to note that a low BGT score does not entirely rule out brain damage because this test is not sensitive to all brain dysfunction. Examples of conditions that could be missed are mild cognitive deficits, language disorders, or a focal lesion. Some researchers believe that the BGT is most sensitive to diffuse, slowly progressive types of brain impairment or to right parietal lobe lesions that interfere with perception of spatial relationships.

Keep in mind that some of these patients with scores of 5 or more may actually have *true* cases of brain damage that the BGT may have correctly classified and the criterion measures may have missed. In this research, most of those misclassified as having brain damage had IQs below 90 or a diagnosis of chronic schizophrenia.

To make a more definitive diagnosis for those who make a borderline score of 4 errors, consider the behavioral observations, the results of other tests, the pattern of symptoms, and the patient's history. You may also need to obtain additional neuropsychological or neurological assessment. If possible, continue to monitor the person for signs of increased impairment.

5. Analyze the patient's specific errors.   In addition to a quantitative analysis of a test, one can attempt a qualitative analysis of pathognomic signs, meaning errors that are particularly indicative of brain impairment. For this scoring system, there is no reliable evidence to allow specific interpretations of individual BGT reproduction errors. It is the sum of the errors that is most diagnostic. However, certain errors are more suggestive of cognitive disorders than others. Based on the data presented in Table 7.6, as well as similar results

Table 9.3   Percent of Incorrect Diagnoses by Number of Errors for Psychiatric Inpatients ($N = 349$)

BGT score	Incorrect diagnoses, %
0–1	0[a]
2	4[a]
3	9[a]
4	18[a]
5	11[b]
6	7[b]
7	3[b]
8	3[b]
9–12	0[b]

[a]Missed cases.
[b]False positives.

Table 9.4   BGT Errors and How Suggestive Each Is of Brain Damage

Especially suggestive	Somewhat suggestive	Not suggestive
Impotence (8)	Simplification (2.6)	Perseveration (1.8)
Fragmentation (3.4)	Angulation Difficulty (2.5)	Overlapping Difficulty (1.7)
Motor Incoordination (3.1)	Rotation (2.4)	Closure Difficulty (1.5)
	Retrogression (2.2)	Cohesion (1.4)
		Collision (1.3)

Note: Numbers in parentheses are multiplication factors. They represent the frequency with which each error occurs in inpatients with brain damage compared to inpatients with no brain damage. For example, the error of Impotence occurs 8 times more often among patients with brain damage than among patients without brain damage.

from Friedt and Gouvier (1989) and Hutt (1985), we can divide the 12 BGT errors into three groups (see Table 9.4). The groups are based upon the relative frequency of each of these errors in the patients with known brain damage in contrast to those without such impairment. The number following each error is the multiplication factor (e.g., Impotence occurs 8 times more often in the group with brain damage than in the group without brain impairment).

In the first group are three errors that appear 3 to 8 times as often in the group with brain damage and so are especially suggestive of a diagnosis of cognitive disorder. The four errors in the middle column are somewhat suggestive, occurring about twice as often. The five errors in the third group are not suggestive at all of brain damage, occurring only about one and a half times as often. In fact, Collision and Collision Tendency, Cohesion, and Closure Difficulty are common errors in all test takers (>30% for each error for nonpatients, >50% each for patients with no brain damage, and >65% each for patients with brain damage) and hence do not discriminate among diagnostic groups.

Note that in the clinical lore, Rotation is considered a pathognomic sign for brain damage. However, in this sample of 349 psychiatric inpatients it occurred only 2.4 times as often in the patients with brain damage as in the patients with no brain damage. The true pathognomic sign for the BGT is the error of Impotence, which occurred 8 times as often. Fragmentation was next, occurring 3.4 times as often.

This information about specific errors cannot be used to confirm a diagnosis but may be one more cumulative piece of data to rule in or rule out brain dysfunction. For instance, if a person had 4 errors that included Impotence, you might want to consider that it is rare for a person without brain impairment to make this error. You should also double-check your scoring to ensure that the patient did indeed make this error. Or if a person had 4 errors and all were in the third group (i.e., not suggestive of brain damage), you could feel more confident that it is unlikely that you have a missed case of brain damage.

6. Note other variables that can affect the test interpretation.   Certain variables complicate the diagnostic picture, lower your confidence in the results, and perhaps also lower the validity and reliability. Extra care should be taken when drawing conclusions about the BGT performance of patients with certain types of characteristics or history. Take particular care if the following variables occur in a protocol with 4 or more errors. For example, exercise more caution in the differential diagnosis of patients with *lower education* or an *IQ below 90*. Patients with these factors may be falsely identified as having brain impairment. But these individuals are also more likely to have some type of previously undetected brain damage, especially conditions that occur early in life or that result in diffuse damage to the brain (Golden, 1990). Reitan and Wolfson (1993), on the other hand, argue that the influence of brain damage is stronger than that of age and education and will consequently minimize the impact of such other factors upon neuropsychological test performance. Consider also that a person with brain impairment who has a high IQ may be able to avoid making 5 or more errors on the BGT.

Sometimes members of other *ethnic groups* have been found to have BGT scores that are statistically higher than those of white test takers. The actual differences, however, have been slight and are generally of no clinical significance. However, with a score of 4 or more errors, consider the possibility that ethnicity or cultural differences may have made a contribution to this person's elevated BGT score.

The most difficult discrimination to make on the BGT is between *chronic schizophrenia* and cognitive disorders. As many as 27% of sampled patients with schizophrenia earn 5 or more BGT errors. Many patients with chronic schizophrenia show cognitive deficits, perhaps because their condition has an organic etiology, they have had prolonged hospitalization, or they have received lengthy courses of antipsychotic medications. However, if the number of errors is 9 or more, schizophrenia is unlikely to explain this many distortions of the BGT designs. More detailed discussions of this dilemma can be found in Chapters 1 and 2.

Another factor that can complicate interpretation is a patient situation that encourages "*faking bad*," such as a court action or an insurance claim. In this case, the examiner may wish to readminister the BGT at a later date to see if the patient is able to repeat the previous error pattern. If the patient commits 9 to 12 errors but does not appear to have obvious brain damage, consider the possibility of malingering. Further discussion of this issue can be found in Chapter 4.

Another complicating factor is *older age*. Older adults do make more errors than younger persons, showing a gradual deterioration in BGT performance over time. However, even into their 80s, 61% of older adults have total BGT scores in the nonimpaired range. With older adults, make sure that errors are not the result of failing eyesight or hearing or a physical disability, such as advanced arthritis.

A final variable that greatly affects results on neuropsychological tests is the *abuse of alcohol* or other substances. It is estimated that 10% of the over 15 million alcohol abusers fulfill the criteria for a cognitive disorder; another 50% exhibit mild to moderate impairment on neuropsychological testing after 3 to 4 weeks of abstinence (Rourke & Loberg, 1996). This fact is particularly true during the detoxification stage, usually the month after withdrawal. During this time, patients may have deficits in multiple areas, including visual-spatial analysis and complex perceptual-motor integration, that may improve over time (Grant, 1987). Some researchers believe that the deficits from the actual consumption of alcohol are small and are more related to other factors associated with the abuse, such as heart and liver disease, head injury, poor nutrition, steady intake versus binge drinking, and age of onset and duration of abuse (Rourke & Loberg, 1996). For example, Tarbox et al. (1986) found that younger drinkers made fewer BGT errors than older abusers (3.61 versus 6.62 errors). Abstinence for at least 2 weeks is necessary to reduce these cognitive deficits (Lezak, 1995).

7. Familiarize yourself with recent research on common diagnostic categories. The reader is referred to Lezak's (1995) excellent chapter on neuropathy that covers head injury and many other diagnoses. The Grant and Adams (1996) book on neuropsychological assessment of neuropsychiatric disorders is also very useful. For other excellent resources on specific diagnoses such as alcoholism or dementia, consult the articles and books briefly reviewed in Chapter 2.

8. Apply scientific decision-making rules. Wedding and Faust (1989) claim that neuropsychologists generally use one of the least reliable interpretation strategies, the clinical and mechanical collection of data combined with interpretation by means of clinical judgment. The proven limitations of humans as judges lead these researchers to argue for more use of actuarial methods in the interpretation of test data.

One of the factors they point to that contributes to judgment error is *hindsight bias,* such as acquiescing to diagnostic consensus or letting your knowledge of details of the case (such as results of medical tests) influence your psychological test interpretation and diagnosis. This type of bias prevents you from capitalizing fully on the unique information provided by neuropsychological measures. Another factor is the underutilization of *base rates.* Clinicians often evaluate their tests by how well they relate to some criterion, such as diagnosis. Few tests achieve high rates of diagnostic accuracy. That fact means that if the rate of occurrence of the event you wish to predict (e.g., a diagnosis of brain damage) occurs rarely in the population in which you work, your test results may actually *lower* your diagnostic success. If the base rate of brain damage is 30% in your work setting, you would need a test accuracy rate of more than 70% to improve upon prediction using the base rate alone. Wedding and Faust (1989) claim that dependence on test indicators that reduce diagnostic accuracy is commonplace among neuropsychologists.

Striving for diagnostic consensus, ignoring base rates, using clinical judgment instead of objective scoring methods, believing that your experience and expertise exempt you from decision-making rules, and many other behaviors all contribute to diagnostic error. Some additional recommendations the authors make to improve diagnostic accuracy are the following:

1. Know the literature on human judgment.
2. Know the diagnostic base rates where you work.
3. Do not depend on insight alone.
4. Remember to take into account regression toward the mean in assessing changes in repeat testing.
5. Begin interpretation with the most valid information you have, because data obtained early in the assessment process tends to influence judgment of data collected later.
6. When possible, make sure you use norms adjusted for age, gender, and education that are appropriate to your setting.

Bender Gestalt Test Screening Report
developed by
Patricia Lacks, PhD

Client Information

Name	**A**	ID Number	
Age	**21**	Education	**12**
Gender	**Female**	Ethnicity	**African American**
Occupation	**Payroll clerk**	Date	**06/28/97**

The following Bender Gestalt Test Screening Report should be viewed as only one source of hypotheses about the client being evaluated. No diagnostic or treatment decision should be based solely on these data. Statements in this report should be integrated with other sources of information about this client, including other psychometric test findings, mental status results, client history, and interview data.

This evaluation is confidential and intended for psychodiagnostic use by qualified professionals only. This summary is for the psychologists' personal files only and is not meant to be shared with the client or any other source.

Bender Gestalt Test (BGT) Screening Report

Client Behavior during Testing

This individual took the BGT in a manner that was serious, cooperative, and careful. The client appeared to be attentive, able to concentrate, and motivated to do well.

1 The time to complete the test was 6 minutes. The average time for individuals without brain impairment to copy the nine BGT figures is 6 minutes ($SD = 2.60$). Overall, there was good rapport between the examiner and the client. Based on the behaviors observed, the results of the BGT appear to be generally valid and reliable. It was noted, however, that this person had some problem in remaining calm during testing.

Bender Gestalt Test Scoring

BGT Error	Figures
Overlapping Difficulty	7
Perseveration	2
Closure Difficulty	A, 4
Cohesion	A

Total errors: 4 (range = 0–12)
Time to complete test: 6 minutes

Analysis of Bender Gestalt Test Results

Using the BGT as a screening measure for brain dysfunction produced the following results. The client made 4 reproduction errors out of a possible 12, based on the Lacks adaptation of the Hutt-Briskin scoring system (Lacks, 1984). With this system, the standard cutoff score for neurological impairment is 5 or more errors.

2 For comparison purposes, the average number of errors for a nonpatient adult of this age and level of education is 1.71 ($SD = 1.43$). For this same age, the average number of errors made by an inpatient with known brain impairment is 5.00 ($SD = 1.41$). Only 21% of inpatients with diagnosed cognitive disorders made a score of less than 5 errors compared to 91% of nonpatient African American females.

Figure 9.1 Computer-assisted screening report for the BGT. (Adapted and reproduced by special permission of the publisher, Psychological Assessment Resources, Inc., Odessa, FL 33556, from the *Bender Gestalt screening software for Windows (V. 1)*, Copyright © 1996. Further reproduction is prohibited without permission of PAR, Inc.)

6 African Americans have sometimes been found to have BGT scores that were statistically worse than those of white test-takers. However, the actual differences were slight and generally of no clinical significance. Consider the possibility that ethnicity or cultural differences may have contributed to this particular client's elevated score.

3 A BGT score of 4 errors indicates a borderline diagnosis of brain impairment. With 4 errors, there is a 21%
4 chance of misclassifying an adult client as not having brain impairment. The client's performance does not include
5 any errors such as Impotence or Rotation that are especially suggestive of brain impairment. However, at the present time, there is no reliable evidence to allow specific interpretations for any particular BGT reproduction errors. It is the sum of the errors that is most diagnostic.

6 It is important to recognize that a diagnosis of brain dysfunction from a screening test does not specify the source of the disorder, nor the degree of impairment. Some neuropsychologists believe that the BGT is most sensitive to diffuse, slowly progressive types of cortical damage or to right parietal lobe lesions that interfere with perception of spatial relationships. To make a more definitive diagnosis, consider the results of the other tests, the pattern of symptoms, and the client's history. For example, it is more likely for a client with a lower education and/or IQ below 90 to be falsely identified as having impairment of cortical functioning. However, these persons may also be more likely to have some type of previously undetected brain damage. Exercise additional caution in the differential diagnosis of persons in the lower IQ or education ranges.

6 Also, this client has a history that includes a prior diagnosis of psychosis. The most difficult discrimination to make on the BGT is between psychosis (especially chronic schizophrenia) and cognitive disorder. As many as 27% of samples of schizophrenics earned a BGT score of 5 or more. Many chronic schizophrenics show cognitive deficits, perhaps because their condition has an organic etiology and/or because they have been on lengthy courses of antipsychotic medications.

If the diagnosis is still unclear, you may want to obtain additional neuropsychological and/or neurological assessment. If possible, continue to monitor the client's progress for signs of deterioration.

No one test, including the BGT, is sufficient for making a diagnosis of brain dysfunction or for clinical decision making. You may wish to clarify the clinical picture through further diagnostic assessment including a referral for a comprehensive neuropsychological battery of tests and/or a neurological examination. To assist in formulating a plan of treatment and rehabilitation, you will need information such as: the kind and location of damage, the specific functions that are impaired, the severity of the deficits, and the type and extent of the client's strengths.

Summary

This client made a BGT score of 4 reproduction errors out of a possible 12. Using the standard cutoff score of 5 errors, the results indicate a borderline diagnosis of brain impairment. With 4 errors, there is some risk of a missed case of brain damage. However, the client's test-taking behaviors and attitudes promote confidence in the validity and reliability of these BGT findings. Certain background information complicates the diagnostic picture in this case, such as the client's ethnic/racial group, a reported history of psychosis, and a low education or IQ. Because the BGT is only a brief screening test, a diagnosis of brain pathology should never be based on such an instrument used alone. Recommendations were made for additional assessment to make a more definitive diagnosis, specify the source and degree of impairment, and provide details to plan for treatment and rehabilitation.

Figure 9.1   (Continued)

CAVEATS   This section reiterates some of the things to avoid when interpreting the BGT. The BGT, as a brief screening test, should be viewed as one test providing one source of hypotheses about the client or patient. No recommendations about diagnosis or treatment should be based solely on this one test. The BGT alone, or for that matter any one psychological test, is not sufficient for making a diagnosis of brain dysfunction. The results of the BGT should instead be integrated with the findings of other measures given as well as mental status, history, and behavioral observations. If the results of this test are unclear, you may want to seek further clarification by administering other neuropsychological measures or by referring the patient for a comprehensive neuropsychological battery of tests or a neurological examination. To formulate a treatment and rehabilitation plan, the psychologist will need much more information than the BGT can provide, such as the type and location of damage to the brain, the specific impaired functions, the severity of the impairment, and the type and extent of the patient's strengths.

COMPUTER-ASSISTED INTERPRETATION OF THE BGT

In recent years, psychologists have turned to computers to aid in the administration, scoring, interpretation, and reporting aspects of psychological assessment (Piotrowski & Keller, 1989). Software is now available to assist with these tasks for many psychological tests, for example, the WAIS and the Rorschach. The reader is referred to Groth-Marnat's (1997) section on this topic for additional details.

As a drawing task, the BGT does not lend itself to electronic assistance with administration or scoring. However, electronic interpretation and report writing are feasible and have recently become available for the Lacks scoring method (Lacks, 1996). In this software, the psychologist enters into the computer the patient's demographic data, behavioral observations, background information, and the BGT scores. The computer assesses the data for six of the eight interpretive steps just outlined. Within minutes, the program then prints a detailed report on the BGT findings. This report is for the psychologist's use only, not to be distributed to others. It is meant to aid the psychologist in analyzing the test findings before integrating the results into the overall psychological report of all the measures used to evaluate the patient. The report can also be customized by the psychologist.

An example of this computer-assisted evaluation of the BGT is shown in Figure 9.1. It is a report of Case A, a 21-year-old African American female, whose test data are reported in Chapter 13. This woman has 12 years of education and an IQ of 81. Numbers in the margin refer to the six interpretation steps (see Table 9.1). Because this person was not hospitalized at the time of testing, she is referred to as "the client."

CHAPTER 10

Use of the Bender Gestalt Test with the Older Adult

As improved health care treatment and access have become available, there are increasing numbers of older adults in the population. This demographic change means that psychologists frequently need to make decisions about older persons. Often, these decisions concern the client's cognitive functioning. Common reasons for neuropsychological evaluation of older persons include the need to evaluate their ability to live independently in the community and to measure cognitive and behavioral changes. Some causes of the latter include cerebrovascular disease, progressive dementias, or medical disorders like diabetes. (Franzen & Rasmussen, 1990).

COGNITIVE IMPLICATIONS OF NORMAL AGING

Previously, there was very little information available about the neuropsychological functioning of the normal older adult. Nor did we know much about the effects of aging upon psychological tests (Lezak, 1987). In fact, much research has systematically omitted individuals over the age of 55. For example, Pascal and Suttell (1951) warned that their Bender Gestalt Test (BGT) norms cannot be used with confidence for clients over the age of 50. To assess accurately the cognitive status of an older person, psychologists must be aware of what kind of changes are a *normal* part of growing older and what kind of changes reflect some *abnormal* condition.

Effects of Age upon Cognitive Functions

Many people, including neuropsychologists, view the latter part of the life span as a time of inevitable decline in physical and mental capability, especially memory. In fact, there are hundreds of studies that document such changes—in the areas of cognitive ability, sensory acuity, and motor responses. However, these declines are not uniform across all functions; some abilities can be retained until late in life. In general, "healthy and active people in their 70s and 80s do not differ greatly in skills or abilities" from younger people (Lezak, 1995, p. 135). There is reduction of capability on timed tasks, and on those that involve memory and active problem solving (Franzen & Martin, 1996). Reductions appear to be more pronounced for those functions related to bilateral frontal-lobe operations (Mittenberg, Seidenberg, O'Leary, & DiGiulio, 1989), rather than to the right hemisphere as was previously believed. As a result of these changes with age, standard cutoff scores may misclassify many normal individuals as having impairment. Yet many neuropsychological tests do not provide norms for the latter part of the age span (Lezak, 1987).

More specific to perceptual-motor performance, the ability to recognize and process perceptual stimuli is retained if the stimuli are familiar ones. Attention abilities do not decline until well into old age unless the task is complex and demanding. There is evidence of increased difficulty with visuoperceptual organization in "old" older adults (Lezak, 1995). The effect of aging on a multidimensional visuoconstructive task such as the BGT is not fully known (Franzen & Martin, 1996); however, the activity of copying simple designs does not seem to be compromised by increased age (Lezak, 1995). Many more details on normal cognitive changes of older persons can be found in Lezak's 1995 book.

Other Variables That Affect Cognitive Performance in Older Persons

When an older person does poorly on a neuropsychological test, it does not necessarily mean that he or she is suffering from brain impairment. Aging is a complex set of interacting factors, including a person's physical and emotional health as well as his or her cognitive abilities. Poor performance of an older adult on a neuropsychological test may result from a host of factors. These can include such medical conditions as diabetes, thyroid imbalance, hypertension, and heart disease, all of which are fairly common in this age group. Other factors are the effects of sleep loss, sedating medications, poor nutrition, and anxious mood. Depression, however, is less likely to result in reduced visuospatial performance. Franzen and Martin (1996) and Franzen and Rasmussen (1990) discuss in more detail the effects of these conditions upon neuropsychological tests.

AGING AND THE BGT

How does this information about the normal aging process apply more specifically to the BGT? First, the BGT is not a timed test, which gives it an added advantage for assessing an older population. The evaluator can allow the person being tested as much time as necessary, even rest periods if required. Second, the BGT is not a memory test, nor does it deal with new material; the stimulus figures are all commonly recognized geometric designs and drawing is a well-known and often-practiced activity. Third, the test involves minimal active problem solving. Fourth, Mittenberg et al. (1989) found that parietal-occipital lobe operations (often considered the main source of perceptual-motor integration) are spared the effects of normal aging. Finally, since 1982, there have been norms for older adults on the BGT against which to evaluate an individual's performance.

Test Administration Issues with the Older Client

Both Davies (1996) and Lezak (1995) address special issues for administering such tests as the BGT to the older person. They urge forethought and planning before beginning the session and a lot of patience after commencing with testing. The most important thing is not to let factors unrelated to brain impairment (such as decreased sensory acuity, speed, and energy) spuriously inflate the number of BGT errors, resulting in inaccurate conclusions. One of the most important factors is the sensory loss that is common in later years. It is estimated that 7% of people ages 65 to 75 and 16% of those older than age 75 have serious visual defects that may lead to disorientation and behavioral deterioration (Bondi et al., 1996) as well as an increase of errors on a visual-motor test such as the BGT. Bright lighting of the stimulus cards might assist with failing eyesight. Before beginning testing, always check to make sure that clients have brought their eyeglasses with them. Also, give instructions in a loud, clear voice while looking directly at the person; do not speak from behind or to the side. Make sure that you have the client's attention before giving any instructions. You may want to repeat directions and ask questions to ensure that they were received and understood. Because of its nonthreatening nature, the BGT is often given first or near the beginning of a test battery.

Many neuropsychological tests have a time component. Because old-older adults especially exhibit general slowing of cognitive and motor performance, a nontimed test like the BGT has an advantage. However, because older persons often fatigue quickly, they may need frequent rest periods and a chance to walk around. It is important not to apply time pressure. Although younger persons average less than 7 minutes to complete the BGT, those who are older may require much more time. It would be wise, also, to take sufficient time and effort to explain fully the purpose of the testing in order to maximize the client's desire to cooperate and put forth the best effort. Finally, Davies (1996) recommends that you not begin testing at all if you cannot meet all of these conditions for a good assessment.

Bender Gestalt Norms for Older Adults

Using the Lacks adaptation of the Hutt-Briskin scoring system, Lacks and Storandt (1982) collected normative BGT data for 334 nonpatient older adults (ages 60 to 87), all living independently in two senior citizen apartment complexes. These older adults came from the middle and lower-middle socioeconomic classes and had education ranging from no formal schooling to completion of college ($M = 8.8$ years). The BGT was given in the standard manner, usually in the person's home, by trained psychologists, graduate students, and research assistants. Scoring was done by an expert and by a trained research assistant with no previous BGT experience. Interscorer reliability was .87 for 163 records.

Table 10.1 presents the mean BGT scores and standard deviations for five age groups. Results show that independent older persons do evidence a gradual decrease in BGT performance across the age span from the sixth through the eighth decade. Mean number of errors for these five age groups ranged from 3.00 to 4.33, all below the brain impairment cutoff score of 5.

In the entire group, 26% had impairment-range scores of 5 or more, from 21% to 39% for the five age groups, with a sharp increase occurring after age 75. As would be expected, greater evidence of brain dysfunction was found in the old-old (above age 75) than in the young-old (ages 60 to 75). Still, even into the eighth decade, more than half (61%) of older adults did *not* earn BGT

Table 10.1 Mean Bender Gestalt Test Scores by Age for Nonpatient Older Adults

Age	N	M	SD	% > 4 errors
60–64	22	3.23	1.67	23
65–69	85	3.00	1.97	21
70–74	100	3.29	1.99	21
75–79	76	3.63	2.02	32
80+	51	4.33	1.85	39

Source: Adapted from Lacks, P., and Storandt, M. (1982). "Bender Gestalt performance of normal older adults." *Journal of Clinical Psychology, 38,* 624–627, Table 1, p. 625. Copyright © 1982. Reprinted by permission of John Wiley & Sons, Inc.

scores that would suggest brain dysfunction. This finding is in contrast to research that has shown a marked effect of age upon a number of commonly used neuropsychological measures (Bak & Greene, 1980). Because the preceding sample of older adults was unscreened for neurological disorders, the chances are good that some of them had undetected brain dysfunction that would account for decreasing perceptual-motor skill with increasing age.

Should the BGT Have Age-Corrected Norms?

Many researchers recommend that older adults be evaluated with age-corrected norms on all tests of cognitive function (e.g., Erickson, Eimon, & Hebben, 1994; Smith, Wong, Ivnik, & Malec, 1997), though Lezak (1987) emphasizes this point mainly for timed tests. However, because older adults perform well on the BGT into the eighth decade, special norms or a higher cutoff score may not be warranted. For example, looking at all the normative data presented in this book, if you make the cutoff score for older adults 6 errors rather than 5, it would halve the number of clients who fall into the impaired range. However, perhaps you would miss something; maybe those people have undetected brain dysfunction. Norms for older adults are usually developed with unscreened participants, some of whom may have early stages of a disorder that affects the brain. Better to keep the norms as they are and follow up with further evaluation of a person who makes five or more errors.

Specific BGT Errors of Older Adults

In terms of specific errors, for all age groups, 50% to 60% of the older participants committed the errors Collision Tendency, Closure Difficulty, and Cohesion. However, these are also the most frequently committed errors of groups with no brain impairment. Another 30% to 40% showed evidence of Overlapping Difficulty, Simplification (usually the less serious problem of drawing circles instead of dots on figure 1), and Perseveration. The remaining six types of errors were found in fewer than 20% of the protocols, with Impotence being the least frequent error (about 8%). Three errors were noted to increase gradually across the five age ranges: Simplification (18% for the youngest group and 52% for the oldest); Perseveration, Type A (14% and 40%); and Angulation Difficulty (9% and 22%).

Thus, it appears that one may have confidence in the use of the BGT, with the Lacks scoring procedures, for the evaluation of neuropsychological functioning of normal older adults. As long as precautions are taken to ensure that a physical disability, such as poor eyesight or hearing or advanced arthritis, does not interfere with the understanding of instructions or the execution of the task, the BGT appears to be an excellent choice as a screening device for brain impairment with the older population.

BGT Case Example of a Normal Older Adult

Figure 10.1 shows the BGT of an 87-year-old man with 12 years of education who worked for many years as a hotel waiter. He served as a nonpatient control in the Memory and Aging project at the Washington University School of Medicine. He took the test in a careful and deliberate manner. This man made only two errors on the BGT: Retrogression on figure 5 and Angulation Difficulty on figure 2. Both were mild versions of these errors. The design gestalts were all well maintained and there were no serious errors, such as Rotation, Fragmentation, or Impotence. This BGT protocol demonstrates that older adults without brain impairment can do very well on the BGT even at very advanced ages.

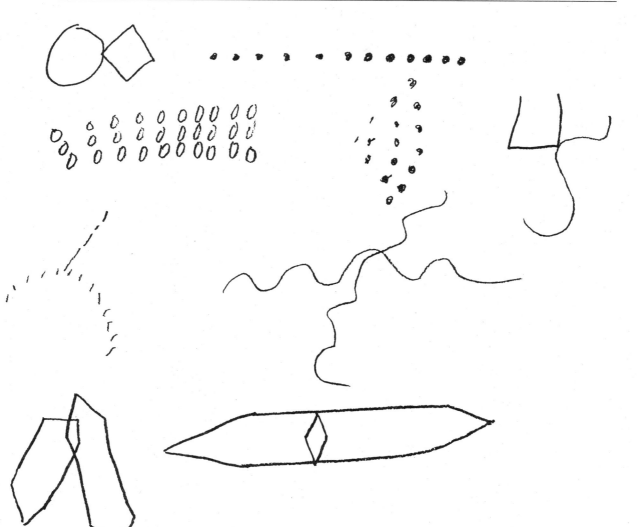

Figure 10.1 Case example of a normal older adult.

The BGT of another older person can be seen in Chapter 13, Case P (Figure 13.17).

Specific Uses of the BGT with an Older Population

Older adults represent a large population for which the BGT could serve a variety of uses. Its brevity, simplicity, and nonthreatening nature make it highly desirable as an assessment device for this group. This section briefly explores some potential uses.

Periodic Neuropsychological Screening. The most obvious use of the BGT with a geriatric population is as a screening instrument for neurological deficits. It could be combined with several other brief instruments (e.g., a memory scale) in the form of regular, periodic monitoring of brain function similar to the yearly check of physical functions with blood work, mammogram, and electrocardiogram. If this were done, each individual would have a baseline no more than a year old against which to compare any changes due to disease, toxic-metabolic disturbance, or accident. Such information could also assist older adults and their caregivers in problem solving and planning treatment management strategies. A yearly BGT could also serve as a baseline to help tease out the complex interaction between age and disease (Albert, 1981). Or the BGT could be used as part of a broader evaluation in cases referred for psychological assessment. Because mental disturbances, in particular depression, may mimic behaviors seen in brain impairment, screening for brain dysfunction is necessary for accurate differential diagnosis.

The BGT and Progressive Dementia.   With the increasing extension of the life span, the prevalence of senile dementia has greatly increased. However, the majority of older persons (perhaps as many as 85%) do not have this illness. Age is not the cause of dementia, but it is a risk factor to its development. Dementia is not a unitary disorder; it varies in cause, course, severity, and pattern of cognitive impairment. Bondi et al. (1996) state that a diagnosis of dementia requires deterioration in two or more of these psychological domains: memory, language, visuospatial skills, judgment or abstract thinking, and emotion or personality. DSM-IV (American Psychiatric Association, 1994) requires memory problems to be one of the domains and impairment must represent a decline in abilities and be so severe that there is significant interference with everyday functioning. Besides age, other variables that increase the risk of dementia are female gender, lower education and occupational achievement, family history, and previous head injury (Bondi et al., 1996).

Alzheimer's disease (AD) may account for as many as 50% of the dementia cases, affecting perhaps as many as 4 million Americans. Vascular dementia is the second most common type, resulting from a series of ministrokes due to cerebrovascular disease. Symptoms of AD are severe memory deficits as well as deterioration of language, executive functions, attention, and visuoconstructive skills (Franzen & Martin, 1996). Final diagnosis of AD requires autopsy; however, diagnostic systems such as DSM-IV (American Psychiatric Association, 1994) correlate well with autopsy results. Brain changes with AD occur first in the hippocampus and entorhinal cortex; as the disease progresses, damage becomes apparent in the frontal, temporal, and parietal cortexes (Bondi et al., 1996).

Because there is no biological marker for AD, neuropsychological assessment plays a large part in the diagnosis of the disorder. It may be especially helpful in detecting mild dementia and in delineating the pattern of deficits that may point to a particular etiology (Franzen & Rasmussen, 1990). For example, although memory deficits are the hallmark of AD, they play a less serious role in dementia from Huntington's disease (Brandt & Butters, 1996). Neuropsychological assessment can document the degree of deterioration and measure the efficacy of various treatments. Testing also provides information that assists in patient management and planning by the family. Finally, this type of assessment can provide baseline levels of functions against which future deterioration can be measured. Generally, measures of learning and memory are most effective in identifying cases of AD. However, measures of language, executive functions, and visuoconstruction have also been useful, especially for tracking the progression of AD, because repeated memory testing is not pertinent with AD sufferers due to early "floor" effects in the measurement of

Table 10.2 **Bender Gestalt Test Performance by Degree of Dementia in Older Adults**

Measure	No dementia ($N = 96$)	Very mild ($N = 48$)	Mild ($N = 72$)	Moderate ($N = 24$)
	Total score			
M	2.40	3.38	4.33	7.42
SD	1.33	1.79	1.90	3.36
Percentage with 5+ errors	7	21	56	79
Percentile				
95th	5	7	7	12
75th	3	4	6	10.5
50th	2	4	5	6.5
25th	1.5	2	3	5
	Percentage of records with each error type			
Rotation	2	4	7	33
Overlapping Difficulty	15	33	42	54
Simplification	19	25	39	58
Fragmentation	4	4	31	83
Retrogression	6	15	17	50
Perseveration	26	46	60	75
Collision	40	46	47	67
Impotence	4	10	15	67
Closure Difficulty	62	73	61	79
Motor Incoordination	15	21	33	50
Angulation Difficulty	5	8	26	58
Cohesion	42	52	56	67

Source: Storandt, M. (1990). "Bender Gestalt Test performance in senile dementia of the Alzheimer type." *Psychology and Aging, 5,* 604–606. Copyright © 1990 by the American Psychological Association. Reprinted by permission of the author.

memory (Kaszniak & Christenson, 1994). Recently, there has been evidence that the cognitive decline of AD may be identifiable in its preclinical phase, up to several years before a clinical diagnosis is evident (e.g., Masur, Sliwinski, Lipton, Blau, & Crystal, 1994).

Because visuoconstruction function is one of the areas of deterioration with AD, psychologists may want to include the BGT in any battery of tests being used to evaluate a person for dementia. Psychologists working in the Memory and Aging research program at the Washington University Medical School in St. Louis use the BGT in their research on AD. Table 10.2 presents the BGT results of their research with 144 individuals with very mild, mild, or moderate AD and 96 healthy older adults (Storandt, 1990). Severe cases of AD were not included because they were generally untestable. Forty percent of the AD cases were verified by autopsy by the time of publication; four of the control participants died and were found by autopsy not to have dementia. Participants were all whites, 97 men and 143 women ranging in age from 63 to 95 years ($M = 73.9$, $SD = 6.3$). Education ranged from 6 to 23 years ($M = 12.7$, $SD = 3.6$). The BGT was given as part of an extensive psychometric battery and was scored with the Lacks system.

The results showed that the nonpatient older adults who had been carefully screened for brain disorder produced mean BGT scores ($M = 2.40$, >5 errors = 7%) below those of relatively unscreened older adult groups (see Table 10.1). As the degree of dementia increased, the average number of errors increased gradually from 3.38 for very mild dementia to 7.42 for moderate dementia. The percentage of persons who made 5 or more errors, the threshold for diagnosis of impairment, ranged from 21% for very mild dementia to 79% for moderate dementia. When comparing individuals with moderate dementia with older adult nonpatients, the overall hit rate was 90%. It was much lower when the contrast was made between nonpatients and those with mild dementia.

The specific errors that most differentiated nonpatients from those with moderate dementia were Rotation, Fragmentation, Retrogression, Impotence, and Angulation Difficulty. The least discriminating errors were Collision, Closure Difficulty, and Cohesion, errors commonly made by other groups with no cognitive impairment.

For an example of the BGT for an AD case from the Memory and Aging program, see Case F in Chapter 13.

The BGT and Basic Living Skills.   Further research needs to be done to provide clinicians with a wide variety of information about the impact of specific deficits on specific activities. This kind of practical information will be very useful for the formulation of meaningful rehabilitation plans for older persons (Diller & Gordon, 1981; Heaton & Pendleton, 1981). In one example of this approach, Wolber and Lira (1981) studied the relationship in older adults between brain damage and behavioral functioning. Participants were 35 geriatric psychiatric inpatients ages 65 to 84 ($M = 72.7$ years). Each was given the BGT (scored unaccountably by the Koppitz method) and the Basic Living Skills Assessment, which taps seven categories of everyday living. They found significant negative correlations between the BGT and five of the seven subscales on the Basic Living Skills Assessment ($r = -.44$ to $-.63$, $p < .004$). These five categories were appearance, personal hygiene, food and drink consumption, motor ability, and motor skills. Ability to communicate and interpersonal skills were not correlated significantly with the BGT. The former group of categories all involve gross motor behaviors but the latter two categories involve fine motor skills.

Perceptual-Motor Functioning in Oxygen Deficiency Disorders.   A continuous and adequate supply of oxygen is critical in maintaining the integrity of the brain functions. Oxygen deficiency disorders are common, especially among the older population. Examples of these disorders are anoxia, or complete oxygen deprivation, as the result of cardiac arrest or stroke, and hypoxemia, or inadequate amounts of oxygen, from chronic obstructive pulmonary disease (COPD) or sleep apnea. Many studies have documented neuropsychological impairment as a result of oxygen deprivation, both between persons with oxygen deficiency and controls and between persons with greater and lesser severity of the condition (e.g., Bedard, Montplaisir, Richer, Rouleau, & Malo, 1991; Grant et al., 1987). A thorough review of the neuropsychological correlates of acute and chronic hypoxemia can be found in a chapter by Rourke and Adams (1996). Perceptual-motor performance has often been found to be one of the functions affected by lack of adequate oxygen. Studies in which this finding has been documented using the BGT are Krop et al. (1973) and Greenberg et al. (1987).

In a number of studies, supplemental oxygen therapy has been used to reverse or improve the observed deficits of oxygen deprivation. For example, Krop et al. (1973) found that short-term oxygenation of a small group of COPD patients resulted in neuropsychological improvements in IQ, memory, finger tapping, and perceptual-motor functioning on the BGT when compared to a group of untreated COPD patients.

In another study with older adults, Jacobs, Winter, Alvis, and Small (1969) measured the effect of increased oxygen on memory in 13 older ($M = 68$ years) "senile" male inpatients. The authors believe that cognitive deterioration and, in particular, impaired recent memory are due at least in part to cortical oxygen deprivation. Each patient received 90 minutes of treatment twice a day for 15 days. Half of the participants served as delayed-treatment controls. The BGT recall administration was given before treatment began and a mean of 12 hours after the last treatment. A weighted scoring system (with a maximum score of 100) that combined number and quality of recalled designs was used. Highly significant changes were found between the men's scores before and after the experimental treatment ($M = 10.00$ and 41.00, respectively; $p < .001$). No significant changes occurred in BGT recall after the control treatment; however, delayed treatment participants who later received the 100% oxygen then showed the same large significant increases in BGT recall. Similar results were found on the Wechsler Memory Scale.

Results of these two studies shows that intermittent hyperoxygenation can greatly improve symptoms of intellectual deterioration, at least for a short period of time. Unfortunately, other investigators have been unable to replicate these findings with short-term therapy. Some have found long-term oxygenation to be more effective; however, some cognitive deficits from acute and chronic oxygen deprivation may be permanent (Rourke & Adams, 1996).

The BGT in a Rehabilitation Setting.   Another study has implications for the treatment and rehabilitation of patients with brain injury, especially stroke victims. Nemec (1978) studied the general and lateralized effects of background interference on the verbal and perceptual-motor functioning of rehabilitation patients who had suffered cardiovascular accidents. Thirty of these patients suffered from right-hemisphere involvement, 30 from left-hemisphere involvement, and 30 had no brain damage. Participants were given a verbal word-naming task and the BGT under standard and background-interference conditions.

Results showed that the individuals with brain damage suffered a greater decrement in performance on either task compared to the group with no brain damage regardless of the site of the cardiovascular accident. However, those patients with left-hemisphere damage were significantly more distracted by verbal interference on a verbal task, compared to those with right-hemisphere involvement. In contrast, patients with right-hemisphere involvement showed more decrements with perceptual interference on a perceptual task than those with left-hemisphere involvement.

The authors concluded that brain damage has both a general and a specific effect. Damage to either side of the brain will increase distractibility regardless of the task; however, verbal distractibility will differentially affect to a greater degree the damaged left side of the brain and perceptual distractibility the damaged right side. In terms of treatment and rehabilitation, this study points to the need for a structured, controlled, and limited degree of stimulation for any patient who is the victim of a cardiovascular accident. But in addition to the general level of distracting environmental stimulation, the rehabilitation therapist must consider what type of background distraction will be particularly destructive to treatment progress, depending on the site of the damage.

In summary, the BGT can be a useful assessment tool in work with the older adult. It can be used in a battery of tests for periodic neuropsychological screening either to monitor the cognitive function of healthy older adults or to document deterioration in persons with known brain impairment, such as dementia. BGT results also show some utility in assessing basic living skills and planning rehabilitation programs. Normative data show that older adults without brain dysfunction can do well on the BGT well into the ninth decade of life.

CHAPTER 11

Use of the Bender Gestalt Test with Children

The focus of this book is on the use of the Bender Gestalt Test (BGT) with adults and the supporting research. However, the BGT is also a popular tool among child psychologists. This chapter discusses some of the issues of employing the BGT with this age group. Several excellent resources for additional details about the BGT with children are Koppitz (1975), Sattler (1992), and Tolor and Brannigan (1980). Chapter 12 discusses the use of the BGT with adolescents.

Since the 1938 publication of Lauretta Bender's book, *A Visual Motor Gestalt Test and Its Clinical Use,* this test has become one of the most popular psychological measures for evaluating children. One survey (Goh, Teslow, & Fuller, 1981) found that 93% of school psychologists use the BGT to assess perceptual-motor functioning. Rosenberg and Beck (1986) reported that 64% of clinical child psychologists and 79% of school psychologists use the BGT to assess hyperactive children, making it their second most used test after the WISC-R. However, the BGT is rarely given alone. Similar to the practice with adults, the BGT is employed as a screening device for perceptual-motor problems within a more extensive battery of tests to assess cognitive and emotional development. Or, it is used as a visuoconstructive measure in a battery of neuropsychological tests to assess brain dysfunction. Part of the reason for the BGT's popularity for evaluating children is that it is inexpensive, brief, easy to administer, and useful in many assessment situations.

THE WORK OF LAURETTA BENDER In 1931, Lauretta Bender, a child psychiatrist at Bellevue Hospital in New York City, became interested in the sidewalk chalk drawings of children. In particular, she came to believe that the variations in drawings done by children of differing ages could shed light on aspects of child development. These observations led her to study the maturation processes of visual-motor function in children. She noted that the earliest drawings of children are scribbles that exhibit pure motor play, the pleasure of motor expression. The patterns at this age do not represent anything, although the child may say that the drawing resembles some object after the fact. Most of the drawings of very young children are whirls that with increasing age differentiate into loops that then evolve into dashes, dots, and zigzags. Perseveration of a particular pattern is also common at this early stage. Eventually, young children may draw these patterns deliberately to portray some object. At age 3 the child can draw circles, arcs, and lines, and by age 4 he or she can arrange them in a line. From the ages of 4 to 7, rapid differentiation of more and more complex forms is evident. To more scientifically study these processes in children, Dr. Bender selected nine gestalt figures from the work of Wertheimer (1923). In her original book, Bender (1938) presents many case examples of copying of the gestalt figures by children at different levels of maturation. From her extensive study of this process, she concluded that the visual-motor gestalt function is a complicated aspect of development that is associated with language ability and "visual perception, manual motor ability, memory, temporal and spatial concepts, and organization or representation" (p. 112).

Bender went on to standardize the test on 800 children ages 3 to 11. A 3-year-old can make a somewhat controlled scribble. At 4, the child can use circles and loops to represent figures. At 5, the child can modify circles and loops into closed squares or ovals. At 6, he or she can begin to draw these forms in relationship to each other—for example, a vertical series of small circles or two crossed wavy lines. From ages 7 to 11, the child improves in the ability to produce more complicated combinations (e.g., BGT Figure 2 is a combination of 11 columns of 3 vertical circles that are also slanted to the left). Bender believed that after the age of 11 individuals only add refinements in details, sizes, and distances. Figure 11.1 is a summary chart of the results of her research, showing typical responses expected at each age from 3 to 11. Printed in the upper left-hand corner of each cell is the percentage of children who could draw a form as well as or better than the one shown. From the beginning, Bender was opposed to any kind of a formal scoring system for this test. Instead, she placed her trust in the evaluator's clinical judgment. She intended that this chart would provide guidelines to the maturation level of any child or "defective" adult. It has no value for anyone whose mental age is above 11 unless that person has "some type of mental disease that tends to distort the visual motor gestalt function" (p. 134).

THE WORK OF ELIZABETH KOPPITZ

Another reason for the test's popularity is the work of Elizabeth Koppitz, who developed the first widely accepted, objective scoring system for the BGT with children. This child psychologist's first book on this instrument, *The Bender Gestalt Test for Young Children* (Volume 1), was published in 1963. In it, she described the Developmental Bender Test Scoring System that has become the preferred scoring procedure for use with children. It was devised to evaluate the maturity of visual-motor perception of children ages 5 to 10, standardized in 6-month steps. By the age of 10 (or 8 or 9 for a bright child), Koppitz believes that a normal child can perform the BGT much as an adult would.

In her work at a child guidance clinic in New York, Koppitz (1963) became aware that many of the children referred to her for learning or emotional problems displayed perceptual problems. Also, schools during that period of time in the United States had begun to have a strong interest in learning problems; many public schools were forming special classes for children with learning disabilities. School psychologists had a serious need for any instrument that might help them to identify children who could benefit from this type of special education. They also wanted to assess school beginners for learning readiness in order to delay entry to school or to provide extra academic assistance. School psychologists found the BGT with Koppitz scoring to be a useful tool for evaluating visual-motor perception in children as part of the effort to eval-

	Figure A	Figure 1	Figure 2	Figure 3	Figure 4	Figure 5	Figure 6	Figure 7	Figure 8
Adult.	100%	25%	100%	100%	100%	100%	100%	100%	100%
11 yrs.	95%	95%	65%	60%	95%	90%	70%	75%	90%
10 yrs	90%	90%	60%	60%	80%	80%	60%	60%	90%
9 yrs.	80%	75%	60%	70%	80%	70%	80%	65%	70%
8 yrs.	75%	75%	75%	60%	80%	65%	70%	65%	65%
7 yrs.	75%	75%	70%	60%	75%	65%	60%	65%	60%
6 yrs	75%	75%	60%	80%	75%	60%	60%	60%	75%
5 yrs	85%	85%	60%	80%	70%	60%	60%	60%	75%
4 yrs	90%	85%	75%	80%	70%	60%	65%	60%	60%
3 yrs	— — — — — — Scribbling — — — — — — — — — — — — — — — — —								

Figure 11.1 Typical BGT responses for ages 3 to 11. Number in each cell indicates the percentage of children of this age group who could draw a form as well as or better than the one shown. (Reprinted, with permission, from *A Visual Motor Gestalt Test and its clinical uses* by Lauretta Bender. Published by the American Orthopsychiatric Association. Copyright © 1938, renewed 1965, by Lauretta Bender and the American Orthopsychiatric Association, Inc.)

uate learning difficulties. The 1963 book also stimulated a large amount of research on the various uses of this test. In 1975, Koppitz published a second volume that summarized this research, made some refinements to her scoring guidelines, and added a new standardization sample. Much of this chapter is devoted to describing her scoring system and summarizing the research that has been done on it.

In the past 20 years, there has been rapid growth of the subspeciality of child neuropsychological assessment. A large number of new instruments have been developed for the task of evaluating the cognitive and emotional functioning of children. And more sophisticated methods have also been developed for use with already well-established tests. Many child and school psychologists still incorporate the BGT into their battery of tests for child assessment. This chapter also describes some of the situations where the BGT is commonly used with children, as well as some innovative uses for it.

ADMINISTRATION OF THE BGT TO CHILDREN

Administration of the BGT to children makes use of the same minimal instructions and noncommittal replies to questions as with adults. More details can be found in Sattler (1992). Children find the test easy and enjoyable to take and also find it nonthreatening, perhaps because it does not resemble school work. Koppitz (1975) found that for elementary-school-age children, the average time to complete the BGT was 6.3 minutes; those with learning and behavior problems worked faster and took an average of 5.3 minutes. Hyperactive children required only 4.7 minutes.

Behavioral Observations

Cummings and Laquerre (1990) emphasize that when testing children one must especially differentiate between the *product* (meaning the objective score earned on the test) and the *process* (the child's behaviors while taking the test). Observations of the latter will lead to greater insights about the child's behavioral style, frustration tolerance, emotional difficulties, and perceptual-motor skills. After years of observing both normal and atypical children, the skilled child psychologist can develop a useful set of internal norms to assist in analysis.

Koppitz believes that the BGT is generally nonthreatening to most children and therefore produces little anxiety. As a result, the child's behavior while taking this test represents his or her typical behavior when faced with a new task, allowing valuable insights into how a child can best learn. For example, a well-adjusted child sits quietly, listens attentively to the instructions, analyzes the problem to be solved, and proceeds with the task, working carefully and deliberately. Even quite young children recognize imperfections in their drawings and spontaneously attempt to improve them. The well-adjusted child is pleased with his or her performance and needs little reassurance. In contrast, the child referred to a psychologist for cognitive, emotional, learning, or behavioral problems demonstrates many problematic behaviors: lack of confidence, seen in constant questions and bids for reassurance; inability to stay seated; difficulty concentrating on instructions; and lack of awareness of incorrect drawings.

Table 11.1 is a compilation of the more frequently mentioned BGT test behaviors to observe in a child (Franzen & Berg, 1989; Koppitz, 1975; Sattler, 1992). The significance of some of these behaviors is discussed following.

Malingering in Children

Early psychologists did not believe that the concept of malingering applied to children. More recently, there has been controversy about whether it is possible for children to fake test responses, perhaps because of the rarity in this age group of situations that elicit such deception in adults (e.g., personal injury lawsuits or relief from punishment for crimes). One of the few deception studies done with children (Faust, Hart, & Guilmette, 1988) used three participants, ages 9 to 12, who were given vague instructions to "fake bad" on the WISC-R and the Halstead-Reitan measures. They were offered a financial incentive for participation plus an additional amount if they could evade detection. Practicing neuropsychologists ($N = 42$) who served as judges were given a brief case history and the test results. The cases were judged as normal by 7% of the neuropsycholgists and as abnormal by 93%. Most of the judges attributed the

Table 11.1   Examples of Child Behavioral Observations with the Bender Gestalt Test

Handedness
Amount of time to complete task
Attention span
Impulsivity
Degree of carefulness of drawing: attention to detail, perfectionism, and erasures
Continued reference to the design versus a quick look and drawing from memory
Use of drawing aids: finger tracing, counting design features, self-verbalizations, and "anchoring" location with nondominant hand
Recognition of errors and attempts to correct
Confidence: expressions of satisfaction or dissatisfaction, frustration tolerance, and need for reassurance and encouragement
Knowledge that errors have been made but inability to correct them even with repeated efforts
Rotations of cards, paper, or drawn designs
Fatigue, illness, or lack of interest
Physical problems—hearing, eyesight, or coordination
Verbal comments by the child

abnormality to brain dysfunction; no test findings were attributed to malingering. However, these findings are not surprising given that the base rate for child malingering is probably very low and judges were not told that malingering was a possibility (Nies & Sweet, 1994). Similar results were found in the same type of study of adolescents (Faust, Hart, Guilmette, & Arkes, 1988). One sign that there may be increasing interest in this topic is a chapter devoted to children and deception in a new book about malingering (Oldershaw & Bagby, 1997).

Variations in Administration for Children

Researchers have described several methods of administering the BGT to children.

Group Administration.   Because one of the primary uses of the BGT is as a screening test, in some situations it is helpful to administer the test to more than one person at a time. Koppitz (1975) describes four different techniques for administering the BGT to groups of school children. In terms of time, testing groups of normal children requires from 15 to 20 minutes but testing groups of children with problems requires as much as 35 minutes.

One group method involves the use of enlarged stimulus cards. This technique, developed by Keogh and Smith (1961), uses 11- by 16¾-inch cards (about three times the size of the standard cards) in a special holder at the front of the classroom. This format makes the procedure very similar to other classroom activities and allows testing of 5 to 15 children at a time. All other aspects of the testing remain the same as the standard administration (pencils, papers, instructions, etc.). Some experimenters use a test booklet and have the child draw each design on a separate page. The disadvantage of the booklet approach is the loss of information about the child's planning ability, organizational skills, and judgment. In using the method of enlarged stimulus cards, one also loses the valuable information provided from observing the execution of the test. However, one can later individually retest anyone whose performance raises questions.

A second group administration technique that does allow for examiner behavioral observations is the use of individual decks of BGT cards to test 2 to 4 individuals at a time (e.g., Dibner & Korn, 1969). All persons being tested draw the design on each card and turn the cards over themselves as they are ready for them. The other aspects of the test remain standard. This method can be used even with very young children or psychiatric patients. It can also be used with larger groups of 15 to 20 persons, but this eliminates the possibility of behavioral observations.

Special BGT copying booklets have also been used for group testing. These booklets contain nine pages (8½ by 11 inches) with a single stimulus figure reproduced in the standard size on the top third of each page. Each figure is to be copied on the bottom two thirds of each page. This method has the same advantages and disadvantages as the enlarged card method, with the added expense of printing the booklets.

The fourth group testing method uses the projection of the BGT designs onto a screen by a slide, opaque, or overhead projector. This technique has the advantage of accommodating the largest number of individuals at one time (20 to 30). The main problem, however, is that the figures must be drawn in a darkened room, with whatever lowered accuracy of reproduction that factor might bring.

The adequacy of these techniques has been verified empirically. For example, Keogh and Smith (1961) explored the feasibility of group administration by using two different group methods and comparing each to the standard individual administration. They found no differences among kindergarten children using the standard individual method, the enlarged stimulus group method, or the copying booklet group method. Other researchers found no differences between slide projection of stimuli and using a separate deck of stimulus cards for kindergarten through fourth grade students (Brannigan & Brannigan, 1995; Dibner & Korn, 1969). Becker and Sabatino (1971) found a correlation of .85 between individual and group administration scores for children ages 5 to 9.

Group testing of children with the BGT appears to be feasible. Group administration has successfully been used to study children's visual-perceptual development and to inexpensively screen large numbers of children to predict school performance and reading achievement. It has also been employed to identify children at high risk for such problems as learning disabilities or emotional maladjustment (Koppitz, 1975).

In the case of diagnostic work with individuals who have already been identified as having problems or who may be too young to work in a group, most clinicians still prefer the standard individual testing procedure. This method allows ample opportunity for establishment of rapport, encouragement to comply with instructions and to complete testing, and observation of the process of reproducing the BGT designs. These advantages far outweigh the savings of time accomplished by group methods.

Other Administration Methods.   Recall, tachistoscopic, and background-interference methods have already been described in Chapter 4 with regard to administration methods for adults. None have been extensively used for children. What little research has been done on these formats has not shown particularly promising results with children. Imm, Foster, Belter, and Finch (1991) provided normative data for BGT recall from a population of 270 child and adolescent psychiatric inpatients. To be considered correct, the recalled figure could not contain any major distortions or omissions. The number of correctly recalled figures increased with age and decreased with lower IQ. Children ages 8 and 9 recalled an average of 3.3 designs ($SD = 1.8$); children ages 10 and 11 recalled 4.5 ($SD = 4.5$). However, Koppitz (1975) states that until the validity of the recall method has been well established, there is little justification for its continued use with children.

The Background Interference Procedure (BIP) appears not to be suitable for use with children. Adams and Canter (1969) found that most children could not copy successfully with the BIP until age 13. Research with children's BIP performance has had mostly disappointing results (Koppitz, 1975). Further details about variations in the administration of the BGT can be found in Koppitz (1975) and Tolor and Brannigan (1980). Koppitz also describes some other modifications to use with preschool children. For example, you can explore motor coordination alone by having the child trace the BGT figures and explore visual perception alone by using a multiple-choice format (Wedell & Horne, 1969).

Testing the limits.   It may sometimes be useful to test the limits of a child's abilities on the BGT. For example, Sattler (1992) suggests asking a child to compare any problematic drawings with the stimulus figures. You can ask the child to express how the two are alike or different. The child can then be given a second opportunity to draw one or more of the designs. This procedure may aid in understanding whether the child recognizes his or her errors, can distinguish them from the original model, and is able to correct errors when given a second chance. It may allow analysis of whether errors are due to such factors as "poor attention to detail, carelessness, impulsiveness, poor organization, fear of completing a difficult task, fatigue, or lack of interest" (p. 360). Testing the limits may also provide information that targets whether a poor BGT performance is due primarily to perceptual or motor aspects or due more to perceptual-motor integration.

KOPPITZ SCORING SYSTEM FOR THE BGT

In 1963, Elizabeth Koppitz published formal scoring procedures that allow a more standardized and objective evaluation of children's BGTs than the more intuitive approach of Lauretta Bender (1938). Although its official name is the Developmental Bender Test Scoring System, it is commonly referred to as the *Koppitz system.* She clarified and extended her system somewhat in 1975, and it is now the most frequently used child BGT scoring method. A second part of this system allows assessment of emotional indicators. The procedures are easy and quick to use, taking only 3 to 5 minutes. The Koppitz system is designed to determine the level of maturity of visual-motor perception for children ages 5 through 11 years. Koppitz believed that by age 10 a child can copy the BGT designs without difficulty. Attempts to use the scoring methods with children younger than 5 have been mostly unsuccessful.

DEVELOPMENTAL SCORING

In the Developmental scoring phase of the Koppitz system, the evaluator examines each of the nine BGT designs for four types of errors:

Distortion of shape
Rotation of the whole design or part of it by at least 45 degrees
Failure to integrate the parts of the design
Perseveration, or repetition of the elements of some designs

The examiner uses the scoring manual to check for the presence or absence of 30 possible errors; 2 to 4 of the types of errors are possible on each of the nine designs. Each error is clearly described and illustrated with multiple examples. Figure 11.2 is taken from her scoring manual (Koppitz, 1975, p. 181) and illustrates the four errors possible for BGT figure 6. Note that on figure 6, there are two types of distortion errors possible, as well as one integration error and one perseveration error. Failure to integrate is not a potential error for this figure. One point is given for each error for a total of 30 points; however, according to Koppitz, scores higher than 20 are rarely seen. A perfect score would be 0. Figure 11.3, also taken from the 1975 book (p. 186) shows the normative distribution (in 6-month increments) of the range and mean of scores for 975 school children. The average number of errors for a 5-year-old child is 13.1 ($SD = 3.3$) and for an 11-year-old child is 1.4 ($SD = 1.4$). She also provides age equivalents for each number of errors and percentile scores for each age level.

To illustrate the Koppitz scoring of the BGT, a test protocol from Jerome Sattler's *Assessment of Children, Third Edition* is presented in Figure 11.4. This BGT was drawn by a female, age 8 years 10 months, who suffers from seizures, learning disability, and speech problems due to an inoperable lesion since birth in her right cerebral hemisphere. She was cooperative, motivated, and friendly during testing. Her WISC-R results were Verbal IQ = 88, Performance IQ = 60, and Full Scale IQ = 72. Scale scores ranged from a 10 on Similarities to a 3 on Mazes and a 1 on Block Design. On the Wide Range Achievement Test (WRAT) her standard scores were 71 in reading, 79 in spelling, and 68 in arithmetic.

On the BGT, she made a total of 10 errors, as described in Table 11.2. The mean number of errors expected for her age would be 3. Ten errors result in a standard score of 58 and place her below the 5th percentile.

VALIDITY OF THE KOPPITZ SCORING SYSTEM

Researchers have assessed the validity of the Koppitz system on a number of criteria, including normative data, relationship of scores to other variables, ability to predict school readiness, and success in detecting learning disabilities and brain damage.

Standardization

Koppitz *standardized* her scoring system on 1,104 school children in 1963 and on another 975 children in 1975. She presented the results of the two groups in her 1975 book. Few details are known about the original sample except that it was 98% white. The 1975 sample, most of whom were from the Northeast (83%), consisted of 86% white, 8.5% African American, 4.5% Hispanic American, and 1% Asian American children. Other characteristics of her sample were not reported. Her 1975 book also presented the results of hundreds of studies on the validity and reliability of the Koppitz scoring system. For example, in reference to the effects of *gender*, she cited 18 studies, in addition to her original normative data, in which girls and boys (ages 5 to 11) showed no differences in their mean BGT scores. No gender differences have been found whether the children being studied were typical school children or those with emotional or learning problems. Consequently, she has chosen to give only one set of normative data for her scoring system.

Relationship of BGT Performance to Other Variables

There are many other variables that can be related to performance on the BGT, such as level of *intelligence*. Koppitz (1975) reviewed 13 studies with children revealing correlations between IQ and BGT scores ranging from −.19 to

Distortion

18a. Distortion of shape; three or more distinct angles or points instead of curves; in case of doubt do *not* score.
Examples:

18b. Straight lines; less than two complete sinusoidal curves or no curves at all in one or both lines.
Examples:

19. *Integration*
Two lines crossing not at all or at extreme end of one or both lines or less than one complete sinusoidal curve from end of line; two interwoven lines.
Examples:

20. *Perseveration*
Six or more complete sinusoidal curves in either direction.
Example:

Figure 11.2 Possible Koppitz errors for children on BGT figure 6. (From Elizabeth M. Koppitz, *The Bender Gestalt Test for young children, Volume II: Research and application 1963–1973.* Copyright © 1975 by Allyn and Bacon. Reprinted by permission.)

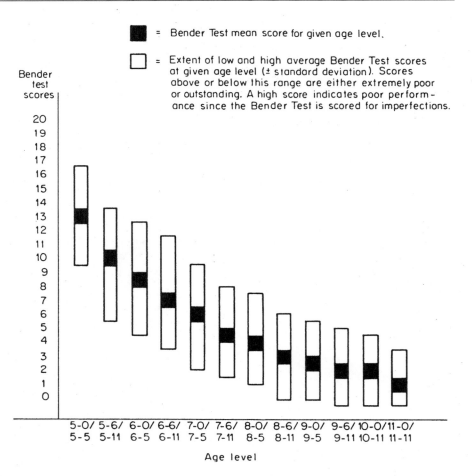

Figure 11.3 Distribution of Bender Gestalt Test mean scores and standard deviations for children. These data are from Koppitz's 1974 normative sample (*N* = 975). (From Elizabeth M. Koppitz, *The Bender Gestalt Test for young children, Volume II: Research and application 1963–1973.* Copyright © 1975 by Allyn and Bacon. Reprinted by permission.)

−.66. All the studies of children with average mental ability showed a significant relationship; those studies of children with superior intelligence did not.

Another variable, *ethnicity,* has been consistently shown to influence children's BGT scores. Review of the research reveals that African American children performed more poorly on the BGT than did white children, even disadvantaged white children. American Indian and Hispanic American children showed a slower rate of visual-motor maturity than white children, but this difference disappeared as the children got older (Koppitz, 1975). Moore and Zarske (1984) evaluated the BGTs of 452 Navajo children (ages 6 to 16) and found that their scores compared favorably to those of white children. Much of the research on ethnic differences in performance on the BGT is based on small samples. However, Sattler and Gwynne (1982) examined seven age groups and three ethnic groups of California children in the System of Multicultural Pluralistic Assessment (SOMPA) standardization sample (*N* =

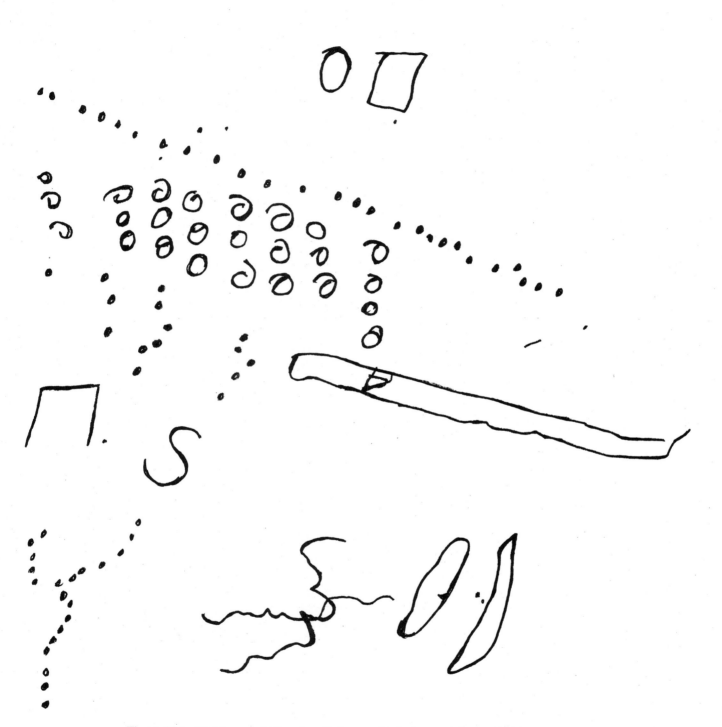

Figure 11.4 Eight-year-old female with inoperable lesion in right cerebral hemisphere.

Table 11.2 Description of Koppitz BGT Errors for a Child (Age 8 Years 10 Months) with Brain Damage

Figure	Description of error	Type of error	Error #
A	Failure to join the circle and diamond	Integration	3
1	Rotation of line by 45 degrees or more	Rotation	5
	More than 15 dots in a row	Perseveration	6
2	No errors	—	—
3	Rotation of axis by 45 degrees or more	Rotation	11
4	Rotation of figure by 45 degrees or more	Rotation	13
	Curve and box more than ⅛ inch apart	Integration	14
5	Rotation of figure by 45 degrees or more	Rotation	16
6	No errors	—	—
7	Hexagons excessively misshapen	Distortion	21b
	Hexagons do not overlap	Integration	23
8	Both shapes excessively misshapen	Distortion	24

Source: Sattler, J. M. (1992). *Assessment of children* (3rd ed.), p. 709. San Diego, CA: Author. Reprinted with permission.

1938, ages 5 to 11, divided evenly among three ethnic groups). They found that African American children had lower performance than the white children (making twice as many errors) at every age level and had lower performance than Hispanic American children at most age levels. The latter group generally performed at the same level as the white children. Possible explanations given for the lowered performance of African American children included slower perceptual-motor development, delayed maturation, insufficient motivation, and cognitive deficits. Taylor and Partenio (1984) found the same results in a Florida SOMPA sample of 652 children equally divided among the three ethnic groups.

The latter researchers, as well as Zuelzer, Stedman, and Adams (1976), found that much of the ethnicity effect could be reduced or eliminated by controlling for IQ. Children who were in the average IQ range had the highest correlations between age and BGT score. This may mean that one can have higher confidence in the BGT results of African American children who fall in the midrange of IQ.

None of the preceding studies, however, have taken into account the enormous number of variables on which various ethnic groups may differ. Research seems to show that the child-rearing practices in some countries (e.g., China and Japan) favor an earlier development of perceptual-motor coordination. Helms (1992) describes the *cultural aspects* of being African American that could influence test performance. Puente, Mora, and Munoz-Cespedes (1997) explore the complexities of neuropsychological assessment of Spanish-speaking children. For example, they note that different cultural environments may lead to the development of a different pattern of skills. Also, a different sociocultural background often means a different language as well as different communication strategies. Straightforward translations, especially of complicated tests, are often incorrect and may introduce as much error as would evaluating the child in English. Few translated tests provide normative data for the translated version of the test. Sattler (1992) concludes that, overall, the BGT is less culturally loaded than other cognitive tests. This test may also have a special advantage for assessing various ethnic groups because the instructions are relatively simple and the task is brief and nonverbal.

Prediction of School Readiness and Academic Achievement

One of the original purposes of using the BGT with children was to measure perceptual-motor development that, in turn, could be used as a *predictor of school readiness* and *academic achievement* (Koppitz, 1975). Educators have good reasons to identify as early as possible those children who need special attention to learn at their age level. It is important to detect cognitive impairment at an early age to curtail the development of further intellectual and emotional sequelae. Contemporary psychoeducational testing usually incorporates measures of a variety of functions, often including a test of perceptual-motor development such as the BGT.

Research has shown a positive correlation between BGT scores and school achievement. In her 1975 book, Koppitz presents 54 such correlations that range from .13 to .58. However, she advises that the relationship is not high enough to use the BGT alone to predict achievement for an individual child. She also believes that when a pupil does well on this test, it does forecast good school achievement. However, because poor school achievement is dependent on so many factors, the BGT does not do as good a job of predicting failure in school (though Hartlage & Golden, 1990, do review research showing better prediction with younger children). Lesiak (1984), in her review of 32 studies of the BGT as a predictor of reading achievement, concludes that this test is inferior to specific reading readiness measures; the test alone was not able to consistently differentiate good from poor readers. These findings are not surprising because perceptual-motor ability constitutes only one aspect of the necessary skills for school success in general and reading achievement in particular. For example, Malatesha (1986) explains that reading skill is dependent upon the ability to process verbal information both in a discrete, *sequential* manner as well as in a *simultaneous* way, that is, by processing gestalts. Deficiencies in either skill can result in reading problems, but the BGT is only relevant to the skill of simultaneous processing. Three groups of third graders (normal readers, sequentially deficient readers, and simultaneous-deficient readers) were given the BGT. The predicted results were obtained; that is, the normal readers produced Koppitz scores of 3.2; those deficient in sequential processing had scores of 6.4; and those deficient in simultaneous processing had scores of 10.3. In this case, the BGT was able to identify problem readers whose difficulty was related to a specific skill measured by this test.

In another study, Nielson and Sapp (1991) compared children of low and normal birth weight on reading and math achievement. As predicted, BGT standard scores for the low-birth-weight children were lower than those from children with normal birth weight. The BGT was also able to do a better job of predicting school achievement for the low-birth-weight students, perhaps because their premature births left them with some form of brain dysfunction or developmental lag. Furthermore, Koppitz (1975) believes that because female students are more able than males to compensate for lower perceptual-motor ability, a poor BGT score for boys is more likely to predict school problems. She also found that BGT errors are more associated with arithmetic achievement than with reading and are most predictive of overall school functioning.

The conclusion is that the BGT is unsatisfactory as a single measure of school readiness or achievement for all groups of school children. However, it appears to be useful as a measure of a specific function within a group of tests.

Also, there is preliminary evidence that the BGT can identify subgroups of pupils who have deficiencies in skills that are measured by the test and that are relevant to school success. As an example, a child with a language deficiency is much less likely to be identified by the BGT than a child with difficulties in visual-spatial processing (Franzen & Berg, 1989).

Detection of Learning Disabilities

Recent surveys indicate that the numbers of school children with mental retardation and speech impairment are decreasing, although cases of learning disability are rapidly increasing. Estimates of children with learning disabilities are as high as 20%, with many going undiagnosed. This increase is attributed variously to increased awareness, medical advances that increase survival rates of infants at high risk, increased in-utero exposure to narcotics, and other causes (Bigler, Nussbaum, & Foley, 1997). We now know that the diagnostic category of learning disability is not a uniform disorder.

Earlier research determined that there are different types of learning disability based on the specific areas of academic deficiency (reading, spelling, writing, and math). More recently, subtypes have also emerged within each of those areas. These subtypes differ in symptoms, neuropsychological results, and neurological patterns (James & Selz, 1997). Some of the subtypes are differentiated by whether they have difficulties in the perceptual-motor sphere. For example, through their extensive research, Rourke and his colleagues identified three subgroups of learning disabilities. Only one of these includes poor visual-spatial skills (Rourke, 1985). In the area of arithmetic disability, he found two subgroups of poor performance on arithmetic tasks—one resulting from reading deficits and the other from visual-spatial impairment. The latter involved spatial organization, visual detail, and graphomotor skills (Rourke, 1993).

Snow and Desch (1988, 1989) reported on two investigations of children who were referred to a university pediatric clinic for academic and behavioral difficulties. These children could be cluster-analyzed into several groups that differed greatly on BGT scores, IQ, medical and developmental history, and social or adaptive behavior. Their research was conducted on a group of 1,204 children and adolescents (mostly white, 72% male, mean age = 9.75) who were given extensive evaluation by a multidisciplinary staff. Cases in their second study fell into five subgroups:

1. Above average IQ, few BGT errors (mean = 4.36), few medical or developmental indicators
2. Similar to number 1 but with lower IQ, mean BGT errors = 5.05
3. Performance IQ (PIQ) < Verbal IQ (VIQ), high BGT errors (8.38), congenital anomalies
4. PIQ > VIQ, borderline IQ, mean BGT errors = 7.14, speech development delays
5. Mild retardation, highest number of BGT errors (mean = 12.03), history of medical and developmental delays

Their results help explain why use of the BGT alone would not identify every case of learning disability. Although some children have perceptual-motor deficiencies at the heart of their learning difficulties, many other academically deficient pupils have impairment in other brain functions.

In an innovative study related to child learning difficulties, Locher and Worms (1977) used BGT visual scanning strategies to examine the visual encoding processes of those with perceptual and neurological disabilities. Participants were 8 each of children ages 6 to 12 with perceptual impairment, neurological impairment, and no impairment. Enlarged stimulus figures were displayed on a rear-projection screen attached to a wide-angle polymetric eye-movement recorder. The stimulus display was reflected on the child's right eye and recorded by a video camera placed in the viewing port of the eye-movement recorder. Resulting low peripheral acuity forced the child to scan the stimulus. Attention shifts then took the form of eye movements.

Participants were asked to view each stimulus until they believed they could draw it on a piece of paper. A few days prior to the scanning procedure each child had been administered the copy phase of the BGT in the standard manner. To analyze eye movements, the videotapes were played back at slow speed. The complete sequence of fixations and the viewing time were recorded on a copy of each design.

Clear and consistent differences were found in the scanning strategies or encoding processes of these three groups of children. The unimpaired children used fixations in an efficient way to scan most or all of the salient structural features of the designs. They examined the whole stimulus, ignored areas of low information content, and directed their fixations to areas of high information content (see Figure 11.5). Examples of these informative areas are changes of contour or points of contact between parts of a design. The systematic selection for encoding of stimulus parts high in information content leads to the greatest internal *organization* of the stimulus.

In contrast, the scanning strategies of the children with perceptual impairment were more a matter of degree than of kind. They required more time to encode and were much less organized and efficient. These children used more fixations, refixated areas previously examined, encoded fewer salient features of each design, and frequently fixated on areas of low information content, including positions that were off the stimulus (see Figure 11.5).

The encoding processes of children with neurological impairment were different in both degree and kind from those of the children with no impairment or perceptual impairment. Not only did they focus off the stimulus but they were frequently completely off the screen. They also stared at low information stimulus points for periods of 2 to 5 seconds in between random scanning of the display at a rapid rate.

Clear differences in scanning strategies were observed between children with no impairment and those with perceptual impairment; however, there were no differences in BGT copying performance. In contrast, the copy performance of children with neurological impairment was clearly discernible from that of the other two groups. Each design on each BGT protocol was rated for "goodness of reproduction" of all the structural components on a 5-point scale (5 = very accurate reproduction). The mean rating for all designs was 3.29 (SD = .76) for the children with no impairment, 3.25 (SD = .93) for those with perceptual impairment, and 1.81 (SD = .88) for those with neurological impairment.

The authors of this study suggest that the information provided by examining the BGT visual scanning patterns of children allows evaluation of visual perception independent of motor functioning. Because motoric function was not affected in children with perceptual impairment, information about visual encoding processes may be useful in detecting the presence and type of a child's learning disability. The more problems a child has with focusing on a

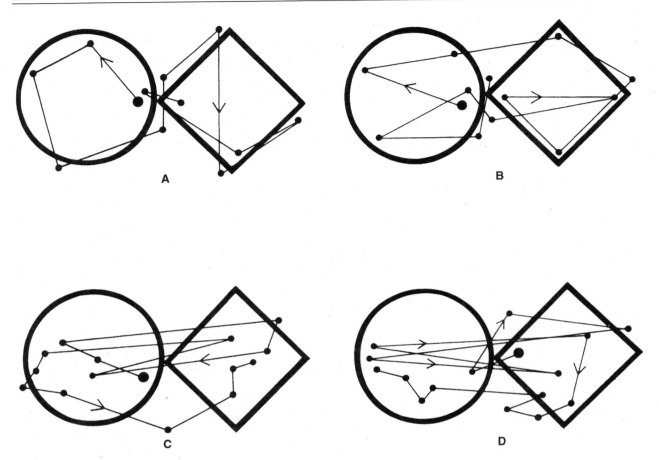

Figure 11.5   Eye-movement scanning patterns of two children with no disabilities (A & B) and two children with perceptual impairment (C & D) viewing Bender Gestalt design A. (From P. Locher and P. Worms, (1977). "Visual scanning strategies of neurologically impaired, perceptually impaired, and normal children viewing the Bender Gestalt designs." *Psychology in the Schools, 14,* 151. Copyright © 1977 by John Wiley & Sons. Reprinted by permission of John Wiley & Sons, Inc.)

task and attending to relevant structural features of visual stimuli, the more likely it is that the child will have difficulty perceiving and interpreting sensory stimuli; therefore, there is a higher chance that he or she will exhibit a learning disability (Pirozzolo, Campanella, Christensen, & Lawson-Kerr, 1981). Learning such complex skills as reading requires efficient scanning strategies. Both groups of children with impairment in this study exhibited major deficiencies in their encoding skills, although of a different type. Information about these processes could be used to plan individualized visual-motor training strategies to overcome inefficiencies (Heaton & Pendleton, 1981; Satz & Fletcher, 1981).

In conclusion, assessing learning disabilities is a complex task because of the likelihood of many different subtypes of deficiencies. Research shows that the best approach is to use a variety of measures that tap various functions of the brain. Because perceptual-motor function appears to play a role in a number of subtypes of learning disability, a measure of this function should be included in the battery (D'Amato et al., 1997; Franzen & Berg, 1989). The BGT has been found to be successful in identifying some children who have certain subtypes of learning disability.

Brain Damage   Within the modern neuropsychology movement, there are two diverse camps that advocate the use of quite different approaches to the assessment of children. One relies primarily upon specialized neuropsychological tests, such as the Halstead-Reitan and the Luria batteries, that have been modified for use with children. The other, more widespread, group consists of psychologists who prefer to use a neuropsychological focus while employing traditional psychological tests. The latter group questions the use of tests not originally constructed for children and that do not take into account the developmental aspects of brain injury (D'Amato et al., 1997). Cognitive functioning in children is quite different from that of adults. Deficient cognitive functions are not necessarily linked to damage in a specific region of the brain. Higher-level cognitive abilities can be sensitive to the effects of brain damage in many different sites of the brain. (Franzen & Berg, 1989). Therefore, although the BGT is considered to be a test that specifically measures right parietal impairment, it may be useful with children who have dysfunction not specific to that particular brain site. What follows are descriptions of several studies that have used the BGT in innovative ways to measure some aspects of brain dysfunction in children.

Shapiro, Shapiro, and Clarkin (1974) investigated the etiology of Gilles de la Tourette syndrome, a rare and insidious illness that starts between the ages of 2 and 13. Symptoms include tics, coprolalia, and complicated movements, noises, or words. In 1974, many clinicians believed that the etiology of Tourette syndrome was psychological; others subscribed to a biological causation viewpoint.

The BGT was given to 30 patients with Tourette syndrome (14 under age 16 and 16 over age 16), along with an IQ test, an EEG, and both a neurological and a psychiatric evaluation. The BGT was scored with the Koppitz system for those patients under age 11 and with the Hutt-Briskin (1960) system for all others. The data from all sources supported the hypothesis of some central nervous system abnormality among individuals with Tourette syndrome. The BGT identified 83% with brain impairment, compared to 37% for the IQ test. Based on the combined psychological tests, 77% of the patients were rated as having mild to marked brain dysfunction. This number contrasts with the approximately 50% who were rated as having brain impairment by either the EEG, neurological evaluation, or psychiatric evaluation.

Another study used the BGT to evaluate the differential effect of two amphetamine optical isomers on children with minimal brain dysfunction (MBD); Arnold, Huestis, Wemmer, & Smeltzer, 1978). Both levoamphetamine and dextroamphetamine had previously been shown to have a beneficial effect on the behavior and in-vitro metabolic activity of children with MBD, hyperactivity, or learning disability. However, the effects of these two drugs upon visual-motor function, an important element in school performance, had not been examined previously.

These researchers examined BGT performance as part of a double-blind, crossover, randomized Latin-square comparison of these two drugs and a placebo. Participants were 26 boys and 5 girls ages 4 to 12 ($M = 8$ years) diagnosed as having MBD. BGTs were obtained at four points: predrug and at the end of each of the three 4-week drug conditions. A "blind" scorer used the Koppitz system.

Behaviorally, both drugs were significantly superior to the placebo and roughly comparable to each other. However, perceptual-motor function was significantly improved by only one of the drugs, dextroamphetamine. The authors suggest that amphetamine's effect on visual-motor performance is mediated through a different neuropharmacological mechanism than its effect on behavior. They emphasize the importance of monitoring more than just changes in behavior in studies of drug efficacy.

Two other studies measured perceptual-motor functioning as part of an investigation of the long-term effects of having alcoholic parents (Werner, 1986) or of exposure in utero to the mother's chronic use of narcotics (Davis & Templer, 1988). In the former study, 49 Hawaiian offspring of alcoholic parents were given, over several years, extensive evaluations that included the BGT. Participants were divided into those who had serious coping problems and those who did not. Also, the effects were measured of the gender of the child and whether the alcoholic parent was the mother or father. The resilient group was disproportionately composed of females who were the offspring of alcoholic fathers. The resilient offspring at ages 10 and 18 made significantly fewer errors on the BGT than the offspring with serious coping problems (1.4 versus 2.8 errors at age 18). Especially vulnerable were a group of children whose mothers used alcohol during their pregnancy. Of these, 33% earned BGT scores indicative of brain impairment.

In the Davis and Templer (1988) study, 28 narcotics-exposed children, ages 6 to 15, were compared to an equal number of nonexposed children. Evaluations included the WISC-R, BGT, Quick Neurological Screening Test, and behavior rating scales. The narcotics-exposed group had significantly lower Performance and Full Scale IQs, higher number of BGT errors (6.95 versus 3.42), and more serious behaviors. The two groups did not differ on the BGT emotional indicators. Children exposed to methadone in utero showed more impairment than those exposed to heroin.

In summary, a number of studies with the BGT have gone beyond a simple focus on diagnostic accuracy. Researchers have used this test to study a wide variety of behaviors in previously unexplored areas, from evaluating surgical procedures to examining children's visual encoding processes. More work in such innovative areas will expand the usefulness of the BGT to clinicians.

RELIABILITY OF THE KOPPITZ SYSTEM

As for reliability, Koppitz (1975) reports a range of *test-retest reliability* from .53 to .90, depending upon age and retest interval (from same day to 8 months). However, Sattler (1992) states that the median reliability ($r = .77$) of these studies is not high enough to warrant diagnostic decision making about the perceptual-motor functioning of a child; instead, results should be used to formulate hypotheses that must be confirmed from other data.

The scoring techniques appear relatively easy to master. Morsbach, Del Priori, and Furnell (1975) found that four undergraduates with no testing experience were able to learn to score reliably by reading the Koppitz instructions. Their results matched those of four experienced psychologists. For 31 studies, *interscorer reliability* has ranged from .79 to .99, with 89% of the studies achieving .89 or better. Both Koppitz and Tolor and Brannigan (1980) do caution clinicians, however, to rely on total scores in making classifications, rather than on the four types of specific errors that all show lower reliabilities. For example, Neale and McKay (1985), analyzing the protocols of 200 6-year-olds, found interrater agreement of 92% for total score; for individual scores it ranged from 71% for distortion of shape on figure A to 94% for rotation on figure A.

OTHER OBJECTIVE SCORING SYSTEMS FOR THE BGT WITH CHILDREN

During the 1960s and 1970s, a number of other BGT scoring systems were developed for use with children. However, none of them have met the test of time and they will not be reviewed here. During the past 30 years, there have been continuing differences of opinion about the relative merits of a strictly objective evaluation method (e.g., Koppitz) and one that allows more input from the clinician's intuitive judgment. Some psychologists think that the latter approach allows a richer analysis of the perceptual, motor, and developmental factors essential to reproducing the BGT designs. A recently published scoring scheme attempts to integrate quantitative and qualitative components. The Qualitative Scoring System (QSS; Brannigan & Brunner, 1989) uses only six of the original BGT figures: A, 1, 2, 4, 6, and 8. These figures are the ones thought to be less difficult and therefore most appropriate for evaluation of young children. For the QSS, each of the six designs is assigned a score from 0 to 5, ranging from a random drawing to a perfect representation, based on criteria provided in a scoring manual. Initial research on this approach is promising. Much of the preliminary research has been done by the authors of the method. For example, Brannigan, Aabye, Baker, and Ryan (1995) found higher correlations between the QSS with the Metropolitan Achievement Test (measuring math, reading, and language skills in first through fourth graders) than were achieved between the Koppitz scoring system and the same achievement test.

EMOTIONAL INDICATORS

The second part of the Koppitz scoring system addresses the child's emotional stability. Children with problems in perceptual-motor coordination (as measured by the Koppitz Development score) may be vulnerable to emotional problems but do not always suffer from them. Koppitz originally designated 10 indicators of emotional problems on the BGT in 1963, adding two more in 1975. She believed the indicators were independent of the developmental level of perceptual-motor function. Examples of the 12 Emotional Indicators are *small size* (drawing is half the size or less of stimulus figure), *fine line* (drawing line so thin it requires effort to observe), *careless overwork or heavily reinforced lines, second attempts* (second drawing without removal of first attempt), and *expansion* (use of two or more sheets of paper to draw the nine designs). Rossini and Kaspar (1987) compared the BGT Emotional Indicators of 7- to 10-year-old normal children and children with adjustment disorders or behavior disorders. Controlling for developmental level, they found that both clinical groups produced more indicators (2.12 for adjustment disorders and 2.57 for behavior disorders) than did the normal children (1.42 indicators), although the two clinical groups were not different from each other.

For each of her emotional indicators, Koppitz summarizes research findings relative to diagnosis, personality, and school behavior. In general, the amount and type of research is inadequate to inspire confidence in the use of these indicators. Koppitz believes that a single emotional indicator does not necessarily mean that the child has any serious emotional problem. Some research has shown that at least three indicators are necessary to raise suspicion of serious emotional disturbance. Rossini and Kaspar (1987) found that two or more indicators warrants considering a diagnosis of psychopathology. The three indicators that they found to be most related to degree of psychopathology were: (1) figures drawn in a *confused order* on the paper, (2) *large size* (drawings at least twice as large as the stimulus figures), and (3) a *box* drawn around figure(s). Five of the indicators were less frequent in the control group (see the five described in the previous paragraph) and the remaining indicators were rarely produced in any of the groups. In any case, Koppitz recommends that any such hypotheses be validated against other test data and observations of the child.

In addition to these formal Emotional Indicators, many child psychologists single out the amount of time to complete the BGT as a useful indicator of personality factors. For example, Sattler (1992) talks about the child who takes inordinate amounts of time for the BGT as one who might have an overly slow and methodical problem-solving approach or may be compulsive or depressed. Those who are overly quick in completing the designs may be overly impulsive in problem solving.

INTERPRETATION OF CHILDREN'S BGT RESULTS

Research and clinical experience show that the BGT is a valuable asset in evaluating elementary-school-age children for school readiness, learning disability, perceptual-motor deficits, brain damage, and emotional problems. However, its value is not as a *single test,* but as an indicator of the maturity of the child's *perceptual-motor development* when used within a battery of other tests measuring other factors. These tests must also be used in combination with information on history of development, physical health, social interactions, school progress, and typical behavioral patterns. Interpretation of BGT results also assumes some basic knowledge of perceptual-motor processes in the child (see Williams, 1983, for a complex paradigm of sensory-perceptual processes). A final key ingredient for diagnosis is the clinician's careful observations of the *process* used by the child to reproduce the nine figures. All of these elements are important and must be integrated for a thorough assessment.

Some general principles of interpretation of the BGT have been put forth by Sattler (1992). Skills related to the accurate reproduction of the BGT designs include "appropriate fine motor development, perceptual discrimination ability, and ability to integrate perceptual and motor processes" (p. 361). However, difficulty with the task may also involve such deficiencies as inability to shift attention between the stimulus and the copied figure, misperception of the input information, execution problems, or faulty storage and retrieval of memory. "Inadequate visual-motor performance may be associated with maturational delay, limited intellectual stimulation, unfamiliarity with testing situations, or neurological impairment" (p. 361). Sattler also gives some clues for differentiating whether poor performance can be attributed to output (motor or expressive) functions or input (perceptual or receptive) functions. If the child appears to struggle to draw the designs, the possibility of an output problem is greater; ease with drawing that nonetheless produces unrecognized errors most likely indicates an input problem. Ability to recognize errors but inability to correct them may signal output difficulties; inability to see errors may indicate faulty input.

Other factors that the psychologist must rule out before interpreting a poor BGT performance as brain dysfunction or learning disability include physical disabilities, such as poor visual acuity, illness, fatigue, stress, and mental retardation; environmental deprivation; and lack of motivation.

Although the BGT is viewed widely as a useful tool for the diagnosis of many childhood difficulties, no specific signs that are indicative of specific diagnoses have stood the test of time or of scientific investigation. For children ages 5 to 10, the BGT seems most useful in assessing perceptual-motor maturation. If perceptual-motor difficulties are found on this test, that knowledge will have to be integrated with many other sources of information about the child to arrive at an accurate diagnosis. Excellent child case examples detailing this process—integrating information from tests and other sources, arriving at a diagnosis, and making recommendations—have been provided by Sattler (1992).

CHAPTER 12

The Bender Gestalt Test with Adolescents

As the reader can see from the previous chapter, there is a wealth of clinical information and research on the use of the Bender Gestalt Test (BGT) with children. Koppitz (1975) designed her widely used scoring system to measure the level of maturity of visual-motor perception in children only. She believes that the perceptual-motor skills of developmentally normal children are fully mature by age 10. After this age, there is no longer a need to assess maturity of this cognitive function. The Koppitz norms (1975) show evidence of such a plateau of development; by ages 10 and 11, children average fewer than 2 BGT errors out of a possible 30. Therefore, Koppitz believes that the BGT has limited or no use in the evaluation of adolescents. Consequently, her scoring norms go only through age 11.

For the primary adult scoring systems (see Chapter 3), norms begin at age 18. As a result, there is created a kind of adolescent limbo with very little information about using this test with individuals ages 12 through 17. Clinically, psychologists have sometimes been advised to use the Koppitz system for younger teens and an adult method for older teens. However, until recently, there was no research to form a basis for this practice. Unfortunately, in the absence of well-executed and widely disseminated research, many psychologists rely on their subjective judgment to interpret adolescent BGT scores.

In this chapter, the reader will find the results of recent studies aimed at providing more objective data for the evaluation of adolescents' BGTs. For teenage clients, there now are preliminary norms for both the Koppitz and Lacks methods. Two case examples are provided at the end of this chapter to demonstrate the use of these methods. In general, procedures for administration and behavioral observations should conform to the specific scoring system used. However, if the adolescent client is in the older age range, the instructions for testing adults will be more appropriate.

BGT SCORING FOR ADOLESCENTS

A brief review of BGT normative data for adolescents and the effects of demographic variables follows.

Adolescent Normative Data

Three sets of investigators studied the validity of the Koppitz system (1963, 1975) with both nonpatient adolescents and those with psychiatric or neurological disorders. In 1988, McIntosh et al. applied the Koppitz scoring system to the BGTs of 337 adolescents (ages 12 to 16). Of these, 150 were nonpatient students in a regular public school, with no known history of receiving special education or mental health services. Another 140 were "emotionally disturbed" inpatients with such diagnoses as affective disorders (37%), conduct disorders (29%), adjustment disorders (18%), and psychosis (4%). A third group consisted of 47 inpatients with mental retardation, neurological impairment, or both. The sample composition was 54% female and 19% African American.

Table 12.1 presents the results of McIntosh et. al. (1988) for the Koppitz scoring system by age and diagnostic subgroup. Results show a significant effect for both age and diagnosis. The group with neurological impairment made more errors than did either of the other two groups, which did not differ from each other. There was a trend for errors to decrease with increasing age.

Bolen, Hewett, Hall, and Mitchell (1992) conducted a study very similar to the McIntosh et al. (1988) research. They used only adolescents who had never received any special education services. There were 311 students (52% female, 59% African American), ages 11.5 through 15. They found results very similar to those of McIntosh et al. (1988). Mean number of Koppitz errors ranged from 1.83 ($SD = 1.10$, range 0 to 4) in the youngest group to 1.42 ($SD = 1.14$, range 0 to 6) for the oldest group. Shapiro and Simpson (1995) conducted the third study of the Koppitz system with 87 adolescent inpatients who had behavioral and emotional disturbances (ages 12 through 17, 49% female, 44% African American). They also found results very comparable to those of McIntosh et al. (1988). Mean number of errors ranged from 2.57 ($SD = 1.99$, range 0 to 6) in the youngest group to 1.00 ($SD = 1.00$, range 0 to 3) for the oldest group. Error scores did not differ significantly among diagnostic categories of mood, conduct, and adjustment.

In the same study, McIntosh et al. (1988) also contrasted the Koppitz scoring with the Lacks (1984) adaptation of the Hutt-Briskin scoring system. The Lacks method results can be seen in Table 12.2. There was a strong connection between diagnosis and number of BGT errors; the adolescents with neurological impairment had significantly more errors than did the other two groups, which did not differ from each other. The trend for scores to decrease with increasing age was not as evident for the Lacks system as it was for the Koppitz

Table 12.1   Koppitz Score Means and Standard Deviations by Age and Subgroups

Age	Nonpatient			Emotional disturbance			Mental retardation/ neurological impairment		
	M	*SD*	*N*	*M*	*SD*	*N*	*M*	*SD*	*N*
12 years	3.50	2.84	30	2.74	2.16	19	5.13	3.04	9
13 years	1.83	1.49	30	1.93	1.94	29	5.63	4.75	8
14 years	1.27	1.76	30	1.38	1.39	26	6.63	4.57	8
15 years	1.27	1.39	30	1.53	1.85	30	3.25	2.59	16
16 years	1.67	1.52	30	1.28	1.75	36	3.29	2.87	7
Total	1.91	2.03	150	1.69	1.86	140	4.55	3.62	47

Source: McIntosh, J. A., Belter, R. W., Saylor, C. F., Finch, A. J., and Edwards, G. L. (1988). "The Bender-Gestalt with adolescents: Comparison of two scoring systems," *Journal of Clinical Psychology, 44,* 226–230, Table 1, p. 228). Copyright © 1988. Reprinted by permission of John Wiley & Sons, Inc.

Table 12.2 Lacks Score Means and Standard Deviations by Age and Subgroups

Age	Nonpatient			Emotional disturbance			Mental retardation/neurological impairment		
	M	SD	N	M	SD	N	M	SD	N
12 years	2.67	1.49	30	3.32	2.03	19	4.87	2.59	8
13 years	2.43	1.43	30	2.52	1.82	29	5.63	2.26	8
14 years	2.30	1.44	30	2.65	1.94	26	5.00	2.51	8
15 years	2.27	1.48	30	2.10	1.32	30	3.94	2.46	16
16 years	2.17	1.29	30	2.00	1.93	36	3.57	1.72	7
Total	2.37	1.42	150	2.43	1.84	140	4.51	2.38	47

Source: McIntosh, J. A., Belter, R. W., Saylor, C. F., Finch, A. J., and Edwards, G. L. (1988). "The Bender-Gestalt with adolescents: Comparison of two scoring systems," *Journal of Clinical Psychology, 44,* 226–230, Table 2, p. 229. Copyright © 1988. Reprinted by permission of John Wiley & Sons, Inc.

scores. Interrater reliability was excellent for both the Koppitz ($r = .97$) and the Lacks ($r = .93$) scoring systems. Scores on the two systems agreed moderately with each other ($r = .71$).

Demographic Variables and the BGT

Each of the preceding studies found a significant relationship between test performance and *age,* but not *gender.* Generally, adolescents continued to improve their performance on the BGT as they got older. Bolen et al. (1992) were the only ones to look at *ethnicity;* they did not find differences between European American and African American performance. Tindall (1991), however, did find that special education students from Spanish-speaking homes made more errors (with both scoring systems) than did those from homes where only English was spoken.

BGT Recall Method

Only one study has examined use of the BGT Recall format with adolescents (Imm et al., 1991). The researchers used 194 psychiatric inpatients, ages 12 through 16. Participants first took the copy phase of the BGT and then reproduced as many designs as possible from memory. Drawings were correct if they had no major distortions, omissions, or variations of the design. Rotations did not disqualify a drawing. Based on 20 records, interscorer reliability for the recall scoring was .98. Those patients ages 12 and 13 ($N = 68$) recalled an average of 5.4 ($SD = 1.6$) designs, and those ages 14 through 16 ($N = 126$) recalled 5.9 ($SD = 1.7$). In an analysis of these adolescents combined with 76 children ages 8 through 11, those with IQs less than 90 recalled significantly fewer designs than did those with IQs above 90 (4.6 versus 6.0 errors, respectively). The authors concluded that the BGT Recall score is a useful measure of short-term visual memory.

ASSESSMENT OF EMOTIONAL DISTURBANCE

Both Hutt (1985) and Koppitz (1975) proposed methods for assessing emotional disturbance on the BGT, although Koppitz intended her approach to be used only with children. Belter, McIntosh, Finch, Williams, and Edwards (1989) compared these two emotional-assessment approaches using the same 337 adolescents (see the preceding for a description) they used to assess BGTs for perceptual-motor skill (McIntosh et al., 1988). Each BGT was scored for the 12

Koppitz *Emotional Indicators* that are described in Chapter 11. Each was also scored for Hutt's 17-factor *Psychopathology Scale,* which rates items from 1 to 10 depending on the severity and frequency of occurrence. In addition, ratings were made with Hutt's *Adolescent Configuration Scale,* which gives weights of 1 or 2 points to seven items of the Psychopathology Scale if they fall above a certain score. Their results showed no support for the use of Hutt's two scales for identifying adolescents with emotional disturbances. There were no differences between the scores of the normal group and those of the group with emotional disturbances (see Table 12.3). However, the group with mental retardation or neurological impairment had significantly higher scores than either of the other two groups. Perhaps this result is due to the fact that the Psychopathology Scale includes 9 of the 12 errors used in the Lacks scoring method for brain impairment (1984). Hutt's scale may be measuring brain impairment rather than emotional disturbance.

As for the results of using the Koppitz measure of emotional disturbance, Table 12.4 presents the mean Emotional Indicator scores by age and by group. The researchers believe that their results provide some support for the usefulness of the Emotional Indicators. Statistical analysis shows that the scores were related to the diagnostic subgroup but not to age. The nonpatient group had the lowest number of indicators, the group with mental retardation or neurological impairment the highest, and the group with emotional disturbance fell in between. There was no correlation of the number of Emotional Indicators to IQ, nor to results from self-report inventories of psychopathology (e.g., depression, anxiety, or anger). The latter finding raises the question of whether this scale is clearly measuring emotional disturbance. Table 12.5 displays the percentage of Emotional Indicators by group, showing the same pattern that was found with the actual scores. However, note that there is considerable overlap among the three diagnostic groups. Koppitz (1975) believes that it is not the total score of Emotional Indicators, but instead the presence of any three or more signs that is strongly indicative of emotional disturbance. At least for the data of this study, the standard of three signs is too low; it was met by 23% of the controls, 60% of those with emotional disturbance, and 43% of those with neurological impairment. Table 12.5 shows some support for the Koppitz emotional signs if you use a cutoff score of *more than* three signs. Only 5% of the

Table 12.3   Mean Psychopathology Scale and Adolescent Configuration Scores by Age and Group

Diagnostic group	N	Psychopathology scale		Adolescent configuration	
		M	SD	M	SD
Nonpatient	150	61.31	13.34	6.61	2.34
Emotional disturbance	140	62.19	15.44	6.83	2.42
Mental retardation/ neurological impairment	47	83.55	20.56	9.34	2.76

Source: Belter, R. W., McIntosh, J. A., Finch, A. J., Williams, L. D., and Edwards, G. L. (1989). "The Bender Gestalt as a method of personality assessment with adolescents." *Journal of Clinical Psychology, 45,* 414–422. Copyright © 1989. Reprinted by permission of John Wiley & Sons, Inc.

Table 12.4 Mean Emotional Indicator Scores by Age and Group

Age	Nonpatient			Emotional disturbance			Mental retardation/ neurological impairment		
	M	SD	N	M	SD	N	M	SD	N
12 years	1.73	.98	30	2.58	1.07	19	3.87	.83	8
13 years	1.83	1.15	30	2.62	1.08	29	2.37	1.92	8
14 years	1.80	1.06	30	2.04	.96	26	3.00	1.31	8
15 years	1.83	1.09	30	2.30	1.02	30	2.25	.93	16
16 years	1.37	0.85	30	1.81	1.04	36	3.86	.69	7
Total	1.71	1.03	150	2.23	1.07	140	2.91	1.33	47

Source: Adapted from Belter, R. W., McIntosh, J. A., Finch, A. J., Williams, L. D., and Edwards, G. L. (1989). "The Bender Gestalt as a method of personality assessment with adolescents." *Journal of Clinical Psychology, 45,* 414–422, Table 5, p. 420. Copyright © 1989. Reprinted by permission of John Wiley & Sons, Inc.

nonpatients had more than three Emotional Indicators, a number that was obtained by 11% of the patients with emotional disturbance and 34% of the patients with mental retardation or neurological impairment. Further research will be needed to determine if this standard is valid with other samples of adolescents.

Oas (1984) chose to investigate BGT emotional signs specific to the behavior of impulsivity. From clinical and research sources, he developed a list of 12 BGT variables designated as being typical of impulsive adolescents and 12 typical of nonimpulsive adolescents. One hundred inpatient adolescents were rated as impulsive or nonimpulsive based on three other measures. The two groups were then compared on the BGT and Draw-A-Person tests. Impulsive adolescents showed significantly more of the impulsive BGT signs than did nonimpulsive patients; the reverse was true for the nonimpulsive signs. The results were then cross-validated on a second group of nonhospitalized ado-

Table 12.5 Frequency Distribution for Koppitz Emotional Indicators by Group

Number of emotional indicators[a]	Percent of indicators		
	Nonpatient	Emotional disturbance	Mental retardation/ neurologically impairment
0	9	3	2
1	38	23	11
2	30	34	30
3	18	29	23
4	5	10	21
5	0	1	11
6	0	0	2
Total	100	100	100

[a]Presence of three or more indicators suggests emotional disturbance.

Source: Adapted from Belter, R. W., McIntosh, J. A., Finch, A. J., Williams, L. D., and Edwards, G. L. (1989). "The Bender Gestalt as a method of personality assessment with adolescents." *Journal of Clinical Psychology, 45,* 414–422, Table 6, p. 420. Copyright © 1989. Reprinted by permission of John Wiley & Sons.

lescents. Discriminant analysis showed that the most successful BGT signs of impulsivity in both samples were overall quality of the drawings, discontinuity, and omissions. Similar results were found for the Draw-A-Person test. Unfortunately, these errors were not fully described in the article.

TWO ADOLESCENT CASE EXAMPLES

Figure 12.1 shows the BGT of Kate, a white female, age 14 years 2 months. Kate is an inpatient for whom there is "probable evidence of neurological impairment." Her overall IQ is estimated to be 88. Her scores on the two scoring systems are listed following (figure numbers in parentheses):

Koppitz Developmental System			Lacks System	
1a	Distortion of shape	(A)	Overlapping Difficulty	(7)
6	Perseveration of dots	(1)	Perseveration, Type B	(1, 2)
12a	Integration—lost shape	(3)	Closure Difficulty	(A, 8)
20	Perseveration of curves	(6)	Angulation Difficulty	(2, 3)
21b	Distortion of shape	(7)	Cohesion	(2, 6 & 3, 4)
23	Integration—no overlap	(7)		
24	Distortion of shape	(8)		
	Total errors: 7		Total Errors: 5	

Currently, there is no way to adequately characterize these scores. For Koppitz scores, a child of 11 (the oldest age in her norms) is expected to make 1.4 errors. Kate's score of 7 errors places her well above that number. The age equivalent for 7 errors is 6 years 6 months to 6 years 11 months. So, from the viewpoint of Koppitz, it is apparent that Kate shows serious developmental immaturity on this test. For the Lacks method, a score of 5 errors indicates brain impairment across the age span of 17 to more than 80 years old. McIntosh et al. (1988) found that 14-year-olds in the group with neurological impairment made an average of 6.63 errors. Therefore, Kate's score of 5 errors certainly raises questions about brain dysfunction that should be more fully assessed. In terms of emotional factors, Kate was found to have only one of the Koppitz Emotional Indicators: small size on figures A, 3, 4, and 5. According to Koppitz (1975), fewer than three of these signs indicates an absence of emotional disturbance. This particular sign has been associated with constriction and timidity.

The BGT of Terrell can be seen in Figure 12.2. He is an African American inpatient, age 12 years 3 months. His IQ is estimated to be 80. He was found to have "positive evidence of brain impairment." His scores on the two scoring systems are listed following (figure numbers in parentheses):

Koppitz Developmental System			Lacks System	
1a	Distortion of shape	(A)	Retrogression	(A, 1, 3, 5)
6	Perseveration of dots	(1)	Perseveration, Type B	(1)
18b	Distortion of shape	(6)	Collision Tendency	(A, 5)
19	Integration of crossing	(6)	Impotence	(A)
21a	Distortion of size	(7)	Closure Difficulty	(A, 4, 8)
21b	Distortion of shape	(7)	Angulation Difficulty	(2, 3)
24	Distortion of shape	(8)		
	Total errors: 7		Total Errors: 6	

Figure 12.1 Kate, a 14-year-old female inpatient with "probable evidence of neurological impairment."

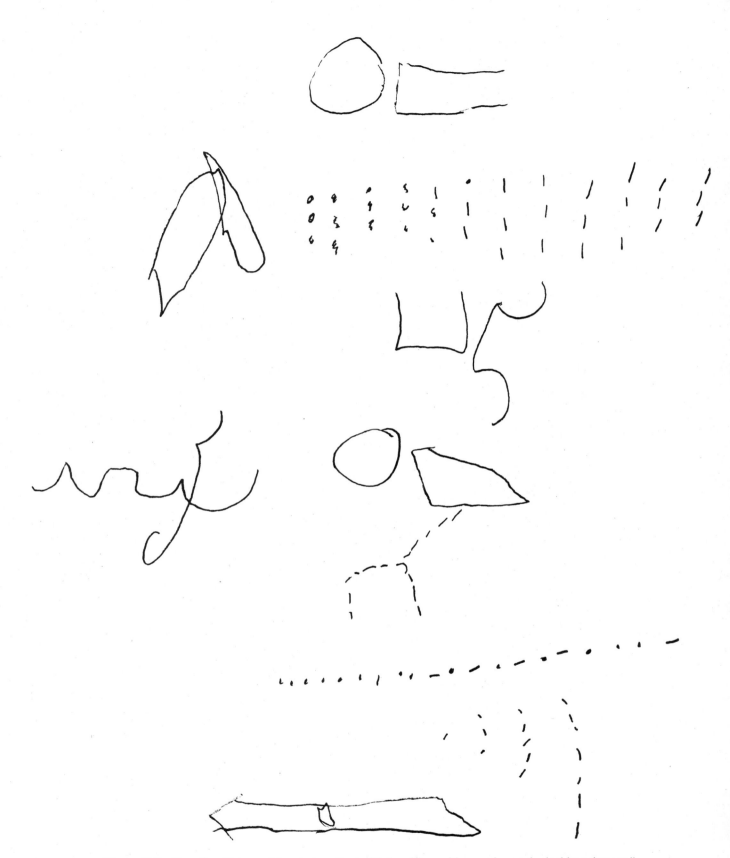

Figure 12.2 Terrell, a 12-year-old male inpatient with "positive evidence of neurological impairment."

For Koppitz scores, a child of 11 is expected to make 1.4 errors. Just as with Kate, Terrell's score of 7 errors places him well above that number. The age equivalent for 7 errors is 6 years 6 months to 6 years 11 months. Therefore, Terrell also shows serious developmental immaturity on this test. For the Lacks scoring, a score of 5 errors indicates brain impairment across the age span of 17 to more than 80 years old. McIntosh et al. (1988) found that 12-year-olds in the group with neurological impairment made an average of 5.13 errors. Therefore, his score of 6 errors raises serious questions about brain dysfunction that should be further evaluated. In terms of emotional factors, Terrell has four of the Koppitz Emotional Indicators: confused order of drawings; dashes for circles on figure 2; increasing size of dots on figures 1, 2, and 3; and a second attempt to draw figure A. According to Koppitz (1975), three or more of these signs indicates emotional disturbance. She mentions that some research associates these particular signs with lack of planning ability, impulsivity, and low frustration tolerance.

SUMMARY

Koppitz's belief that perceptual-motor development is essentially complete by age 10 or 11 may not be true. Three recent studies show that the number of errors on the BGT continue to decrease after age 12 for both patient and nonpatient groups. That is, perceptual-motor integration skills appear to continue to develop beyond the age of 11. All of the studies found significant correlations between BGT performance and age in the range of 12 to 16 years old. From the currently available studies, it appears that, for now, the clinician may use either the Koppitz or the Lacks scoring method when evaluating the perceptual-motor performance of an adolescent. However, more research needs to be done for clinicians to have sufficient confidence in either scoring system for this age group.

Although all three studies showed remarkably congruent results, they each also had shortcomings. No systematic evaluation has been made of the ability of either of these two methods to detect brain dysfunction in adolescents. Furthermore, all three adolescent validity studies of these two systems were done in the same geographical region, using small samples of adolescents in each subgroup. Although each study contained a good representation of African Americans, other ethnic groups were not included. "Normals" were usually selected solely because they had no known problems rather than through any screening process; therefore, "normal" groups may contain teens who have emotional or neurological problems. Additional analyses are required to clarify the relationships between the adolescent BGT scores and other variables, such as gender, ethnicity, IQ, and education. Finally, there is much less support for the usefulness of the personality indicators of Hutt (1985) and Koppitz (1975) than has been found for the perceptual-motor aspects of the BGT.

CHAPTER 13

Selected Clinical Cases

In this chapter, the reader will find 12 selected clinical cases with Bender Gestalt Test (BGT) protocols and an explication of the scoring for each. Only one of these cases is from the sample cases of the first edition of the book; the others are all new examples. An attempt has been made to provide a variety of clinical examples and to replicate the population that a clinician is likely to encounter when using this test to screen for organic brain dysfunction. The following cases were selected as examples:

Schizophrenia (2)
Dementia (4)
Other cognitive disorders (4)
Nonpatients (2)

Each case includes a brief history; intelligence test results when available; observations of Bender Gestalt test-taking behavior; a list of the scorable errors and the figures on which they appear; an explanation of the scoring, including why certain errors were not scored; and diagnoses from the test and elsewhere (e.g., a hospital discharge diagnosis). The protocols were scored by the author.

Study these 12 cases carefully, noting not only the errors that are scored but also the ones that remain unscored. The latter will be just as instructive as the former. Figure numbers for the BGT stimulus designs can be seen in Figure 4.1, on page 42. When these example cases have been absorbed, move on to the second half of the chapter where another 10 cases of similar variety are included without the scoring. These cases are meant to serve as opportunities for practice. Feedback on the scoring of this second group of cases appears at the end of the chapter.

SCORED EXAMPLES
Case A

Personal Data.   A is a 21-year-old, African American female with a high school education who has worked as a payroll clerk. This woman was 8 months pregnant and living in a home for unwed pregnant women, awaiting delivery and adoption of the baby. A was referred for outpatient testing because she was feeling fearful and was too afraid to sleep. She refused to take her vitamins and instead baked and ate dirt. During evaluation, A revealed that she hears voices, feels some force trying to make her harm herself, and senses a presence in her room at night. She admitted to similar symptoms, including "visions," twice before in her life at times of extreme stress. However, she has never been hospitalized. A also denied any kind of drug use at any time. Because the psychological tests indicated a psychotic disorder, A was hospitalized in an acute psychiatric treatment center. The WAIS at this time showed a Full Scale IQ of 81.

Behavioral Observations.   This woman was very cooperative, compliant, and seemed motivated to do her best. Results appear generally valid. At times, however, she did appear somewhat agitated. Testing time was 6 minutes.

BGT Scoring

Error	Figure
Overlapping Difficulty	7
Perseveration, Type A	2
Closure Difficulty	A, 4
Cohesion	A

Total errors: 4

Test Analysis.   Overlapping Difficulty can be seen on figure 7 in the reworking and distortion of the drawing at the point of overlap (see Figure 13.1). Because the patient was able to improve the drawing by a second attempt, it is not scored Impotence. Some scorers may see figures 1, 3, and 5 as made up of circles rather than dots. However, there was some attempt to fill them in so Simplification is not scored. But when A continues to use these dots of figure 1 on figure 2 instead of the circles that should be used, Perseveration, Type A is scored. One significant problem with bringing two adjacent parts together can be seen on figure 4. In addition, A demonstrates some Closure Difficulty in joining the two parts of figure A. Although the protocol does indicate some problem with angulation in figures 2 and 3, it is not severe enough to be a scorable error. Finally, this protocol contains a dramatic example of Cohesion, with figure A much larger than all the rest.

Test Diagnosis.   A total of 4 errors is not enough to make a definite test diagnosis of brain dysfunction. However, because A performed in a borderline fashion on another test for brain dysfunction, it was recommended that she be reevaluated following the delivery of her child. The dirt she had been eating, a possible chemical imbalance from pregnancy, or any past use of drugs may have been causing some interference with brain functioning.

Diagnosis.   The hospital discharge diagnosis was Schizophrenia, Paranoid Type.

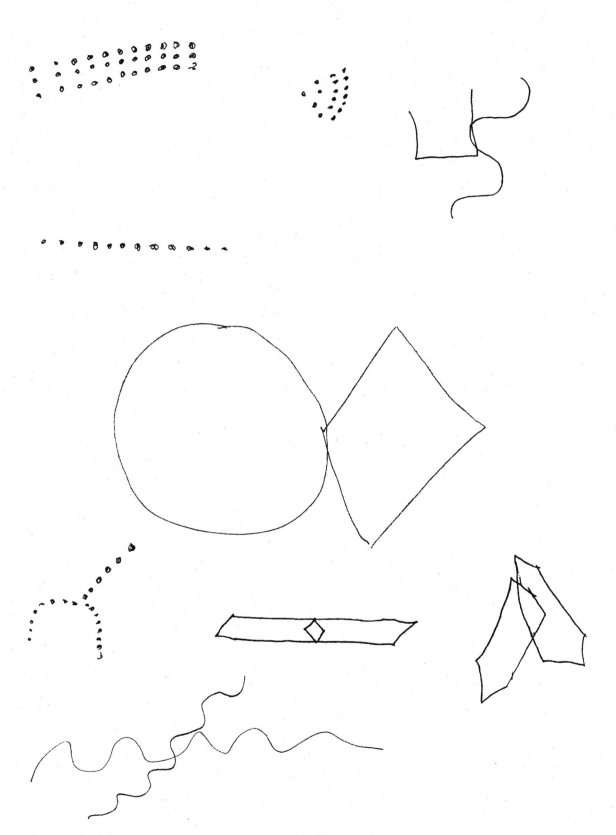

Figure 13.1   Case A.

Case B   *Personal Data.*   B is a 12-year-old, female American Indian who is currently in the sixth grade. She was part of a normative sample of students, chosen because they had no known history of or need for special education or mental health services.

Behavioral Observations.   B was cooperative and put forth a good effort on the test. The results appear to be reliable and valid. Testing time was 6.5 minutes.

BGT Scoring

Error	Figure
Rotation	A, 1, 2
Collision	4 & 6
Closure Difficulty	4, 8
Cohesion	A

Total errors: 4

Test Analysis.   This young woman rotated the first three figures of the BGT, including rotating the columns of figure 2 as well as the whole figure (see Figure 13.2). She also overlapped figures 4 and 6, earning the error of Collision. Figures 1 and 2 are close enough to indicate Collision Difficulty. However, the error of Collision is a more serious flaw and therefore takes precedence in the scoring. On both figures 4 and 8, this student had to use an additional line to get the two parts of each design to join. This action fulfills one of the conditions for the error of Closure Difficulty—"consistent but not significant joining problems on two out of the three" of figures A, 4, and 8. The fourth error is Cohesion, seen on figure A where the diamond is significantly smaller than the circle when the two should be of equal size.

Test Diagnosis.   A total of 4 errors results in a conclusion of borderline organic brain involvement based on the BGT alone. Norms show that the average BGT score for an adolescent of her age is 2.67 errors.

Diagnosis.   This female pupil has no known history of cognitive problems.

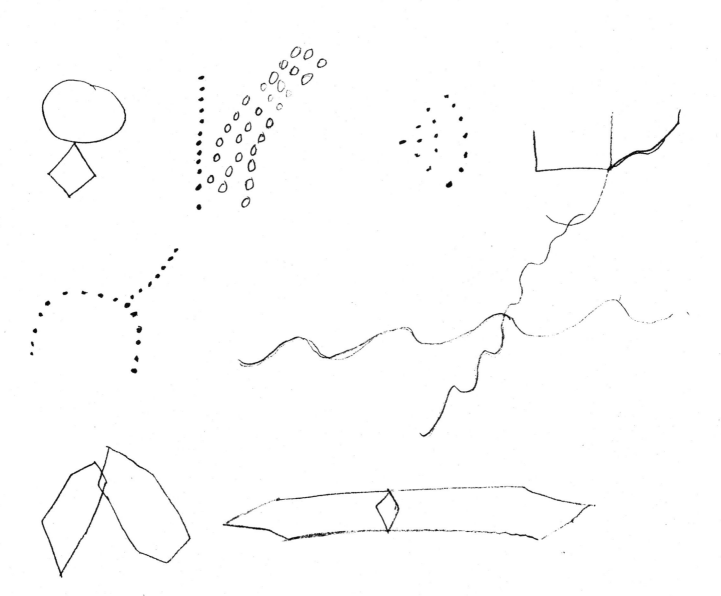

Figure 13.2   Case B.

Case C   ***Personal Data.***   At the time of testing, *C* was an inpatient in a large mental health hospital in the eastern United States. This white female is 28 years old, a high school graduate, and has worked as a nursing home attendant. She was brought to the hospital emergency room by police who found her shouting obscenities in the middle of a busy street. Her IQ was estimated to be in the average range.

Behavioral Observations.   *C* was unkempt in appearance and surly in behavior. However, once rapport was established, she worked diligently (BGT time = 6 minutes) and seemed motivated to do her best.

BGT Scoring

Error	Figure
Overlapping Difficulty	6
Simplification	A
Collision Tendency	3 & 6
Cohesion	3 & 6

Total errors: 4

Test Analysis.   This patient makes the two elements of figure 6 overlap at the wrong place on the vertical wavy line (Overlapping Difficulty; see Figure 13.3). The large distance between the adjacent parts of figure A is scored Simplification. This error is not scored for figure 5 because C was able to correct the original simplified figure. In her second attempt, she was also able to correct the Fragmentation, or incomplete drawing. It is a judgment call as to whether figure 1 is composed of circles or dots. They appear more dotlike, as there is some attempt to fill them in; otherwise this would be declared Simplification also. Figures 3 and 6 are drawn within ¼ inch of each other, resulting in Collision Difficulty. Cohesion can be found in the large relative difference in size of figures 3 and 6. Retrogression is not scored for the distorted left hexagon of figure 7; because hexagons are difficult to copy, some leeway is given in scoring. Impotence is not scored on figure 5, because the second attempt is greatly improved. Although the stars for dots on figures 4 and 5 are distortions, they do not constitute one of the 12 errors of this scoring system. In the author's experience, this type of substitution of stars for dots occurs most often in cases of schizophrenia.

Test Diagnosis.   The total of 4 errors results in a BGT diagnosis of borderline brain dysfunction. None of the errors were of the type especially suggestive of brain impairment.

Diagnosis.   The hospital discharge diagnosis was Schizophrenia, Undifferentiated Type.

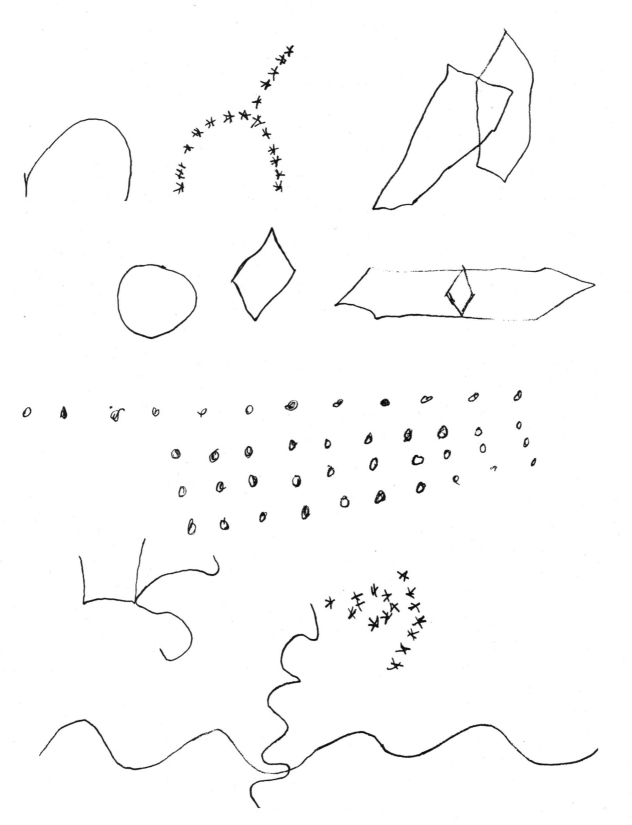

Figure 13.3 Case C.

Case D   *Personal Data.*   *D* is a 78-year-old, white female who is a retired employment agency worker. She is a high school graduate with estimated IQ in the bright normal range. She sought evaluation of a hand tremor of many years duration associated with more recent changes of tremulous voice. The shaking is not evident at rest, only when she attempts to write or hold materials, such as the newspaper. She also has a moderate problem with diabetes, for which she takes insulin; however, the tremor predates the diabetes. Otherwise, she is in good health.

Behavioral Observations.   This woman was very motivated to do well and took the BGT in a quite serious and attentive way. She showed average levels of carefulness and persistence. She also demonstrated a moderate hand tremor during testing. It took her 7 minutes to complete the test. Based on these behaviors, the results of the BGT appear to be valid and reliable.

BGT Scoring

Error	Figure
Perseveration, Type A	2
Collision Tendency	4 & 6, 5 & 6
Closure Difficulty	A, 4, 7, 8
Motor Incoordination	All figures

Total errors: 4

Test Analysis.   In general, this woman shows good preservation of the gestalt for all nine designs (see Figure 13.4). However, she continued the dots of figure 1 onto figure 2 instead of using circles for the latter. This error constitutes Perseveration, Type A. Several drawings were placed within ¼ inch of each other, figures 4 with 6 and 5 with 6, resulting in Collision Difficulty. It is possible to make the error of Closure Difficulty on four designs: A, 4, 7, and 8. This woman shows consistent, though not substantial, difficulty merging the joining parts of all four of these figures. Consistent with the reported tremor, she also demonstrates Motor Incoordination on all figures.

Test Diagnosis.   From the norms for older adults, a person of this age would be expected to make 3.63 errors. The client made 4 errors, one of which was related to her tremor. There is no other history to indicate a cognitive disorder. Therefore, the test diagnosis is no brain dysfunction.

Diagnosis.   Her family physician gave her the diagnosis of Essential Tremor.

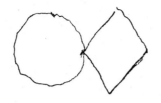

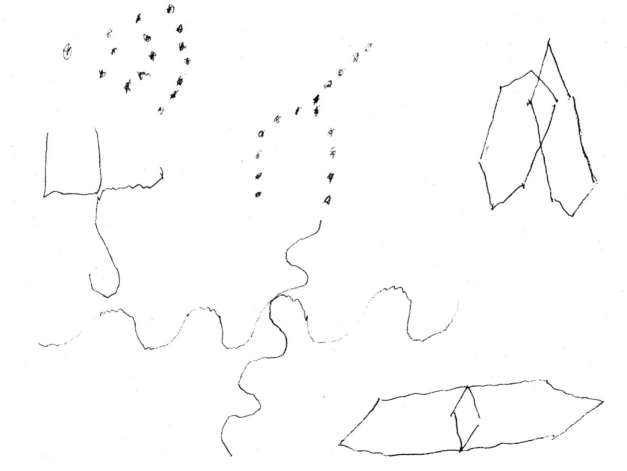

Figure 13.4 Case D.

Case E *Personal Data.*   *E* is a 22-year-old, white male outpatient. He completed 8 years in a special education program, has a Full Scale WAIS IQ of 50, and has never been employed. He also has a history of seizures.

Behavioral Observations.   This man completed the BGT in 6 minutes, drawing the figures in a serious, persistent, and methodical way. He was calm and compliant. The psychologist noticed that *E*'s eyes did not focus properly and that he displayed a mild hand tremor. He drew a first attempt at figure A on the reverse side of the paper; he then turned the paper over and made a second drawing with the same distortion. He also commented that figure 3 was incorrectly drawn but that he was not sure how to correct it. Amount of time to complete testing is unknown.

BGT Scoring

Error	Figure
Simplification	6
Fragmentation	2, 3
Impotence	A, 3
Closure Difficulty	A, 4, 8
Motor Incoordination	6
Cohesion	A & 7 or 8

Total errors: 6

Test Analysis.   Figure 6 is drawn in a much easier form, omitting most of the waves, and earning the error of Simplification (see Figure 13.5). Design 2 is incomplete, containing only one of the three lines; on number 3, the figure is broken into parts, distorting the drawing so that it is unrecognizable. These two errors are examples of Fragmentation. Although figures A, 1, 4, 5, 7, and 8 all show distortions, they are not sufficient to earn the error of Retrogression or any other one. For example, the dashes on 1 are not extreme enough. Also, on figure 7, considerable leniency is allowed in scoring because it is a difficult design to reproduce. The two behaviors of drawing a figure twice without being able to correct the errors (figure A) or of recognizing errors but expressing inability to correct them (figure 3) are both instances of Impotence. A significant problem with Closure Difficulty can be seen on figures A and 8; a less serious example is found on figure 4. Consistent with the behavior observations of tremor, Motor Incoordination is apparent on figure 6. The fact that figure A is much smaller than either figure 7 or 8 is classified as Cohesion. Note that sometimes a drawing is so distorted that you are not able to judge whether a certain error was made; for example, we cannot judge figure 3 for Angulation Difficulty.

Test Diagnosis.   Six errors lends some evidence for a test diagnosis of brain disorder. Such a diagnosis is consistent with *E*'s history.

Diagnosis.   This young man was diagnosed with both Mental Retardation and epilepsy.

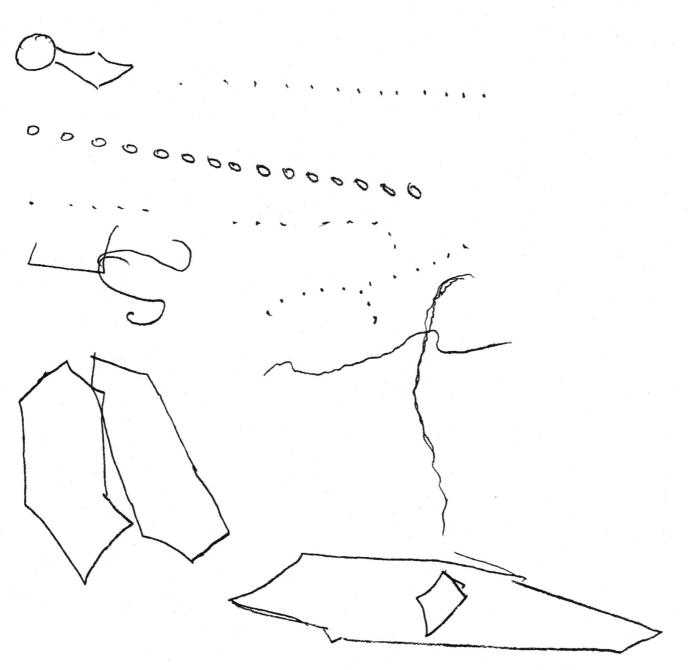

Figure 13.5 Case E.

Case F (Time 1)   *Personal Data.*   *F* is a 75-year-old, married white female who was a participant in a research project on memory and aging at a large medical school. She has an eighth-grade education and has always been a homemaker. At the time of testing she was estimated to have average intelligence. She also had some history of confusion and memory difficulties. *F* was tested twice, 2½ years apart.

Behavioral Observations.   *F*'s test-taking behavior was exemplary, with high levels of cooperation, carefulness, persistence, and rapport with the examiner. As such, the results are considered valid and reliable. Even though she was careful, she did complete the BGT in less than 3 minutes.

BGT Scoring

Error	Figure
Overlapping Difficulty	6, 7
Simplification	1
Collision Tendency	1 & 2, 2 & 3
Impotence	7
Closure Difficulty	7, 8
Angulation Difficulty	2
Cohesion	A, 5, 7

Total errors: 7

Test Analysis.   Figures 6 and 7 both show major Overlapping Difficulty (see Figure 13.6). In the first of these, the lines overlap in three places instead of one. In the second instance, there are multiple attempts and reworking to accomplish the overlap. Circles drawn for dots on figure 1 are an example of Simplification. Although some dots and circles are missing from figures 2, 3, and 5, the gestalts are still preserved; therefore, the error of Fragmentation is not scored. Figures 1 and 2 and 2 and 3 each come within ¼ inch of each other, resulting in Collision Tendency because the figures do not touch each other. The client had major problems drawing figure 7 and repeated attempts did not lead to improvement (Impotence). On this same figure and on number 8, *F* demonstrates Closure Difficulty or inability to get adjacent parts of the design to connect. Although the lower part of figure 4 is distorted, she was able to connect the two parts. The slope of the columns on figure 2 is haphazard, with only three leaning in the correct direction, showing Angulation Difficulty. Finally, on figures A and 7, one part of the design is disproportionately smaller than the other part. This error is Cohesion. Another version of this error can be seen on figure 5, where the whole figure is smaller than others, such as figure A.

Test Diagnosis.   Seven errors on the BGT represent strong evidence for brain impairment of some type. The normative number of errors for a person of this age is only 3.63.

Diagnosis.   After extensive psychological and neurological evaluation, as part of the research study, *F* was given the diagnosis of mild dementia.

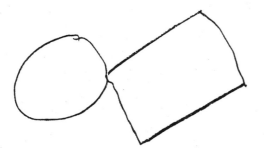
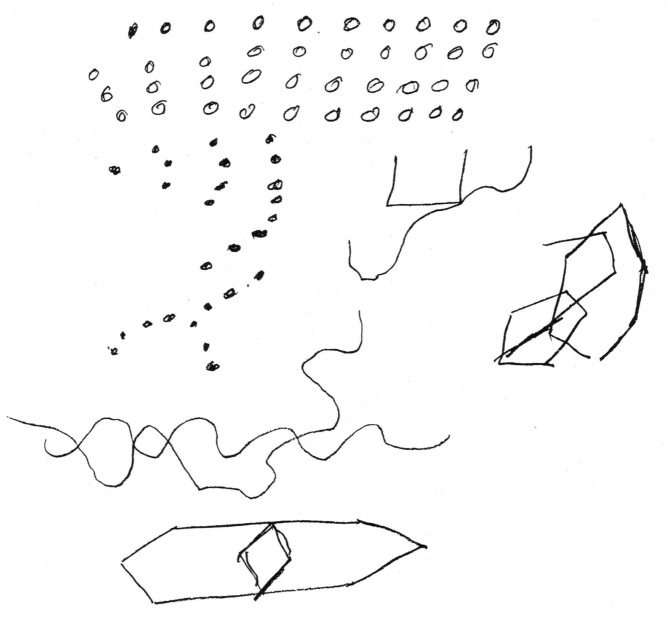

Figure 13.6 Case F (Time 1).

Case F (Time 2)   *Personal Data.*   As part of the memory and aging research project, *F* was retested 2½ years later, just before she turned 78.

Behavioral Observations.   On her second testing, *F* continued to be serious, methodical, and persistent in her approach to the BGT. However, she was also somewhat anxious and showed some fatigue. In addition, she expressed dissatisfaction with her poorly drawn designs though she was unable to improve her performance. She took 5 minutes to complete the test.

BGT Scoring

Error	Figure
Rotation	4
Simplification	A, 1
Retrogression	A
Fragmentation	2, 3, 5, 6, 7
Collision Tendency	All
Impotence	3 through 8
Closure Difficulty	A, 4
Cohesion	A

Total errors: 8

Test Analysis.   *F* had great difficulty drawing these figures (see Figure 13.7). In some ways, a protocol like this one is more difficult to score than one that does not have as many serious distortions. *F* rotated figure 4 by 90 degrees. The excessive distance between the two parts of figure A and the use of circles for dots on figure 1 are errors of Simplification. The triangle for a diamond in figure A and the diamond for a hexagon on figure 7 are instances of Retrogression, substituting a more primitive form than that of the stimulus. Figures 2, 3, 5, 6, and 7 are all incomplete to the point of destroying the gestalt, earning the error of Fragmentation. This woman's awareness of her errors and her repeated unsuccessful attempts to improve some designs is a very good example of Impotence. All drawings are within ¼ inch of each other for Collision Tendency. All the joining parts of A and 4 show Closure Difficulty. Cohesion can be seen in the greater comparative size of figure A. The client was unable to make the errors of Overlapping Difficulty and Angulation Difficulty because she did not draw enough of the figures to meet the criteria for these errors (e.g., figure 6 has only one line and figure 7 only one hexagon and so cannot overlap with the missing parts).

Test Diagnosis.   Although *F* only made one additional error on her second time of testing, her test protocol looks much worse. She showed more instances of errors and more serious distortions. Her attempts show primitive drawings with little retention of the original gestalt. There appears to be a good deal of deterioration of her condition. Eight errors again is strong evidence of brain damage. In addition, *F* made two of the three errors that are especially suggestive of brain damage: Impotence and Fragmentation.

Diagnosis.   At the time of this second testing, *F* was judged to have severe dementia of the Alzheimer's type. The diagnosis was confirmed by autopsy after her death. The two BGTs, given 2½ years apart, demonstrate the serious progression of her dementia.

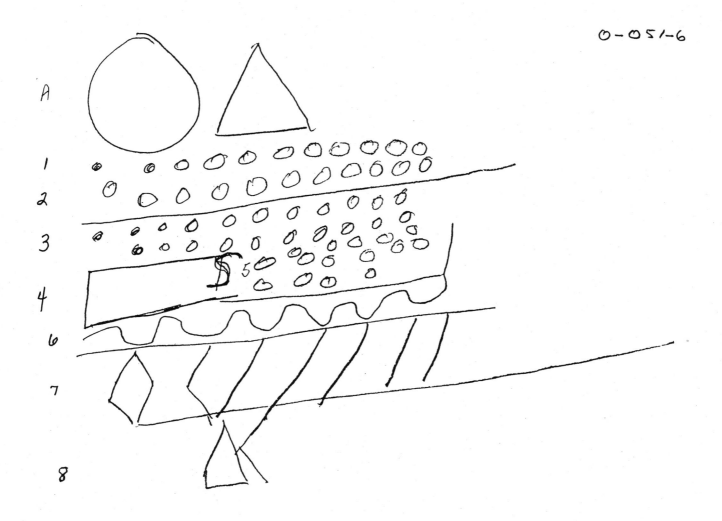

Figure 13.7 Case F (Time 2).

Case G   *Personal Data.*   G is a 73-year-old, married white homemaker who completed 1 year of college. Her IQ is 81. She suffered several strokes about 1 year before this testing was done. Her complaints include confusion, moderate memory problems, planning difficulties, and intermittent paranoid delusions.

Behavioral Observations.   This woman put forth a good effort on the BGT in spite of some symptoms of depression, anxiety, and fatigue. She was serious, attentive, and motivated. However, she did express some dissatisfaction with the quality of her drawings. She took 20 minutes to complete the BGT.

BGT Scoring

Error	Figure
Rotation	2
Overlapping Difficulty	7
Fragmentation	2, 3, 4
Retrogression	7
Perseveration, Type A	3, 5
Collision Tendency	A & 1, 1 & 2
Impotence	A, 2, 4
Closure Difficulty	A, 4, 7, 8
Cohesion	5 & 8

Total errors: 9

Test Analysis.   Rotation can be seen on figure 2 (see Figure 13.8). The reworking of number 6 indicates Overlapping Difficulty. Figures 2, 3, and 4 all have missing parts that seriously compromise the figures' gestalt; that indicates Fragmentation. The maturationally more primitive diamond drawn for the hexagon of figure 7 indicates Retrogression. Figures 3 and 5 are drawn with circles instead of dots, which is a Perseveration (Type A) of the circles from figure 2. Figures A and 1, as well as 1 and 2, are drawn close enough to warrant the error of Collision Tendency. Despite multiple attempts at drawing figures A, 2, and 4, G's lack of improvement indicates Impotence. All four figures where Closure Difficulty is possible (A, 4, 7, and 8) show multiple examples of trouble getting parts of figures to join. Contrasting the relative sizes of figures 5 and 8 shows the error of Cohesion.

Test Diagnosis.   Nine errors indicates very strong evidence of brain dysfunction. The 9 errors are even more striking given that this woman needed 20 minutes to draw all the figures. Also, her errors include two that are especially suggestive of brain impairment: Impotence and Fragmentation. Older adults of this age without brain impairment can be expected to average only 3.29 errors.

Diagnosis.   G's history shows that she suffered several strokes a year before testing. It appears that she sustained considerable brain impairment as a result. The diagnosis was Vascular Dementia.

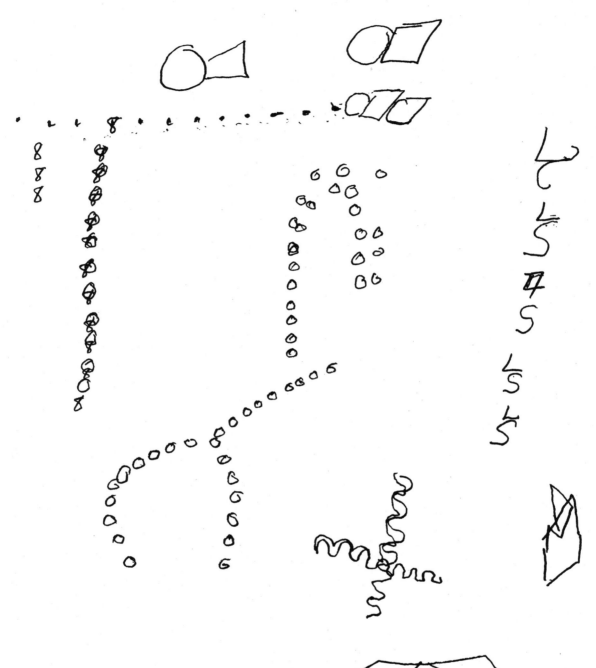

Figure 13.8 Case G.

Case H   ***Personal Data.***   *H* is a 45-year-old, white divorced male with 10 years of education. Three years before testing, he sustained a severe, diffuse head injury during an automobile accident. He was in a deep coma at first and had a 3-month period of amnesia after the accident. Upon discharge from the hospital, he was noted to have significant cognitive deficits of memory, insight, judgment, and intellectual functioning. He also showed mood lability and episodes of agitation. Previous to the injury, *H* worked at unskilled labor. His premorbid IQ was estimated at average to low average; currently he was tested at the borderline mental retardation level. He now is unable to live alone. The client's status was evaluated through extensive psychological testing.

Behavioral Observations.   During testing, *H* struggled to pronounce words and needed continual reminding to stay focused on any task. However, the client took the test with considerable care and deliberation. Testing time was 7 minutes. He was motivated and attentive but also fairly agitated. He was also observed to have a moderate hand tremor. Test results are thought to be an accurate assessment of his level of functioning.

BGT Scoring

Error	Figure
Perseveration, Type A	3, 5
Closure Difficulty	A, 4, 7, 8
Motor Incoordination	A, 4, 6, 7
Angulation Difficulty	2

Total errors: 4

Test Analysis.   *H* began at the bottom of the page and worked up (see Figure 13.9). Note that there were two attempts to draw figures A and 1; however, the second attempts are both improvements so are not evidence of Impotence. He correctly used dots in figure 1 but then switched to circles on figures 3 and 5. This is an example of Perseveration, Type A or inappropriate substitution of the circles of figure 2. Many of the drawings (e.g., A, 4, 7, and 8) also show difficulty getting parts of figures to meet, or Closure Difficulty. Tremor or Motor Incoordination was noted behaviorally and is apparent on several drawings (A, 4, 7, and 8). On figure 2, the client angled the entire drawing about 45 degrees to try to accomplish the column slant. This is one of the criteria for Angulation Difficulty. This amount of rotation is not enough to earn the error of Rotation. Note also that several drawings lack the complete number of dots or circles; however, not enough are missing to meet the criterion for Fragmentation. All figures are drawn to a relatively small scale and so there is no evidence of Cohesion.

Test Diagnosis.   A score of 4 errors shows borderline evidence for brain damage. Only one of these errors, Motor Incoordination, is especially suggestive of impairment. He also showed mild impairment on other similar tests. However, the Recall portion of the BGT (seen in Figure 4.3) shows major memory deficits.

Diagnosis.   This person has well-documented evidence of continued and fairly extensive neuropsychological impairment across many ability domains. His diagnosis is Dementia from Head Trauma. However, results of the BGT and other tests showed only mild impairment in the visuoconstructive realm. Although this man has definite brain damage, it appears not to interfere equally with all his cognitive functions.

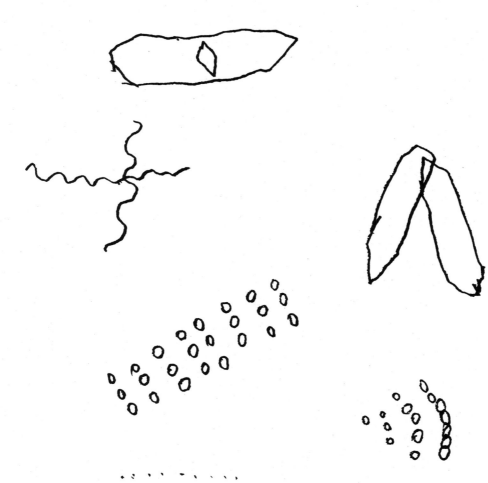
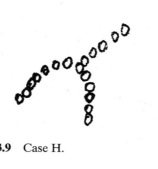

Figure 13.9 Case H.

Case I   *Personal Data.*   This 20-year-old, Asian American man has 11 years of special education and an estimated IQ of 77. Academic skills are believed to be moderately to severely limited. He is currently unemployed. He is described as a social isolate who complains that the world is against him.

Behavioral Observations.   During testing, this young man was quite anxious and showed only moderate levels of attention, compliance, and persistence. He was somewhat careless in his work. He took 15 minutes to complete the BGT.

BGT Scoring

Error	Figure
Perseveration, Type B	2
Collision	2 & 7
Closure Difficulty	A, 4, 7, 8
Cohesion	A & 6

Total errors: 4

Test Analysis.   In general, the gestalt of all the figures was preserved (see Figure 13.10). The first error is the rather obvious long line of three columns that is a Perseveration (Type B) of the elements of figure 2. There is also a Collision where figure A just touches the end of figure 2. There are consistent but not serious joining problems or Closure Difficulty on figures A, 4, 7, and 8. Cohesion can be seen where figure A is relatively much smaller than the largest figure 6. Although figure 5 is somewhat distorted, it does not meet the criteria for any of the 12 specific errors. On figure 1, he tends to use something other than a dot, a kind of squiggle. However, this distortion does not meet the criteria for Retrogression or for any other of the errors in this system. He does show ability to draw dots in figures 3 and 5. Figures 3 and 6 are very well drawn.

Test Diagnosis.   A score of 4 shows borderline evidence of brain impairment. The normative number of errors for this age and amount of education is 2.20. Information that might argue toward brain dysfunction is this man's low IQ and history of special education. However, there is no history of specific brain damage. Also, all four of his errors are ones that are commonly made and are least suggestive of impairment. Finally, this man's somewhat indifferent behavior during testing may have contributed to lower his score.

Diagnosis.   After a complete psychological assessment, the clinician gave this person a diagnosis of Schizoid Personality Disorder and Severe Learning Disability.

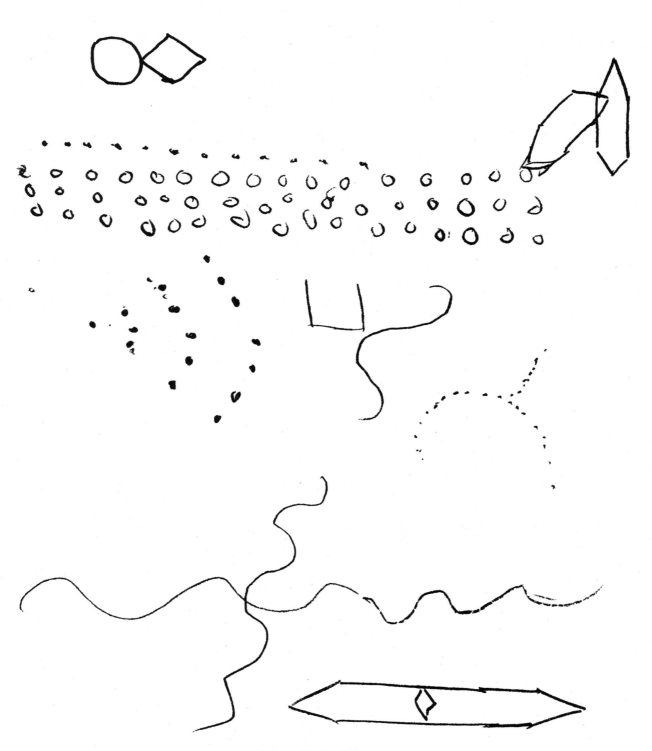

Figure 13.10   Case I.

Case J   *Personal Data.*   *J* is a 78-year-old, white psychiatric inpatient who was admitted for symptoms of confusion, belligerence, and extreme neglect of hygiene. In the hospital, he was often confused and was aggressive with the staff and other patients. He lived alone with no apparent friends or relatives; little background history could be determined.

Behavioral Observations.   *J* required 15 minutes to complete the test. He seemed moderately cooperative, careful, and persistent. At times he became agitated, but could be calmed fairly quickly. He did not appear to have any vision or hearing problems, although hand tremors were noted.

BGT Scoring

Error	Figure
Overlapping Difficulty	6, 7
Simplification	4
Fragmentation	7
Retrogression	A, 8
Perseveration, Type A	3, 5
Perseveration, Type B	2
Collision	A & 8, 2 & 7
Impotence	A, 5, 8
Closure Difficulty	A, 8
Motor Incoordination	6, 7

Total errors: 9

Test Analysis.   Figure 6 shows reworking of the lines; the other example of Overlapping Difficulty is on figure 7 where one hexagon is distorted at the point of overlap (see Figure 13.11). On figure 4, *J* took the easy way out when trying to join the two parts of the drawing, resulting in the error of Simplification. Figure 7 is incomplete, demonstrating Fragmentation. Both figures A and 8 show a triangle substituted for the more advanced diamond, which is evidence of Retrogression. Both types of Perseveration are evident on this protocol. Type A occurs with the continuation of the circles from figure 2 onto 3 and 5, having correctly made dots on figure 1. Type B occurs because the patient drew 16 columns of circles instead of 11 on figure 2. There are two obvious instances of Collision on this protocol and several others of Collision Tendency. When both problems are present, score only for the former, which is considered more serious. Notice how this man made three attempts to draw figure A and to situate the diamond in figure 8. He was unable to correct his errors through these multiple attempts, thus earning the error of Impotence. Closure Difficulty occurred on figures A and 8 and Motor Incoordination or tremor on figures 6 and 7.

Test Diagnosis.   These nine errors are a very strong indication of brain damage. A healthy man of 78 years should make on average 3.63 errors; only 32% of a sample of this age group made 5 or more errors. Furthermore, he made all three of the errors that are especially suggestive of brain damage.

Diagnosis.   After extensive evaluation, both psychological and neurological, this man was diagnosed as having Cognitive Disorder with frontal lobe lesion.

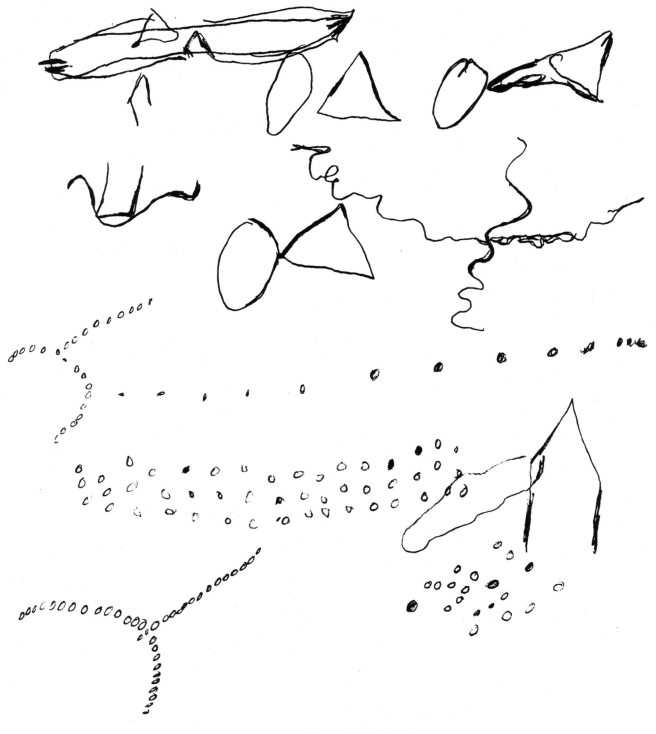

Figure 13.11 Case J.

Case K   ***Personal Data.***   *K* is a 31-year-old Hispanic woman, and is employed as a housekeeper and baby sitter. She has a sixth-grade education and an estimated IQ of 57. She was referred for testing to determine her intellectual capability.

Behavioral Observations.   During testing, *K* was noted to be scattered, perplexed, and garrulous. Nonetheless, she was able to cooperate with testing. Her results appear to be valid and reliable.

BGT Scoring

Error	Figure
Simplification	A, 4, 7
Retrogression	7
Perseveration, Type A	3
Collision Tendency	7 & 8
Impotence	4

Total errors: 5

Test Analysis.   Figure 2 started out as a Rotation, which the patient then corrected (see Figure 13.12). A figure whose joining parts are drawn more than ⅛ inch apart is an example of the error of Simplification (seen on figures A, 4, and 7). The substitution of a more primitive form, such as a diamond for a hexagon as seen on figure 7, is the error of Retrogression. Figure 1 correctly uses dots but figure 3 inappropriately continues the circles from figure 2. This mistake is called Perseveration, Type A. Figures 7 and 8 are drawn within ¼ inch of each other (Collision Tendency). The person drew figure 4 twice. Again she corrected the Rotation, but she still had the error of Simplification. This behavior probably represents Impotence; however, without detailed behavioral observations, it is difficult to be certain. Note that there is not much angulation on figure 3; however, this is not scored as Angulation Difficulty because the scoring allows much leniency on this figure.

Test Diagnosis.   With a score of 5 errors, there is evidence of brain dysfunction on this test. However, one of these errors—in fact, the most serious one— is somewhat in question. The other four errors are not in the group especially suggestive of brain damage. Other factors from the person's history that are sometimes associated with brain damage are low IQ and little education. A psychologist needs to carefully examine the other tests given to make a final diagnostic determination.

Diagnosis.   The woman's diagnosis was Mild Mental Retardation of unknown cause.

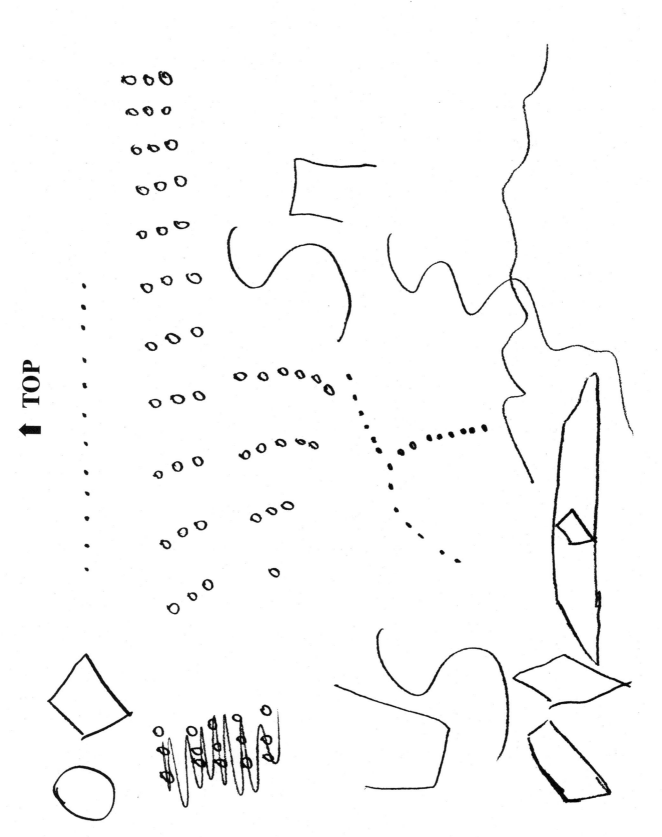

Figure 13.12 Case K.

PRACTICE SCORING
EXERCISES
Case L

Personal Data.   L is a 31-year-old, single, African American male with 9 years of education. From the WAIS Vocabulary subtest, his Verbal IQ was estimated to be 87. This was his second admission to an urban inpatient psychiatric hospital for symptoms such as hearing electric buzzing noises and voices and delusions of being killed. At admission, he was pleasant and well dressed but frightened and distractible with circumstantial and tangential thinking.

Behavioral Observations.   His execution of the BGT was careful, taking 7 minutes. He turned card A upside down and drew it in this position, so it is not considered a Rotation error. Based on his behavior, the results of the test appear to be valid and reliable. (See Figure 13.13.)

Figure 13.13 Case L.

Case M   ***Personal Data.***   M is a 36-year-old Asian American man with an irregular job history of mostly janitorial work. He graduated from a special education high school and has an IQ of 77. As a result of a birth injury he has cerebral palsy. Neuropsychological testing was requested as part of vocational rehabilitation counseling.

Behavioral Observations.   M was very cooperative and well motivated during testing, drawing the BGT designs with a good deal of care and deliberation. However, he did exhibit some drawing difficulty due to his physical disability. Testing took 15 minutes. (See Figure 13.14.)

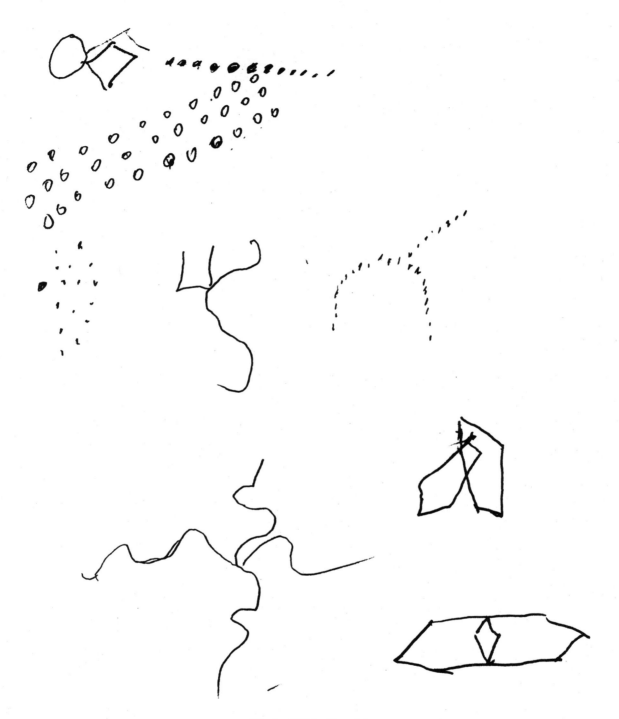

Figure 13.14 Case M.

Case N   *Personal Data.*   N is a 39-year-old single male and is an immigrant from southern Asia. He has a high school education and formerly worked as an office clerk. He was referred by his physician for psychological testing because of suspected brain dysfunction. Symptoms of declining cognitive performance included memory, organization, and judgment problems. His WAIS IQ was 77.

Behavioral Observations.   N took the test in a very cooperative, careful, and attentive manner. He was, however, quite anxious during testing. He took 12 minutes to draw the BGT designs. (See Figure 13.15.)

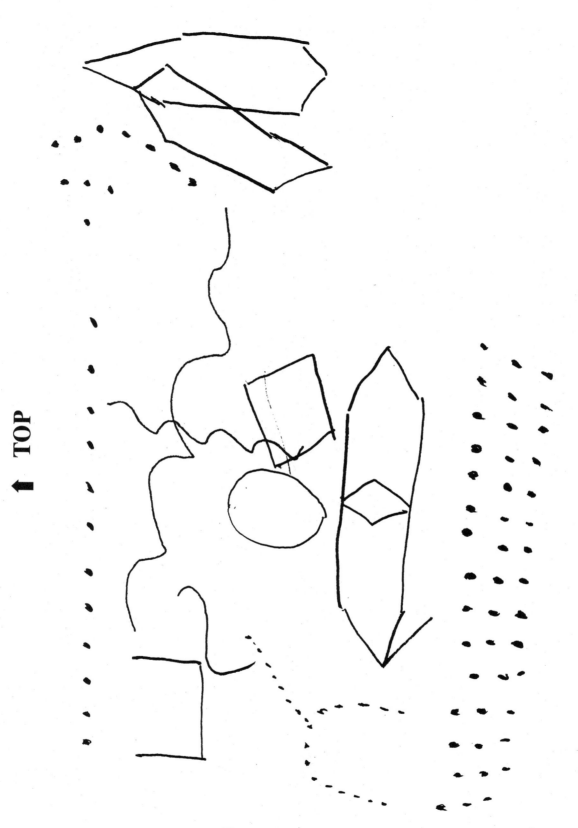

Figure 13.15 Case N.

Case O   *Personal Data.*   *O* is a 45-year-old white man with a 20-year history of alcoholism. He has a tenth-grade education and an estimated IQ of 88. His work history has been erratic for many years. He was brought to the emergency room of an acute psychiatric hospital intoxicated, behaving in a "wild" manner, and experiencing visual hallucinations. Although, he had been hospitalized multiple previous times for alcoholism, there was never any history of psychotic symptoms.

Behavioral Observations.   The BGT was given to this man 5 days after he was admitted to the hospital. At that time, he was still somewhat agitated and suspicious. He was adequately careful and cooperative, though he appeared fatigued and took 13 minutes to complete the test. Moderate hand tremors were observed during the drawing task. The patient also showed perplexity at his inability to draw figure 7 correctly. (See Figure 13.16.)

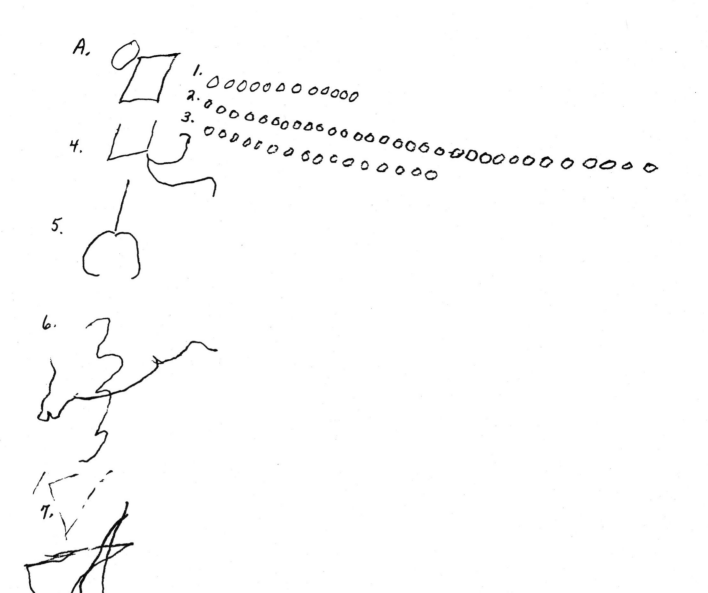

Figure 13.16 Case O.

Case P ***Personal Data.*** *P* is a 64-year-old, white, widowed homemaker who served as a nondemented control for a research project on memory and aging. She has 8 years of education and was estimated to have above-average intelligence.

Behavioral Observations. She worked very quickly (time = 2 minutes) but not carelessly. She was serious, persistent, and attentive. She showed no evidence of problems with hearing or vision. (See Figure 13.17.)

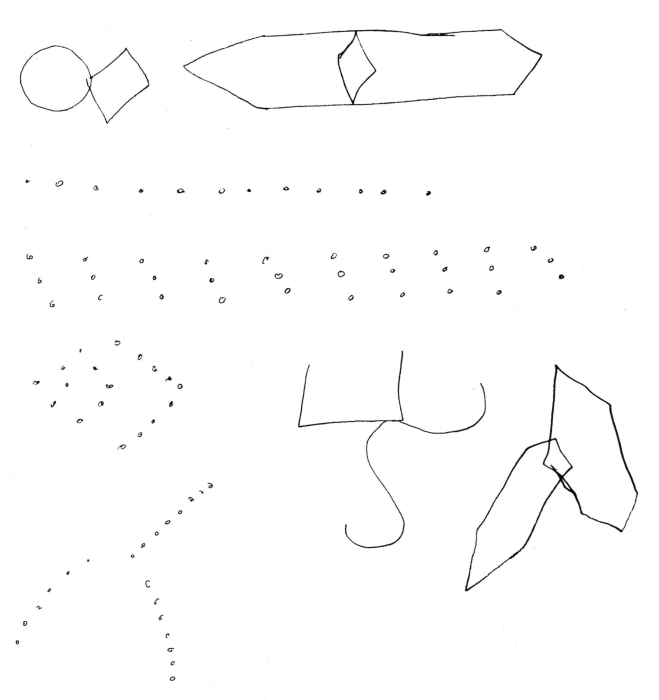

Figure 13.17 Case P.

Case Q   ***Personal Data.***   This was the fourth psychiatric hospitalization for *Q*, a 41-year-old, married, African American female. She is a high school graduate who is now unemployed but has worked as a nurse's aide. Her Verbal IQ, estimated from the WAIS Vocabulary subtest, was 88. In the emergency room of an acute psychiatric treatment center she was bizarrely dressed and exhibited flight of ideas, grandiose delusions, and auditory and visual hallucinations. She had at least an 8-year history of such symptoms, including trying to set her home on fire. She was brought to the hospital by the police, who found her beneath a bridge "working in a teletype station." *Q*'s memory and orientation were intact but she demonstrated no insight or judgment.

Behavioral Observations.   During testing *Q* was delusional but worked quickly (test time = 3.5 minutes) and cooperatively. (See Figure 13.18.)

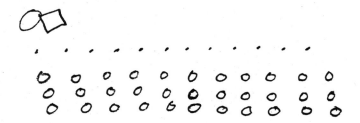

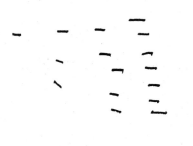

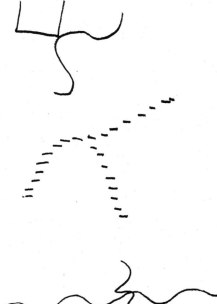

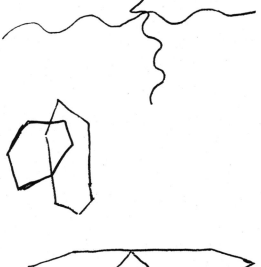

Figure 13.18 Case Q.

Case R   ***Personal Data.***   *R* is a 48-year-old, divorced, white male who was brought to an acute psychiatric treatment center dirty and unkempt; his speech was slurred, and he had an odor of alcohol. He has a 25-year drinking history with heavy alcoholic abuse (two fifths of whiskey per day) for the past 4 years. He admitted to previous blackouts and possible DTs. He has a sixth-grade education, an estimated Verbal IQ of 96, and currently works as a truck driver.

Behavioral Observations.   The patient was given the BGT 3 days after admission. No remarkable behavior was observed. *R* was cooperative, generally careful, and completed the test in 5 minutes. No hand tremors were noted. (See Figure 13.19.)

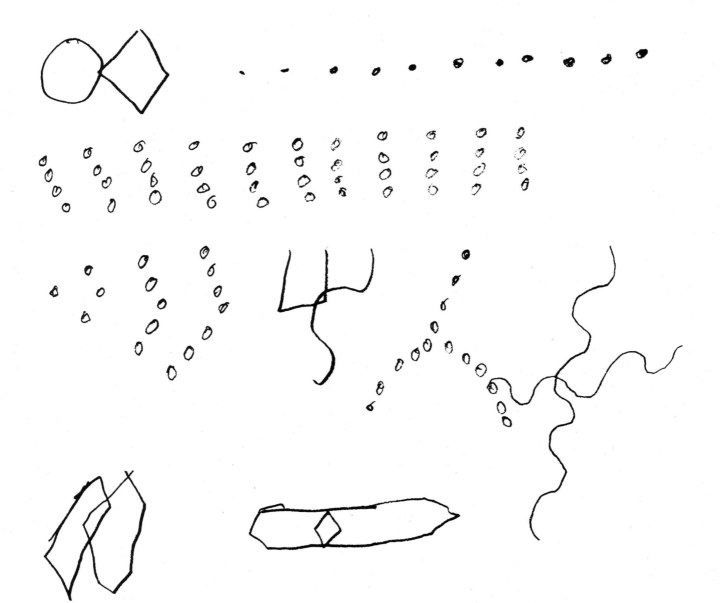

Figure 13.19 Case R.

Case S   ***Personal Data.***   This woman is an outpatient who was sent to a clinic for cognitive evaluation. *S* is 19 years old, graduated from a special education high school, and works as a nursery school aide. In infancy she suffered from a stroke; her current WAIS IQ is 68.

Behavioral Observations.   *S* was very cooperative with testing, working carefully and concentrating on the task. However, her pace was slow, requiring 18 minutes to complete the BGT. On several figures, she erased multiple times, trying unsuccessfully to make her drawings more accurate. (See Figure 13.20.)

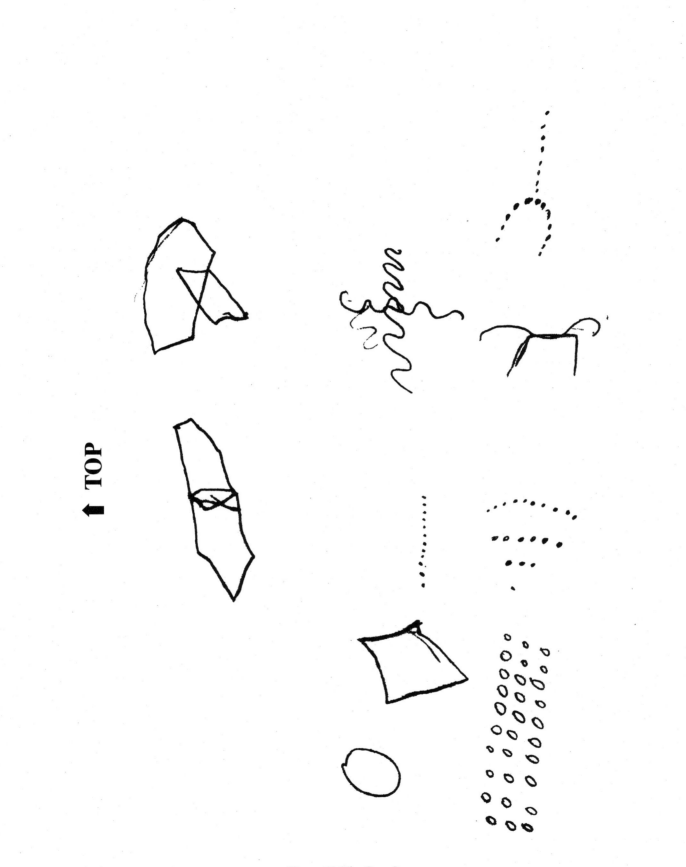

Figure 13.20 Case S.

Case T   ***Personal Data.***   *T* is a 14-year-old Hispanic American inpatient. He was considered "emotionally disturbed," exhibiting acting-out and defiant behaviors that rendered his parents unable to control him. On the ward, he was considered to be angry and unwilling to follow the rules. Although his WISC IQ is 82, he is doing failing work in school.

Behavioral Observations.   *T* took the BGT in a careless manner, rushing through it in 2 minutes. He often glanced at the test stimuli for a short time and then dashed off his copy. He did not seem motivated to do his best and gave up easily when he encountered difficulty. He also seemed somewhat agitated. His test-taking behaviors raise questions about the validity and reliability of the results. (See Figure 13.21.)

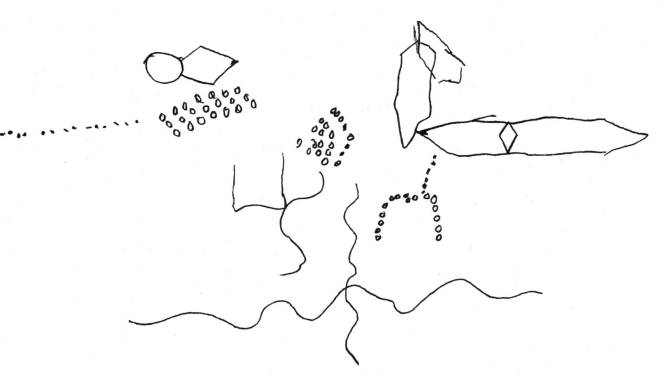

Figure 13.21 Case T.

Case U   *Personal Data.*   *U* is a 65-year-old, white widow with a history of depression and abuse of alcohol and prescription drugs. She is currently a psychiatric inpatient who has a low mood and some confusion. Although she has 14 years of education, her current IQ is only 90. Psychological evaluation was requested to determine the extent of any cognitive decline and whether she is capable of caring for herself. Hearing and vision appeared adequate.

Behavioral Observations.   The patient was anxious during testing and eager to get it over with. However, she was compliant, fairly careful, and attentive. She exhibited a moderate hand tremor. She took 7 minutes to complete the BGT. (See Figure 13.22.)

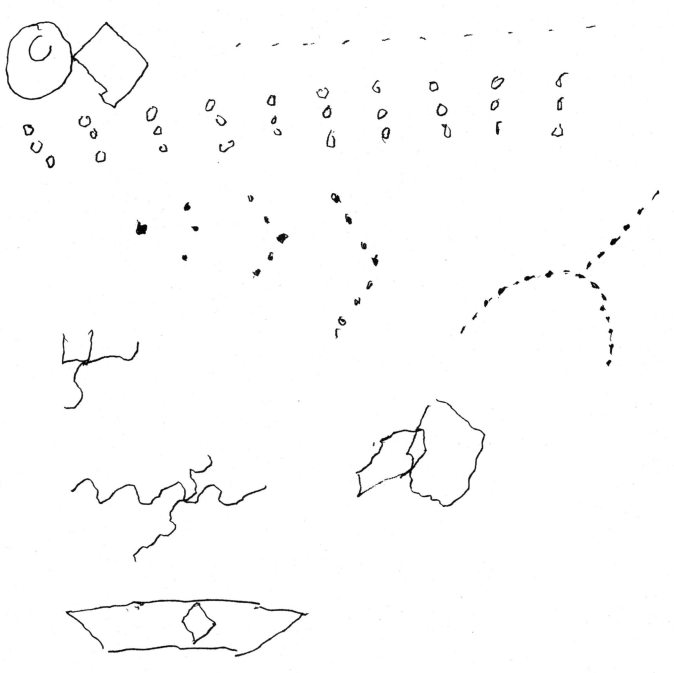

Figure 13.22 Case U.

SCORING FOR PRACTICE CASES

Case L   *BGT Scoring*

Error	Figure
Perseveration, Type B	2
Collision Tendency	4 & 5
Closure Difficulty	4
Cohesion	A & 4

Total errors: 4

Test Analysis.   Figure 2 is drawn so that each of the 11 columns of circles has four rather than three circles, an example of Perseveration, Type B (see Figure 13.13). Figures 4 and 5 are drawn close enough together to score Collision Tendency. Also, on 4, the intrusion of the wavy line so far into the body of the three-sided box is significant enough by itself to score Closure Difficulty, even though the joinings on other figures are adequate. The tiny size of figure 4 compared to A is scored as Cohesion. Also, the diamond of A is comparatively larger than the circle. The fact that *L* spontaneously corrected his simplified figure 5 means that he is not penalized with the error Simplification.

Test Diagnosis.   A score of 4 errors is a borderline indicator of brain dysfunction. However, nothing in *L*'s history, behavior, or type of BGT errors suggests such a conclusion. Consider the possibility that ethnic or cultural differences, lower education, and a prior diagnosis of psychosis may have contributed to the number of errors.

Diagnosis.   The hospital discharge diagnosis was Schizophrenia, Paranoid Type.

Case M   *BGT Scoring*

Error	Figure
Overlapping Difficulty	6, 7
Collision Tendency	1 & 2
Closure Difficulty	A, 4, 7, 8
Motor Incoordination	4, 5, 6, 7
Angulation Difficulty	2

Total errors: 5

Test Analysis.   Both figures 6 and 7 show distortion at the point of overlap, or Overlapping Difficulty (see Figure 13.14). Figure 2 almost collides with number 1, which is Collision Tendency. Four figures show that *M* had trouble joining parts of the designs, or Closure Difficulty. A tremor or Motor Incoordination is evident on four of the drawings. Also, *M* exhibits Angulation Difficulty; rather than angle the columns of figure 2, he angles the whole drawing by about 45 degrees.

Test Diagnosis.   *M*'s BGT score of 5 errors indicates a diagnosis of brain damage. Some aspects of his performance suggest that the effect on perceptual-motor functioning is not severe. Many of the errors appear to be motor in nature rather than perceptual. Three of his five errors are from the *not suggestive of brain damage* type.

Diagnosis. The psychologist's diagnosis from a full battery of tests was Cognitive Disorder, cerebral palsy, and Severe Learning Disability.

Case N *BGT Scoring*

Error	Figure
Fragmentation	3
Perseveration, Type A	2
Perseveration, Type B	2
Collision	A & 6
Closure Difficulty	A, 4, 7, 8
Angulation Difficulty	2

Total errors: 5

Test Analysis. Figure 3 is missing one wing of dots, a sign of Fragmentation (see Figure 13.15). Figure 2 demonstrates both types of Perseveration: Type A because the dots from the previous figure were inappropriately carried over to figure 2; Type B because there are 15 columns of dots when the stimulus has 12. Collision is evident where figures A and 6 overlap. There are also many instances of Collision Tendency between figures A and 8, 1 and 6, 3 and 7, and 4 and 5. However, because Collision is the more serious error, it alone is scored. Significant examples of Closure Difficulty can be seen in the failure to join the adjacent parts of figures A and 4. Less serious but consistent joining problems can be seen on figures 7 and 8. Angulation Difficulty is evident on figure 2, where more than half of the columns are tilted to the right instead of to the left. If all the columns were tilted in this way, it would be scored as a Rotation. Figure 2 is also a good example of how one drawing can have more than one error, in this case both Perseveration and Angulation Difficulty. Although *N* did use some dashes instead of dots on figure 5, they are not extreme or persistent enough to warrant the error of Retrogression.

Test Diagnosis. From the adult nonpatient norms, we can see that the average number of errors for a man of this age and education is 1.23. Only a small percentage of this group earn a score of 5 errors or more. In addition, this man made one error (Fragmentation) that is among the three most suggestive of brain impairment. Therefore, the diagnosis from this test alone is brain dysfunction.

Diagnosis. The psychologist, based on a complete clinical analysis, gave *N* a diagnosis of Cognitive Disorder, etiology unknown.

Case O *BGT Scoring*

Error	Figure
Simplification	1, 5
Fragmentation	2, 3
Retrogression	7, 8
Collision Tendency	1 & 2, 2 & 3, 3 & 4
Impotence	7
Closure Difficulty	A, 4
Motor Incoordination	6, 7, 8
Cohesion	A

Total errors: 8

Test Analysis. The drawings of figures 1 and 5 are classic examples of the error of Simplification (see Figure 13.16). Fragmentation can be seen on figures 2 and 3, where drawing just a line of circles destroys the gestalt of the design. It is interesting to note that on both of these drawings he copied the correct number of circles but eliminated the shape of the figure. Also, on both these figures we cannot assess for the error of Angulation Difficulty because he has totally removed any opportunity to demonstrate his ability to draw such angles. Circles for dots on figure 3 are not scored as Perseveration from figure 2 because they were also used in figure 1 and scored as Simplification. Drawing a maturationally more primitive design, as in the triangles instead of hexagon or diamond of figures 7 and 8, is an example of Retrogression. Although the parts of figure 7 are more primitive, they do overlap correctly. Figures 1, 2, 3, and 4 are all drawn within ¼ inch of one another, resulting in Collision Tendency. This patient made several unsuccessful attempts to draw figure 7, and was confused by his inability to do so. This is an example of Impotence. Note that on figures A and 4, *O* did not draw the adjacent parts as touching and then drew small lines to connect one part to the other. These are both significant examples of Closure Difficulty. The hand tremor or Motor Incoordination observed during testing can also be seen in the drawings for figures 6, 7, and 8. The last error is Cohesion, observed on figure A, where the circle is drawn much smaller than the diamond.

Test Diagnosis. With 8 errors on the BGT, there is strong evidence of brain impairment. Also, *O* committed all three of the errors that are especially suggestive of brain dysfunction: Impotence, Fragmentation, and Motor Incoordination.

Diagnosis. This patient was discharged after 12 days with the diagnoses of Alcohol Induced Psychotic Disorder and Alcohol Dependence.

Case P   ***BGT Scoring***

Error	Figure
Simplification	1
Cohesion	A & 6

Total errors: 2

Test Analysis. This woman drew circles for dots on figure 1, which is an instance of Simplification (see Figure 13.17). The circles on figures 3 and 5 are other instances of this error, not of Perseveration of the circles of figure 2. She also drew figure A relatively smaller than number 6, demonstrating Cohesion. There is a small Closure Difficulty on figure A, but the joinings on other figures are done well, so there is not enough evidence to score this error. All the other figures were drawn accurately with good preservation of the gestalt.

Test Diagnosis. Based on the BGT alone, 2 errors indicate no sign of brain impairment. In fact, this woman was retested 10 years later and she made the exact same two errors on the BGT. Her performance on the second testing was almost identical to that on the first.

Diagnosis. Based on a thorough neurological examination and a battery of neuropsychological tests, this woman was found to have no cognitive impairment.

Case Q *BGT Scoring*

Error	Figure
Retrogression	3, 5
Angulation Difficulty	3
Cohesion	A, 7

Total errors: 3

Test Analysis.   Persistent dashes instead of dots on 3 and 5 are maturationally more immature and so are classified as Retrogression (see Figure 13.18). These dashes on figure 3 are drawn in a straight line, for an error of Angulation Difficulty. Figure 3 therefore demonstrates that you can make two separate errors on the same figure. The relatively small size of A compared to the other figures and the shorter length of the left hexagon on 7 are both examples of Cohesion. All the other figures are drawn well with good preservation of the gestalt. On figure 6, the low placement of the vertical line is a borderline example of Overlapping Difficulty. When not certain about an error, do not score. The minor difficulties with closure of adjacent parts of several figures are not quite scorable errors with this system.

Test Diagnosis.   With only 3 errors, the BGT diagnosis is no brain pathology.

Diagnosis.   After 74 days in the hospital, Q was transferred to a long-term hospital for chronic care. Her discharge diagnosis was Schizophrenia, Undifferentiated Type.

Case R *BGT Scoring*

Error	Figure
Perseveration, Type A	3, 5
Perseveration, Type B	2
Collision	5 & 6
Closure Difficulty	4
Cohesion	3

Total errors: 4

Test Analysis.   Both kinds of Perseveration (A and B) can be seen on this protocol, although it still only counts as one error (see Figure 13.19). First, as an example of Type A, the circles of figure 2 are continued inappropriately onto 3 and 5. Although it appears that R also used circles for dots on figure 1 (which would be the error of Simplification), he recognized that they should be dots and tried to fill them in. Second, as an example of Type B, each column of circles on figure 2 has an extra circle, making four rows rather than three. In addition, on figure 2, several of the columns are not slanted in the correct direction; however, more than half are correctly slanted, so there is no error of Angulation Difficulty. Figures 5 and 6 touch, earning an error of Collision. Although there are many examples of minor problems with joining designs, the problem on figure 4 is significant enough by itself to warrant scoring Closure Difficulty. Figure 3 is drawn relatively larger than several others for Cohesion. Although some of the straight lines do look a bit tremulous, no hand tremors were noted at the time of testing, so no error is scored. Also, although the hexagons on figure 7 are missing a few angles, the scoring for this figure is rather lenient because of the difficulty of the design.

Test Diagnosis.   A score of 4 errors does not give clear-cut evidence of brain dysfunction. With this number of errors, there is a 21% chance of misclassifying an adult patient as nonimpaired. Because of the long drinking history and low education, this score may be considered borderline. Continued heavy use of alcohol is likely to result in a future diagnosis of brain pathology.

Diagnosis.   *R* was discharged after 6 days with a final diagnosis of Alcohol Dependence.

Case S   *BGT Scoring*

Error	Figure
Rotation	2, 4, 5, 7
Overlapping Difficulty	7
Simplification	A, 4
Retrogression	7, 8
Impotence	A, 4, 7, 8
Cohesion	A, 1, 7

Total errors: 6

Test Analysis.   There are numerous Rotations on this protocol (see Figure 13.20). Figure 2 is a mirror image; figures 4, 5, and 7 are each rotated 90 degrees. The two designs of figure 7 show Overlapping Difficulty, intersecting at the wrong place. Two versions of Simplification are evident. On figure A, the two parts are reproduced far apart. On figure 4, the two parts join in an overly simple way, avoiding the complexity of the task. Although this scoring system allows liberal distortion of hexagons, those in figures 7 and 8 are quite distorted, as is the diamond in figure 8. This type of substituting of a more immature figure is called Retrogression. Multiple erasures without improvement in the product on figures A, 4, 7, and 8 indicate the error of Impotence. Cohesion can be seen in several places in this BGT. One part of both figures A and 7 is much smaller than the other part. Also, figure A is much larger than figure 1. Some might want to score the error Angulation Difficulty on figure 3; however, this system is fairly lenient on this design because its angulation is especially difficult to reproduce.

Test Diagnosis.   A score of 6 errors on the BGT shows evidence of brain dysfunction on this test. The normative number of errors for nonpatients of this age is 1.47, and very few of this group make 5 or more errors. In addition, *S* committed the error of Impotence, which is eight times more frequent in those with brain damage than in those without.

Diagnosis.   The clinic diagnosis was Cognitive Disorder due to stroke in infancy and Mild Mental Retardation.

Case T *BGT Scoring*

Error	Figure
Perseveration, Type A	3, 5
Perseveration, Type B	1, 3
Collision	7 & 8
Closure Difficulty	A, 8
Cohesion	3 & 6, 7

Total errors: 4

Test Analysis. This adolescent correctly used dots on figure 1 but switched to circles on 3 and 5 (see Figure 13.21). This pattern is considered a Perseveration (Type A) of the circles from figure 2. He also demonstrated Type B Perseveration by drawing figures beyond the limits in the stimulus. On figure 1, he drew 15 dots instead of 12; on figure 3, he added an extra row. Figures 7 and 8 touch, for the error of Collision. Several others are close enough to illustrate Collision Tendency. A significant example of Closure Difficulty between two adjacent parts of a figure can be seen in figure A; other minor examples can be seen in 4, 7, and 8. The fourth error is Cohesion. Note the relative difference in size between figures 3 and 6. Also, the two parts of figure 7 are sufficiently different in size. You might think that figure 2 is a Fragmentation. However, the definition for this error on this figure is "6 or fewer columns of circles," whereas this one has 7 columns. Also, you might consider scoring Angulation Difficulty on this same drawing because the figure is tilted; however, it is not tilted to the criterion of 45 degrees or more and good angulation ability is shown on figure 3, which is more difficult to draw. Some of the lines in the drawings look tremulous. However, no behavioral tremors were seen during testing and the figures were drawn carelessly. The more conservative approach is not to score an error unless you are certain. Some of the elements in figure 1 are somewhat dashlike, though not enough to earn the error of Retrogression.

Test Diagnosis. This young man earned 4 errors on the BGT, a borderline impaired score. The normative number of errors for a nonpatient of this age is 2.30 and for an inpatient with no brain damage is 2.65. Several of his behaviors may have unrealistically inflated his number of errors, such as carelessness, insufficient attention to the test designs, and lack of interest in the task. For this one test, the score is most likely in the no-brain-impairment range.

Diagnosis. This boy was given the diagnoses of Oppositional Defiant Disorder and Learning Disorder.

Case U *BGT Scoring*

Error	Figure
Retrogression	1
Closure Difficulty	4, 7, 8
Motor Incoordination	All figures
Cohesion	3 & 4, 7

Total errors: 4

Test Analysis. The patient opens by starting to draw a small circle, which she then corrects to a larger circle without erasing the first attempt (see Figure 13.22). Because she improved her first effort, this is not considered Impotence. Also, many of the drawings have distortions (A, 4, and 8); however, they are not serious enough to earn errors; they seem to be primarily due to lack of motor control from her widespread Motor Incoordination. The extreme and persistent use of dashes for dots is an example of Retrogression. Many of the drawings do have persistent, though not serious, acts of Closure Difficulty. The relative size difference between figures 3 and 4 indicates Cohesion, as does the smaller size of the left hexagon on figure 7 compared to the one on the right.

Test Diagnosis. A score of 4 errors on the BGT is a borderline indicator of brain damage. Although this woman does not have a clear-cut diagnosis of brain impairment, there are a number of factors that could have elevated her score: her age, substance abuse, and cognitive decline. None of her errors were of the type especially indicative of brain damage. The results of other tests in the battery will be important in determining her specific condition.

Diagnosis. The psychologist's diagnosis was Major Depressive Disorder.

CHAPTER 14

Summary and Conclusions

Since its introduction by Lauretta Bender 60 years ago, the Bender Gestalt Test (BGT) has developed into one of the most widely used psychological tests. It is brief, inexpensive, nonverbal, and nonthreatening to those being tested. It is useful with children, adolescents, and adults across a wide range of intellectual abilities and cultural backgrounds. Healthy individuals maintain their performance on this test well into their 70s and 80s, making it an effective diagnostic measure of brain function in the older adult. The first edition of this book focused on use of the BGT with adults; however, the current version adds chapters on its use with older adults, children and adolescents. These chapters explore specific BGT issues and practices unique to each of these age groups.

The BGT is employed by psychologists for a broad array of purposes. It often functions as a warm-up procedure or as a buffer between objective and projective batteries. It can be used as a projective personality test. With children it is widely given to assess learning problems and school readiness. However, the major use of this instrument is as a general screening tool for differential diagnosis with adult psychiatric inpatients. As such, it is rarely used in isolation but more often in concert with other tests, such as the WAIS, MMPI, and other brief screening tests for brain dysfunction.

A number of variants on the standard administration of the BGT have been introduced through the years, and they enjoy varying popularity. These include group administration and the recall, tachistoscopic, and background-interference methods. Although the adequacy of group administration has been verified empirically, there is not enough evidence at this time to warrant reliance on the recall and tachistoscopic methods. Use of Canter's Background Interference Procedure is somewhat more controversial. Although early research produced very high hit rates, later studies have not shown consistently high diagnostic accuracy. Answers about the potential usefulness of these variations on the BGT await future methodologically sound research.

Investigations to determine which psychological abilities or functions account for performance on the BGT have not been conclusive. Three factors are assumed to be most relevant: perceptual ability, motor ability, and the integration of the two. In addition, recent research has implicated the role of other factors, such as memory, and such "executive" functions as planning, organization, and level of drive.

In the past 20 years, the growth of the subspeciality of neuropsychology has led to a much more sophisticated understanding of brain function and neuropathology. Neuropsychologists can now deploy a wide variety of measures to assess many aspects of brain function. Evaluators now use a *continuum* of neuropsychological assessment that varies in thoroughness as well as in effort and expense. General screening for brain impairment is on one end of the continuum, with comprehensive clinical neuropsychological evaluation on the other end. As a *screening* test, the BGT can be used in a system of "successive sieves." When general test batteries, or even single screening instruments such as the BGT, indicate the possibility of brain damage and further information is desired, then a battery of carefully selected neuropsychological tests is called for. For the isolation of specific brain functions and extensive evaluation of damage, including location and severity of lesions, more comprehensive neuropsychological assessment can be used, including elaborate test batteries such as the Halstead-Reitan.

The BGT can be used at all points of this continuum. For example, within a comprehensive evaluation, the BGT can be used as a measure of the perceptual-motor or visuoconstructive *domain* of cognitive functions. This book was written for those psychologists who wish to use the BGT as a visuoconstructive test either for screening for brain impairment or to assess a particular cognitive domain.

Although the basis of its usefulness is still not entirely known, a large percentage of clinical psychologists agree that the BGT is useful to them. It is especially helpful in discriminating between cognitive impairment and psychotic disturbance. There is general agreement that the BGT is most sensitive in detecting diffuse, slowly progressive cortical damage rather than localized lesions. However, it now appears that the BGT casts a broader net and it may be sensitive to impairment in many brain areas, including the frontal and parietal lobes.

Early BGT research did not allow successful individual identification. However, with improvements in scoring techniques and research design, more recent studies demonstrate the clinical utility of the BGT, meaning its ability to predict individuals with accuracy. In spite of a number of methodological shortcomings in this research area, the BGT used as a screening measure compares very favorably to other single neuropsychological tests, as well as to more elaborate assessment batteries. Clinicians can use the BGT with confidence for the assessment of brain dysfunction except for patients with chronic or process schizophrenia, who appear to perform much as patients with brain damage do. This group may do poorly on a test to detect brain dysfunction because many of them may have some neuropathy due to a biological etiology for their disorder, prolonged hospitalization, lengthy courses of potent antipsychotic drugs, or all three.

Some neuropsychologists criticize the use of single neuropsychological tests such as the BGT when more comprehensive assessment batteries such as the Halstead-Reitan or Luria-Nebraska are available. They base their criticisms on two issues: (1) use of a single test implies a naive unitary concept of brain dysfunction rather than a specific-deficits concept; and (2) the single test does not allow for a thorough description of an individual's brain dysfunction.

Such criticism ignores evidence favoring a general-effect view of brain dysfunction. It also ignores the reality of the typical testing situation in which psychologists are asked to *screen* for brain impairment in psychiatric clinics or hospitals that have high base rates for schizophrenia. In these more typical settings, the elaborate test batteries have generally not shown high discriminative ability, especially in comparisons between those with brain impairment and those with schizophrenia. In addition, the expense of these batteries is not justified for screening purposes in these settings.

So for the typical referral in a typical psychiatric setting, the BGT used with other tests can serve the valuable function of a brief, inexpensive, low-risk, and low-discomfort screening test or *marker* for brain dysfunction. Results should be integrated with other information about the client or patient: behavioral observations, interview data, and history. If further information is needed after screening, individuals can then be referred for more extensive evaluation.

The first objective scoring system for the BGT was not published until 1951, 13 years after the test was initially developed. That system, developed by Pascal and Suttell, is probably the one most familiar to clinicians, and it has certainly been the one most used in research projects. Regrettably, this approach does not enjoy wide clinical application, most likely because it is cumbersome to use. Since 1951, a number of other scoring systems have been developed, all of which focus on a different set of possible drawing distortions, although there is considerable overlap among the various systems. In 1988, McIntosh et al. demonstrated that both the Koppitz scoring system for children and the Lacks scoring methods for adults could be successfully extended to age 12. Previously, no scoring covered the adolescent age range. Unfortunately, past surveys show that at least half of clinicians do not use one of these objective scoring systems for adult BGTs but instead rely on their less accurate subjective clinical acumen.

The scoring system presented in this book consists of 12 *essential discriminators* for brain dysfunction, originally presented by Hutt and Briskin in 1960 and later modified by Lacks. The BGT protocol is judged for the presence or absence of each of these errors, a procedure that usually takes less than 3 minutes. With the publication in 1984 of a detailed scoring manual for this method, more researchers are now using it in their work. There is no current information about the extent of its use in clinical practice. Research has shown that psychologists can achieve much higher levels of diagnostic accuracy through the use of these brief, easily learned scoring procedures than they can through continued reliance on clinical impressions. This finding is true across all levels of experience with the BGT. A capable psychometrician trained to use this system can achieve the same level of diagnostic accuracy as a BGT expert.

In Chapter 7, covering validity, considerable evidence is presented attesting to the utility of this scoring system in screening for organic brain dysfunction. Clear differences exist among group scores of nonpatients, nonimpaired patients, and individuals with diagnosed neuropathology. In addition, a number of studies show this system to have high discriminative power in predicting the diagnosis of individuals. Cross-validated overall hit rates, using the standard cutoff score, range from 80% to 85% accuracy across different populations and scorers.

Furthermore, the BGT is significantly correlated with other neuropsychological tests. In comparisons of the BGT (with the Lacks scoring) with other tests and with other scoring systems, it emerges as consistently superior. This superiority has been demonstrated regardless of the level of experience of the scorer, from novice through expert.

Statistically significant, though not clinically meaningful, sex and race differences exist for nonpatients. These effects are no longer apparent for patients, suggesting that they may have been overridden by psychopathology. As with other cognitive or information-processing tests, significant age, education, and IQ effects have been found for the BGT with both nonpatients and patients. However, it appears that these effects may only influence diagnostic interpretations when individuals fall in the extreme ranges of these variables.

In addition to validity, the Lacks procedures presented here have demonstrated reliability, both in temporal stability and in interscorer consistency. *Temporal stability* refers to the consistency of test results with repeated administrations over time. Such consistency is important because retesting with neuropsychological tests is common over serial hospitalizations, as a check against equivocal results, or to assess deterioration of function. Based on four different types of samples, test-retest reliability of total scores using the Lacks method ranges from .57 to .79, depending on retesting interval (5 days to 12 months) and on actual patient stability (from very stable to known progressive condition). These figures are comparable to reliabilities published for other BGT scoring systems and even to those for batteries of neuropsychological tests. From a clinical perspective, the reliability of this scoring system is even more encouraging. For the same four samples, agreement on diagnosis ranged from 72% to 93%, the latter achieved for two groups who were expected to be relatively stable due either to short retest intervals or to careful screening.

As for *consistency* among different scorers, two studies show high levels of agreement among evaluators ($r = .87$ to .95 for scores and 86% to 97% for diagnosis) using this system. These results were achieved even when the scorers differed radically in level of general experience and specific background with the BGT. Novice scorers with only 2 hours of training were able to achieve high levels of agreement with very experienced scorers.

To facilitate maximum BGT scoring competency and consistency among the users of the Lacks adaptation of the Hutt-Briskin scoring system, Chapters 6 and 13 of this book present a detailed scoring manual and 22 varied practice cases. If clinicians will devote 3 or 4 hours to reading the manual, understanding the scoring examples, and testing themselves with the practice cases, they should also be able to achieve these high levels of scoring efficiency.

The BGT is used primarily as a brief screening test for brain dysfunction in a psychiatric setting, and the majority of studies have investigated its efficacy for this task. In recent years, however, research on this measure has turned away from studies of diagnostic accuracy to examine new settings, new types of clinical problems, and atypical patient groups for which this instrument might be of use. The BGT has been found helpful in the evaluation of the impact of surgical techniques upon cerebral integrity, the early identification of Huntington's disease victims, and the periodic monitoring of cognitive function in healthy older adults or the documenting of the path of deterioration in persons with dementia. Because of the large increase in number of forensic cases and number of individuals suing for compensation, neuropsychologists have recently begun to investigate methods for detecting malingering or feigned cognitive deficits. Other studies have used the BGT to measure the effect of increased cerebral oxygenation on cognitive functioning, to examine the visual scanning strategies of children with learning disabilities, and to assess differing drug regimens for those with minimal brain dysfunction. Another area of interest uses the BGT and other tests to assess basic living skills and to plan rehabilitation programs for seniors.

The focus of the first edition of this book was on the administration and scoring of the test. This second edition adds a chapter detailing an eight-step approach to interpretation of the BGT results. The interpretation begins with determination of the reliability and validity of the patient's effort and continues through to the application of scientific decision-making rules. In the latest twist for this 60-year-old test, computer software is now available for the electronic interpretation and reporting of the results of the BGT.

References

Acker, M. B., & Davis, J. R. (1989). Psychology test scores associated with late outcome in head injury. *Neuropsychology, 3,* 123–133.

Adams, J., & Canter, A. (1969). Performance characteristics of school children on the BIP Bender test. *Journal of Consulting and Clinical Psychology, 33,* 508.

Adams, R. L., Boake, C., & Crain, C. (1982). Bias in a neuropsychological test classification related to education, age, and ethnicity. *Journal of Consulting and Clinical Psychology, 50,* 143–145.

Albert, M. S. (1981). Geriatric neuropsychology. *Journal of Consulting and Clinical Psychology, 49,* 835–850.

Allen, R. M. (1968). Visual perceptual maturation and the Bender Gestalt Test quality. *Training School Bulletin, 64,* 131–133.

Allen, R. M. (1969). The Developmental Test of Visual Perception and the Bender Gestalt Test achievement of educable mental retardates. *Training School Bulletin, 66,* 80–85.

American Psychiatric Association. (1994). *Diagnostic and statistical manual of mental disorders* (4th ed.). Washington, DC: Author.

American Psychological Association. (1985). *Standards for educational and psychological testing.* Washington, DC: Author.

Anastasi, A. (1996). *Psychological testing* (7th ed.). New York: Macmillan.

Andert, J. N., Hustak, T. L., & Dinning, W. D. (1978). Bender-Gestalt reproduction times for retarded adults. *Journal of Clinical Psychology, 34,* 927–929.

Arbit, J., & Zager, R. (1978). Psychometrics of a neuropsychological test battery. *Journal of Clinical Psychology, 34,* 460–465.

Armstrong, R. G. (1965). A re-evaluation of copied and recalled Bender-Gestalt reproductions. *Journal of Projective Techniques and Personality Assessment, 29,* 134–139.

Arnold, L. E., Huestis, R. D., Wemmer, D., & Smeltzer, D. J. (1978). Differential effect of amphetamine optical isomers on Bender Gestalt performance of the minimally brain dysfunctioned. *Journal of Learning Disabilities, 11,* 127–132.

Bak, J. S., & Greene, R. L. (1980). Changes in neuropsychological functioning in an aging population. *Journal of Consulting and Clinical Psychology, 48,* 395–399.

Baker, R. R. (1968). The effects of psychotropic drugs on psychological testing. *Psychological Bulletin, 69,* 377–387.

Bash, I. Y., & Alpert, M. (1980). The determination of malingering. *Annals of New York Academy of Sciences, 347,* 86–99.

Becker, J. T., & Sabatino, D. A. (1971). Reliability of individual tests of perception administered utilizing group techniques. *Journal of Clinical Psychology, 27,* 86–88.

Bedard, M. A., Montplaisir, J., Richer, F., Rouleau, I., & Malo, J. (1991). Obstructive sleep apnea syndrome: Pathogenesis of neuropsychological deficits. *Journal of Clinical and Experimental Neuropsychology, 13,* 950–964.

Belter, R. W., McIntosh, J. A., Finch, A. J., Williams, L. D., & Edwards, G. L. (1989). The Bender-Gestalt as a method of personality assessment with adolescents. *Journal of Clinical Psychology, 45,* 414–422.

Bender, L. (1938). *A visual motor gestalt test and its clinical use.* New York: American Orthopsychiatric Association.

Bender, L. (1946). *Instructions for the use of the Visual Motor Gestalt Test.* New York: American Orthopsychiatric Association.

Bender, L. (1965). On the proper use of the Bender-Gestalt test. *Perceptual and Motor Skills, 20,* 189–190.

Benson, D. F., & Barton, M. I. (1970). Disturbances in constructional ability. *Cortex, 6,* 19–46.

Benton, A. L., & Tranel, D. (1993). Visuoperceptual, visuospatial, and visuoconstructive disorders. In K. M. Heilman & E. Valenstein (Eds.), *Clinical neuropsychology* (pp. 165–213). New York: Oxford University Press.

Berg, R. A., Franzen, M., & Wedding, D. (1994). *Screening for brain impairment: A manual for mental health practice.* New York: Springer.

Bigler, E. D., & Ehrfurth, J. W. (1981). The continued inappropriate singular use of the Bender Visual Motor Gestalt Test. *Professional Psychology, 12,* 562–569.

Bigler, E. D., Nussbaum, N. L., & Foley, H. A. (1997). Child neuropsychology in the private medical practice. In C. R. Reynolds & E. Fletcher-Janzen (Eds.), *Handbook of clinical child neuropsychology* (2nd ed., pp. 726–742). New York: Plenum Press.

Binder, L. (1993). An abbreviated form of the Portland Digit Recognition Test. *The Clinical Neuropsychologist, 7,* 104–107.

Black, F. W., & Bernard, B. A. (1984). Constructional apraxia as a function of lesion locus and size in patients with focal brain damage. *Cortex, 20,* 111–120.

Boake, C., & Adams, R. L. (1982). Clinical utility of the Background Interference Procedure for the Bender-Gestalt Test. *Journal of Clinical Psychology, 38,* 627–631.

Bolen, L. M., Hewett, J. B., Hall, C. W., & Mitchell, C. C. (1992). Expanded Koppitz scoring system of the Bender Gestalt Visual-Motor Test for adolescents: A pilot study. *Psychology in the Schools, 29,* 113–115.

Bondi, M. W., Salmon, D. P., & Kaszniak, A. W. (1996). The neuropsychology of dementia. In I. Grant & K. M. Adams (Eds.), *Neuropsychological assessment of neuropsychiatric disorders* (pp. 164–199). New York: Oxford University Press.

Brandt, J., & Butters, N. (1996). Neuropsychological characteristics of Huntington's disease. In I. Grant & K. M. Adams (Eds.), *Neuropsychological assessment of neuropsychiatric disorders* (pp. 312–341). New York: Oxford University Press.

Brannigan, G. G., Aabye, S. M., Baker, L. A., & Ryan, G. T. (1995). Further validation of the Qualitative System for the modified Bender-Gestalt Test. *Psychology in the Schools, 32,* 24–26.

Brannigan, G. G., & Brannigan, M. J. (1995). Comparison of individual versus group administration of the Modified Version of the Bender-Gestalt Test. *Perceptual and Motor Skills, 80,* 1274.

Brannigan, G. G., & Brunner, N. A. (1989). *The modified version of the Bender-Gestalt Test for preschool and primary school children.* Brandon, VT: Clinical Psychology Publishing Company.

Brilliant, P., & Gynther, M. D. (1963). Relationships between performance on three tests for organicity and selected patient variables. *Journal of Consulting Psychology, 27,* 474–479.

Brown, G. G., Baird, A. D., Shatz, M. W., & Bornstein, R. A. (1996). The effects of cerebral vascular disease on neuropsychological functioning. In I. Grant & K. M. Adams (Eds.), *Neuropsychological assessment of neuropsychiatric disorders* (pp. 342–378). New York: Oxford University Press.

Bruhn, A. R., & Reed, M. R. (1975). Simulation of brain damage on the Bender-Gestalt Test by college students. *Journal of Personality Assessment, 39,* 244–255.

Butler, M., Retzlaff, P., & Vanderploeg, R. (1991). Neuropsychological test usage. *Professional Psychology: Research and Practice, 22,* 510–512.

Butler, O. T., Coursey, R. D., & Gatz, M. (1976). Comparison of the Bender Gestalt Test for both black and white brain-damaged patients using two scoring systems. *Journal of Consulting and Clinical Psychology, 44,* 280–285.

Canter, A. (1966). A background interference procedure to increase sensitivity of the Bender-Gestalt Test to organic brain disorder. *Journal of Consulting Psychology, 30,* 91–97.

Canter, A. (1971). A comparison of the background interference procedure effect in schizophrenic, nonschizophrenic, and organic patients. *Journal of Clinical Psychology, 27,* 473–474.

Chouinard, M. J., & Braun, C. M. J. (1993) A meta-analysis of the relative sensitivity of neuropsychological screening tests. *Journal of Clinical and Experimental Neuropsychology, 15,* 591–607.

Craig, P. L. (1979). Neuropsychological assessment in public psychiatric hospitals: The current state of the practice. *Clinical Neuropsychology, 1,* 1–7.

Culbertson, F. M., & Gunn, R. C. (1966). Comparison of the Bender Gestalt Test and the Frostig Test in several clinical groups of children. *Journal of Clinical Psychology, 22,* 439.

Cummings, J. A., & Laquerre, M. (1990). Visual-motor assessment. In C. R. Reynolds & R. W. Kamphaus (Eds.), *Handbook of psychological and educational assessment of children: Intelligence and achievement* (pp. 593–610). New York: Guilford Press.

D'Amato, R. C., Rothlisberg, B. A., & Rhodes, R. L. (1997). Utilizing a neuropsychological paradigm for understanding common educational and psychological tests. In C. R. Reynolds & E. Fletcher-Janzen (Eds.), *Handbook of clinical child neuropsychology* (2nd ed., pp. 270–295). New York: Plenum Press.

Davies, S. (1996). Neuropsychological assessment of the older person. In R. T. Woods (Ed.), *Handbook of the clinical psychology of aging* (pp. 441–474). Chichester, UK: John Wiley & Sons.

Davis, B. D., Fernandez, F., Adams, F., Holmes, V., Levy, J. K., Lewis, D., & Neidhart, J. (1987). Diagnosis of dementia in cancer patients. *Psychosomatics, 28,* 175–179.

Davis, D. D., & Templer, D. I. (1988). Neurobehavioral functioning in children exposed to narcotics in utero. *Addictive Behaviors, 13,* 275–283.

Delaney, R. C. (1982). Screening for organicity: The problem of subtle neuropsychological deficit and diagnosis. *Journal of Clinical Psychology, 38,* 843–846.

Dibner, A. S., & Korn, E. J. (1969). Group administration of the Bender Gestalt Test to predict early school performance. *Journal of Clinical Psychology, 25,* 265–268.

Diller, L., & Gordon, W. A. (1981). Interventions for cognitive deficits in brain-injured adults. *Journal of Consulting and Clinical Psychology, 49,* 822–834.

Dodrill, C. B. (1997). Myths of neuropsychology. *The Clinical Neuropsychologist, 11,* 1–17.

Erickson, R. C., Eimon, P., & Hebben, N. (1994). A listing of references to cognitive test norms for older adults. In M. Storandt & G. R. VandenBos (Eds.), *Neuropsychological assessment of dementia and depression in older adults: A clinician's guide* (pp. 183–197). Washington, DC: American Psychological Association.

Erwin, E. F., & Hampe, E. (1966). Assessment of perceptual-motor changes following electroshock treatment. *Perceptual and Motor Skills, 22,* 770.

Essman, W. B. (1973). Psychopharmacology. In H. J. Eysenck (Ed.), *Handbook of abnormal psychology.* London: Pitman.

Fantie, B. D., & Kolb, B. (1991). The problems of prognosis. In J. Dywan, R. D. Kaplan, & F. J. Pirozzolo (Eds.), *Neuropsychology and the law* (pp. 186–238). New York: Springer-Verlag.

Faust, D., Hart, K. J., & Guilmette, T. J. (1988). Pediatric malingering: The capacity of children to fake believable deficits on neuropsychological testing. *Journal of Consulting and Clinical Psychology, 56,* 578–582.

Faust, D., Hart, K. J., Guilmette, T. J., & Arkes, H. R. (1988). Neuropsychologists' ability to detect adolescent malingerers. *Professional Psychology: Research and Practice, 19,* 508–515.

Field, K., Bolton, B., & Dana, R. (1982). An evaluation of three Bender-Gestalt scoring systems as indicators of psychopathology. *Journal of Clinical Psychology, 38,* 838–842.

Fjeld, S. P., Small, I. F., Small, J. G., & Hayden, M. (1966). Clinical, electrical, and psychological tests and the diagnosis of organic brain disorder. *Journal of Nervous and Mental Disease, 142,* 172–179.

Franzen, M. D., & Berg, R. (1989). *Screening children for brain impairment.* New York: Springer.

Franzen, M. D., Iverson, G. L., & McCracken, L. M. (1990). The detection of malingering in neuropsychological assessment. *Neuropsychology Review, 1,* 247–279.

Franzen, M. D., & Martin, R. C. (1996). Screening for neuropsychological impairment. In L. L. Carstensen, B. A. Edelstein, & L. Dornbrand (Eds.), *The practical handbook of clinical gerontology* (pp. 188–216). Thousand Oaks, CA: Sage.

Franzen, M. D., & Rasmussen, P. R. (1990). Clinical neuropsychology and older populations. In A. M. Horton (Ed.), *Neuropsychology across the life-span: Assessment and treatment* (pp. 81–102). New York: Springer.

Friedt, L. R., & Gouvier, W. D. (1989). Bender Gestalt screening for brain dysfunction in a forensic population. *Criminal Justice and Behavior, 16,* 455–464.

Garb, H. N., & Schramke, C. J. (1996). Judgment research and neuropsychological assessment: A narrative review and meta-analyses. *Psychological Bulletin, 120,* 140–153.

Garron, D. C., & Cheifetz, D. I. (1968). Electroshock therapy and Bender-Gestalt performance. *Perceptual and Motor Skills, 26,* 9–10.

Glasser, A. O. (1982). The detection of malingering and the Bender Gestalt Test. *Dissertation Abstracts International, 43*(03), 870B. (University Microfilms No. AAC 82-17692).

Goh, D. S., Teslow, C. J., & Fuller, G. B. (1981). The practice of psychological assessment among school psychologists. *Professional Psychology, 12,* 696–706.

Goldberg, L. R. (1959). The effectiveness of clinicians' judgments: The diagnosis of organic brain damage from the Bender Gestalt Test. *Journal of Consulting Psychology, 23,* 25–33.

Golden, C. J. (1990). *Clinical interpretation of objective psychological tests* (2nd ed.). Boston: Allyn and Bacon.

Golden, C. J., Berg, R. A., & Graber, B. (1982). Test-retest reliability of the Luria-Nebraska Neuropsychological Battery in stable, chronically impaired patients. *Journal of Clinical Psychology, 50,* 452–454.

Goldman, R. S., Axelrod, B. N., & Taylor, S. F. (1996) Neuropsychological aspects of schizophrenia. In I. Grant & K. M. Adams (Eds.), *Neuropsychological assessment of neuropsychiatric disorders* (pp. 504–525). New York: Oxford University Press.

Goldstein, G. (1986). The neuropsychology of schizophrenia. In I. Grant & K. M. Adams (Eds.), *Neuropsychological assessment of neuropsychiatric disorders* (pp. 148–171). New York: Oxford University Press.

Grant, I. (1987). Alcohol and the brain: Neuropsychological correlates. *Journal of Consulting and Clinical Psychology, 55,* 310–324.

Grant, I., & Adams, K. M. (1996). *Neuropsychological assessment of neuropsychiatric disorders.* New York: Oxford University Press.

Grant, I., Prigatano, G. P., Heaton, R. K. McSweeny, A. J., Wright, E. C., & Adams, K. M. (1987). Progressive neuropsychologic impairment and hypoxemia. *Archives of General Psychiatry, 44,* 999–1006.

Greenberg, G. D., Watson, R. K., & Deptula, D. (1987). Neuropsychological dysfunction in sleep apnea. *Sleep, 10,* 254–262.

Gregory, R. J. (1987). *Adult intellectual assessment.* Boston: Allyn & Bacon.

Gregory, R. J. (1996). *Psychological testing: History, principles, and applications.* Boston: Allyn & Bacon.

Griffith, R. M., & Taylor, V. H. (1960). Incidence of Bender-Gestalt figure rotations. *Journal of Consulting Psychology, 24,* 189–190.

Groth-Marnat, G. (1997). *Handbook of psychological assessment* (3rd ed.). New York: John Wiley & Sons.

Groth-Marnat, G. (in press). *Neuropsychological assessment in clinical practice: A practical guide to test interpretation and integration.* New York: John Wiley & Sons.

Hain, J. D. (1964). The Bender Gestalt Test: A scoring method for identifying brain damage. *Journal of Consulting Psychology, 28,* 34–40.

Hammainen, L. (1994). Computerized support for neuropsychological test interpretation in clinical situations. *The Clinical Neuropsychologist, 8,* 167–185.

Hartlage, L. C., & Golden, C. J. (1990). Neuropsychological assessment techniques. In T. B. Gutkin & C. R. Reynolds (Eds.), *The handbook of school psychology* (2nd ed., pp. 431–457). New York: John Wiley & Sons.

Hauer, A. L., & Armentrout, J. A. (1978). Failure of the Bender-Gestalt and Wechsler tests to differentiate children with and without seizure disorders. *Perceptual and Motor Skills, 47,* 199–202.

Heaton, R. K., Baade, L. E., & Johnson, K. L. (1978). Neuropsychological test results associated with psychiatric disorders in adults. *Psychological Bulletin, 85,* 141–162.

Heaton, R. K., & Pendleton, M. G. (1981). Use of neuropsychological tests to predict adult patients' everyday functioning. *Journal of Consulting and Clinical Psychology, 49,* 807–821.

Heaton, R. K., Ryan, L., Grant, I., & Matthews, C. G. (1996). Demographic influences on neuropsychological test performance. In I. Grant & K. M. Adams (Eds.), *Neuropsychological assessment of neuropsychiatric disorders* (2nd ed., pp. 141–163). New York: Oxford University Press.

Heaton, R. K., Vogt, A. T., Hoehn, M. M., Lewis, J. A., Crowley, T. J., & Stallings, M. A. (1979). Neuropsychological impairment with schizophrenia vs. acute and chronic cerebral lesions. *Journal of Clinical Psychology, 35,* 46–53.

Heinrichs, R. W. (1993). Schizophrenia and the brain: Conditions for a neuropsychology of madness. *American Psychologist, 48,* 221–233.

Helms, J. (1992). Why is there no study of cultural equivalence in standardized cognitive ability testing? *American Psychologist, 47,* 1083–1101.

Hiscock, M., & Hiscock, C. K. (1989). Refining the forced-choice method for the detection of malingering. *Journal of Consulting and Experimental Neuropsychology, 11,* 967–974.

Holland, T. R., & Wadsworth, H. M. (1979). Comparison and contribution of recall and Background Interference Procedures for the Bender-Gestalt Test with brain-damaged and schizophrenic patients. *Journal of Personality Assessment, 43,* 123–127.

Horine, L. C., & Fulkerson, S. C. (1973). Utility of the Canter Background Interference Procedure for differentiating among the schizophrenias. *Journal of Personality Assessment, 37,* 48–52.

Hutt, M. L. (1985). *The Hutt adaptation of the Bender-Gestalt Test* (4th ed.). New York: Grune & Stratton.

Hutt, M. L., & Briskin, G. J. (1960). *The clinical use of the revised Bender Gestalt Test.* New York: Grune & Stratton.

Hutt, M. L., & Dates, B. G. (1977). Reliabilities and interrelationships of two HABGT scales in a male delinquent population. *Journal of Personality Assessment, 41,* 353–357.

Hutt, M. L., & Miller, L. J. (1976). Interrelationships of psychopathology and adience-abience. *Journal of Personality Assessment, 40,* 135–139.

Imm, P. S., Foster, K. Y., Belter, R. W., & Finch, A. J. (1991). Assessment of short-term visual memory in child and adolescent psychiatric inpatients. *Journal of Clinical Psychology, 47,* 440–443.

Jacobs, E. A., Winter, P. M., Alvis, H. J., & Small, S. M. (1969). Hyperoxygenation effect on cognitive functioning in the aged. *New England Journal of Medicine, 281,* 753–757.

James, E. M., & Selz, M. (1997). Neuropsychological bases of common learning and behavior problems in children. In C. R. Reynolds & E. Fletcher-Janzen (Eds.), *Handbook of clinical child neuropsychology* (2nd ed., pp. 157–179). New York: Plenum Press.

Johnson, J. E., Hellkamp, D. J., & Lottman, T. J. (1971). The relationship between intelligence, brain damage, and Hutt-Briskin errors on the Bender-Gestalt. *Journal of Clinical Psychology, 27,* 84–85.

Joseph, R. J. (1996). *Neuropsychiatry, neuropsychology, and clinical neuroscience: Emotion, evolution, cognition, language, memory, brain damage, and abnormal behavior* (2nd ed.). Baltimore: Williams & Wilkins.

Kane, R. L., Sweet, J. J., Golden, C. J., Parsons, O. A., & Moses, J. A. (1981). Comparative diagnostic accuracy of the Halstead-Reitan and standardized Luria-Neuropsychological Batteries in a mixed psychiatric and brain-damaged population. *Journal of Consulting and Clinical Psychology, 49,* 484–485.

Kaszniak, A. W., & Cristenson, G. D. (1994). Differential diagnosis of dementia and depression. In M. Storandt & G. R. VandenBos (Eds.), *Neuropsychological assessment of dementia and depression in older adults: A clinician's guide* (pp. 81–117). Washington, DC: American Psychological Association.

Kelly, M. D., Grant, I., Heaton, R. K., Marcotte, T. D., & The HNRC Group. (1996) Neuropsychological findings in HIV infection and AIDS. In I. Grant & K. M. Adams (Eds.), *Neuropsychological assessment of neuropsychiatric disorders* (pp. 403–422). New York: Oxford University Press.

Keogh, B. K., & Smith, C. E. (1961). Group techniques and proposed scoring system for the Bender-Gestalt Test with children. *Journal of Clinical Psychology, 17,* 172–175.

Klonoff, H., Fibiger, C. H., & Hutton, G. H. (1970). Neuropsychological patterns in chronic schizophrenia. *Journal of Nervous and Mental Disease, 150,* 291–300.

Kolb, B., & Whishaw, I. Q. (1990). *Fundamentals of neuropsychology* (3rd ed.). New York: W. H. Freeman.

Koppitz, E. M. (1963). *The Bender Gestalt Test for young children.* New York: Grune & Stratton.

Koppitz, E. M. (1975). *The Bender Gestalt Test for young children. Volume 2: Research and application, 1963–1973.* New York: Grune & Stratton.

Korman, M., & Blumberg, S. (1963). Comparative efficiency of some tests of cerebral damage. *Journal of Consulting Psychology, 27,* 303–309.

Kramer, E., & Fenwick, J. (1966). Differential diagnosis with the Bender Gestalt Test. *Journal of Projective Techniques and Personality Assessment, 30,* 59–61.

Krop, H. D., Block, A. J., & Cohen, E. (1973). Neuropsychologic effects of continuous oxygen therapy in chronic obstructive pulmonary disease. *Chest, 64,* 317–322.

Lacks, P. (1979). The use of the Bender Gestalt Test in clinical neuropsychology. *Clinical Neuropsychology, 1,* 29–34.

Lacks, P. (1984). *Bender Gestalt screening for brain dysfunction.* New York: John Wiley & Sons.

Lacks, P. (1996). *Bender Gestalt screening software for Windows.* Odessa, FL: Psychological Assessment Resources.

Lacks, P. (in press). Visuoconstructive abilities. In G. Groth-Marnat (Ed.). *Neuropsychological assessment in clinical practice: A practical guide to test interpretation and integration.* New York: John Wiley & Sons.

Lacks, P., Colbert, J., Harrow, M., & Levine, J. (1970). Further evidence concerning the diagnostic accuracy of the Halstead organic test battery. *Journal of Clinical Psychology, 26,* 480–481.

Lacks, P., & Newport, K. (1980). A comparison of scoring systems and level of scorer experience on the Bender Gestalt Test. *Journal of Personality Assessment, 44,* 351–357.

Lacks, P., & Storandt, M. (1982). Bender Gestalt performance of normal older adults. *Journal of Clinical Psychology, 38,* 624–627.

Landis, B., Baxter, J., Patterson, R., & Tauber, C. E. (1974). Bender Gestalt evaluation of brain dysfunction following open-heart surgery. *Journal of Personality Assessment, 38,* 556–562.

Lesiak, J. (1984). The Bender Visual Motor Gestalt Test: Implications for the diagnosis and prediction of reading achievement. *Journal of School Psychology, 22,* 391–405.

Lezak, M. D. (1987). Norms for growing older. *Developmental neuropsychology, 3,* 1–12.

Lezak, M. D. (1995). *Neuropsychological assessment.* New York: Oxford University Press.

Lilliston, L. (1973). Schizophrenic symptomatology as a function of probability of cerebral damage. *Journal of Abnormal Psychology, 82,* 377–381.

Locher, P. J., & Worms, P. F. (1977). Visual scanning strategies of neurologically impaired, perceptually impaired, and normal children viewing the Bender-Gestalt designs. *Psychology in the Schools, 14,* 147–157.

Lownsdale, W. S., Rogers, B. J., & McCall, J. N. (1989). Concurrent validation of Hutt's Bender Gestalt screening method for schizophrenia, depression, and brain damage. *Journal of Personality Assessment, 53,* 832–836.

Lyle, O. E., & Quast, W. (1976). The Bender-Gestalt: Use of clinical judgment versus recall scores in prediction of Huntington's disease. *Journal of Consulting and Clinical Psychology, 44,* 229–232.

Malatesha, R. N. (1986). Visual motor ability in normal and disabled readers. *Perceptual and Motor Skills, 62,* 627–630.

Malec, J. (1978). Neuropsychological assessment of schizophrenia versus brain damage: A review. *Journal of Nervous & Mental Disease, 166,* 507–516.

Marley, M. L. (1982). *Organic brain pathology and the Bender-Gestalt Test: A differential diagnostic scoring system.* New York: Grune & Stratton.

Marsico, D. S., & Wagner, E. E. (1990). A comparison of the Lacks and Pascal-Suttell Bender-Gestalt scoring methods for diagnosing brain damage in an outpatient sample. *Journal of Clinical Psychology, 46,* 868–877.

Masur, D. M., Sliwinski, M., Lipton, R. B., Blau, A. D., & Crystal, H. A. (1994). Neuropsychological prediction of dementia and the absence of dementia in healthy elderly persons. *Neurology, 44,* 1427–1432.

Matarazzo, J. D., Matarazzo, R. G., Wiens, A. N., Gallo, A. E., & Klonoff, H. (1976). Retest reliability of the Halstead Impairment Index in a normal, a schizophrenic, and two samples of organic patients. *Journal of Clinical Psychology, 32,* 338–349.

McCann, R., & Plunkett, R. P. (1984) Improving the concurrent validity of the Bender-Gestalt Test. *Perceptual and Motor Skills, 58,* 947–950.

McIntosh, J. A., Belter, R. W., Saylor, C. F., & Finch, A. J., & Edwards, G. L. (1988). The Bender-Gestalt with adolescents: Comparison of two scoring systems. *Journal of Clinical Psychology, 44,* 226–230.

McPherson, S., & Cummings, J. L. (1996). Neuropsychological aspects of Parkinson's disease and parkinsonism. In I. Grant & K. M. Adams (Eds.), *Neuropsychological assessment of neuropsychiatric disorders* (pp. 288–311). New York: Oxford University Press.

Meehl, P. E. (1954). *Clinical versus statistical prediction.* Minneapolis: University of Minnesota Press.

Meehl, P. E., & Rosen, A. (1955). Antecedent probability and the efficiency of psychometric signs, patterns, or cutting scores. *Psychological Bulletin, 52,* 194–216.

Miller, L. J., & Hutt, M. L. (1975). Psychopathology Scale of the Hutt Adaptation of the Bender-Gestalt Test: Reliability. *Journal of Personality Assessment, 2,* 129–131.

Mittenberg, W., Seidenberg, M., O'Leary, D. S., & DiGiulio, D. V. (1989). Changes in cerebral functioning associated with normal aging. *Journal of Clinical and Experimental Neuropsychology, 11,* 918–932.

Moore, C. L., & Zarske, J. A. (1984). Comparison of Native American Navajo Bender-Gestalt performance with Koppitz and SOMPA norms. *Psychology in the Schools, 21,* 148–153.

Morsbach, G., Del Priori, C., & Furnell, J. (1975). Two aspects of scorer reliability in the Bender-Gestalt Test. *Journal of Clinical Psychology, 31,* 90–93.

Neale, M. D., & McKay, M. F. (1985). Scoring the Bender-Gestalt Test using the Koppitz Developmental System: Interrater reliability, item difficulty, and scoring implications. *Perceptual and Motor Skills, 60,* 627–636.

Nemec, R. E. (1978). Effects of controlled background interference on test performance by right and left hemiplegics. *Journal of Consulting and Clinical Psychology, 46,* 294–297.

Nielson, S., & Sapp, G. L. (1991). Bender-Gestalt developmental scores: Predicting reading and mathematics achievement. *Psychological Reports, 69,* 39–42.

Nies, K. J., & Sweet, J. J. (1994). Neuropsychological assessment and malingering: A critical review of past and present strategies. *Archives of Clinical Neuropsychology, 9,* 501–552.

Oas, P. (1984). Validity of the Draw-A-Person and Bender-Gestalt tests as measures of impulsivity with adolescents. *Journal of Consulting and Clinical Psychology, 52,* 1011–1019.

Oldershaw, L., & Bagby, R. M. (1997). Children and deception. In R. Rogers (Ed.), *Clinical assessment of malingering and deception* (2nd ed., pp. 153–166). New York: Guilford Press.

Owen, J. D. (1971). The effects of chlorpromazine on performance of schizophrenic patients on two tests for brain damage and related measures, *Dissertation Abstracts International, 43*(07), 4343B.

Pankratz, L., & Binder, L. M. (1997) Malingering on intellectual and neuropsychological measures. In R. Rogers (Ed.), *Clinical assessment of malingering and deception* (pp. 223–236). New York: Guilford Press.

Parsons, O. A., & Prigatano, G. P. (1978). Methodological considerations in clinical neuropsychological research. *Journal of Consulting and Clinical Psychology, 46,* 608–619.

Pascal, G. R., & Suttell, B. J. (1951). *The Bender Gestalt Test.* New York: Grune & Stratton.

Pauker, J. D. (1976). A quick-scoring system for the Bender Gestalt: Interrater reliability and scoring validity. *Journal of Clinical Psychology, 32,* 86–89.

Pettinati, H. M., & Bonner, K. M. (1984). Cognitive functioning in depressed geriatric patients with a history of ECT. *American Journal of Psychiatry, 141,* 49–52.

Piotrowski, C. (1995). A review of the clinical and research use of the Bender-Gestalt Test. *Perceptual and Motor Skills, 81,* 1272–1274.

Piotrowski, C., & Keller, J. W. (1989). Psychological testing in outpatient mental health facilities: A national study. *Professional Psychology: Research and Practice, 20,* 423–425.

Pirozzolo, F. J., Campanella, D. J., Christensen, K., & Lawson-Kerr, K. (1981). Effects of cerebral dysfunction on neurolinguistic performance in children. *Journal of Consulting and Clinical Psychology, 49,* 791–806.

Price, L. J., Fein, G., & Feinberg, I. (1980). Neuropsychological assessment of cognitive function in the elderly. In L. W. Poon (Ed.), *Aging in the 1980's* (pp. 78–85). Washington, DC: American Psychological Association.

Puente, A. E., Mora, M. S., & Munoz-Cespedes, J. M. (1997). Neuropsychological assessment of Spanish-speaking children and youth. In C. R. Reynolds & E. Fletcher-Janzen (Eds.), *Handbook of clinical child neuropsychology* (2nd ed., pp. 371–383). New York: Plenum Press.

Reitan, R. M., & Wolfson, D. (1993). *The Halstead-Reitan Neuropsychological Test Battery: Theory and clinical interpretation.* Tucson, AZ: Neuropsychology Press.

Retzlaff, P., Butler, M., & Vanderploeg, R. D. (1992). Neuropsychological battery choice and theoretical orientation: A multivariate analysis. *Journal of Clinical Psychology, 48,* 666–672.

Reznikoff, M., & Olin, T. D. (1957). Recall of the Bender Gestalt designs by organic and schizophrenic patients: A comparative study. *Journal of Clinical Psychology, 13,* 183–186.

Robiner, W. (1978). *An analysis of some of the variables influencing clinical use of the Bender Gestalt.* Unpublished masters thesis, Washington University, St. Louis, MO.

Rogers, D. L., & Swenson, W. M. (1975). Bender-Gestalt recall as a measure of memory versus distractibility. *Perceptual and Motor Skills, 40,* 919–922.

Rogers, R. (1997a) Current status of clinical methods. In R. Rogers (Ed.), *Clinical assessment of malingering and deception* (2nd ed., pp. 373–397). New York: Guilford Press.

Rogers, R. (1997b). Introduction. In R. Rogers (Ed.), *Clinical assessment of malingering and deception* (2nd ed., pp. 1–19). New York: Guilford Press.

Rosenberg, R. P., & Beck, S. (1986). Preferred assessment methods and treatment modalities for hyperactive children among clinical child and school psychologists. *Journal of Clinical Child Psychology, 15,* 142–147.

Rossini, E. D., & Kaspar, J. C. (1987). The validity of the Bender-Gestalt emotional indicators. *Journal of Personality Assessment, 51,* 254–261.

Rourke, B. P. (1985). *Neuropsychology of learning disabilities: Essentials of subtype analysis.* New York: Guilford Press.

Rourke, B. P. (1993). Arithmetic disabilities, specific and otherwise: A neuropsychological perspective. *Journal of Learning Disabilities, 26,* 214–226.

Rourke, S. B., & Adams, K. M. (1996) The neuropsychological correlates of acute and chronic hypoxemia. In I. Grant & K. M. Adams (Eds.), *Neuropsychological assessment of neuropsychiatric disorders* (pp. 379–402). New York: Oxford University Press.

Rourke, S. B., & Loberg, T. (1996). Neurobehavioral correlates of alcoholism. In I. Grant & K. M. Adams (Eds.), *Neuropsychological assessment of neuropsychiatric disorders* (pp. 423–485). New York: Oxford University Press.

Sattler, J. M. (1992). *Assessment of children* (3rd ed.). San Diego: Author.

Sattler, J. M., & Gwynne, J. (1982). Ethnicity and Bender Visual Motor Gestalt Test performance. *Journal of School Psychology, 20,* 69–71.

Satz, P., Fennell, E., & Reilly, C. (1970). Predictive validity of six neurodiagnostic tests: A decision theory analysis. *Journal of Consulting and Clinical Psychology, 34,* 375–381.

Satz, P., & Fletcher, J. M. (1981). Emergent trends in neuropsychology: An overview. *Journal of Consulting and Clinical Psychology, 49,* 851–865.

Saykin, A. J., Gur, R. C., Gur, R. E., Mozley, P. D., Mozley, L. H., Resnick, S. M., Kester, D. B., & Stafiniak, P. (1991). Neuropsychological function in schizophrenia: Selective impairment in memory and learning. *Archives of General Psychiatry, 48,* 618–624.

Schretlen, D. (1988). The use of psychological tests to identify malingered symptoms of mental disorder. *Clinical Psychology Review, 8,* 451–476.

Schretlen, D., & Arkowitz, H. (1990). A psychological test battery to detect prison inmates who fake insanity or mental retardation. *Behavioral Sciences and the Law, 8,* 75–84.

Schretlen, D., Wilkins, S. S., Van Gorp, W. G., & Bobholz, J. H. (1992). Cross-validation of a psychological test battery to detect faked insanity. *Psychological Assessment, 4,* 77–83.

Seretny, M. L., Dean, R. S., Gray, J. W., & Hartlage, L. C. (1986). The practice of clinical neuropsychology in the United States. *Archives of Clinical Neuropsychology, 1,* 5–12.

Shapiro, E., Shapiro, A. K., & Clarkin, J. (1974). Clinical psychological testing in Tourette's syndrome. *Journal of Personality Assessment, 38,* 464–478.

Shapiro, S. K., & Simpson, R. G. (1995). Koppitz scoring system as a measure of Bender-Gestalt performance in behaviorally and emotionally disturbed adolescents. *Journal of Clinical Psychology, 51,* 108–112.

Smith, A. (1975). Neuropsychological testing in neurological disorders. *Advances in Neurology, 7,* 49–110.

Smith, G. E., Wong, J. S., Ivnik, R. J., & Malec, J. F. (1997). Mayo's Older American Normative Studies: Separate norms for Wechsler Memory Scale logical memory stories. *Assessment, 4,* 79–86.

Smith, G. P. (1997). Assessment of malingering with self-report instruments. In R. Rogers (Ed.), *Clinical assessment of malingering and deception* (pp. 351–372). New York: Guilford Press.

Snow, J. H., & Desch, L. W. (1988). Subgroups based on Bender-Gestalt error scores. *Journal of Psychoeducational Assessment, 6,* 261–270.

Snow, J. H., & Desch, L. W. (1989). Characteristics of empirically derived subgroups based on intelligence and visual-motor score patterns. *Journal of School Psychology, 27,* 265–275.

Spreen, O., & Benton, A. L. (1965). Comparative studies of some psychological tests for cerebral damage. *Journal of Nervous and Mental Disease, 140,* 323–333.

Stoer, L., Corotto, L. V., & Curnutt, R. H. (1965). The role of visual perception in the reproduction of Bender-Gestalt designs. *Journal of Projective Techniques and Personality Assessment, 29,* 473–478.

Storandt, M. (1990). Bender-Gestalt Test performance in senile dementia of the Alzheimer type. *Psychology and Aging, 5,* 604–606.

Strauss, B. S., & Silverstein, M. L. (1986). Luria-Nebraska measures in neuropsychologically nonimpaired schizophrenics: A comparison with normal subjects. *The International Journal of Clinical Neuropsychology, 8,* 35–38.

Sweet, J. J., Moberg, P. J., & Westergaard, C. K. (1996). Five-year follow-up survey of practices and beliefs of clinical neuropsychologists. *The Clinical Neuropsychologist, 10,* 202–221.

Tarbox, A. R., Connors, G. J., & McLaughlin, E. J. (1986). Effects of drinking pattern on neuropsychological performance among alcohol misusers. *Journal of Studies on Alcohol, 47,* 176–179.

Taylor, R. L., & Partenio, I. (1984). Ethnic differences on the Bender-Gestalt: Relative effects of measured intelligence. *Journal of Consulting and Clinical Psychology, 52,* 784–788.

Tindall, T. C. (1991). Utilization of the Bender-Gestalt Test for an adolescent Anglo-Hispanic population. *Dissertation Abstracts International, 51*(09), 3023A. (University Microfilms No. AAC 91-05260.)

Tolor, A., & Brannigan, G. G. (1980). *Research and clinical applications of the Bender-Gestalt Test.* Springfield, IL: Charles C. Thomas.

Trueblood, W., & Binder, L. M. (1997). Psychologists' accuracy in identifying neuropsychological test protocols of clinical malingerers. *Archives of Clinical Neuropsychology, 12,* 13–27.

Trueblood, W., & Schmidt, M. (1993). Malingering and other validity considerations in the neuropsychological evaluation of mild head injury. *Journal of Clinical and Experimental Neuropsychology, 15,* 578–590.

Vega, M., & Powell, A. (1973). The effects of practice on Bender Gestalt performance of culturally disadvantaged children. *Florida Journal of Educational Research, 12,* 45–49.

Watkins, C. E., Campbell, V. L., Nieberding, R., & Hallmark, R. (1995). Contemporary practice of psychological assessment by clinical psychologists. *Professional Psychology: Research and Practice, 26,* 54–60.

Watson, C. G., Thomas, R. W., Andersen, D., & Felling, J. (1968). Differentiation of organics from schizophrenics at two chronicity levels by use of the Reitan-Halstead organic test battery. *Journal of Consulting and Clinical Psychology, 32,* 679–684.

Webster, J. S., Scott, R. R., Nunn, B., McNeer, M. F., & Varnell, N. (1984). A brief neuropsychological screening procedure that assesses left and right hemispheric function. *Journal of Clinical Psychology, 40,* 237–240.

Wedding, D. & Faust, D. (1989). Clinical judgment and decision making in neuropsychology. *Archives of Clinical Neuropsychology, 4,* 233–265.

Wedell, K., & Horne, I. E. (1969). Some aspects of perceptuo-motor disability in five and a half year old children. *British Journal of Educational Psychology, 39,* 174–182.

Weintraub, D. L. (1991). Comparison of two scoring systems for the Bender-Gestalt Test: Assessment, concurrent validity, diagnostic accuracy. *Dissertation Abstracts International, 52*(02), 1088B. (University Microfilms No. AAC 91-20832.)

Werner, E. E. (1986). Resilient offspring of alcoholics: A longitudinal study from birth to age 18. *Journal of Studies on Alcohol, 47,* 34–40.

Wertheimer, M. (1923). Studies in the theory of Gestalt psychology. *Psychologische Forschung, 4,* 301–350.

West, P. A., Hill, S. Y., & Robins, L. N. (1977). The Canter Background Interference Procedure (BIP): Effects of demographic variables on diagnosis. *Journal of Clinical Psychology, 33,* 765–771.

Williams, H. J. (1983). *Perceptual and motor development.* Englewood Cliffs, NJ: Prentice-Hall.

Wolber, J., & Lira, F. T. (1981). Relationship between Bender designs and basic living skills of geriatric psychiatric patients. *Perceptual and Motor Skills, 52,* 16–18.

Yozawitz, A. Applied neuropsychology in a psychiatric center. (1986). In I. Grant & K. M. Adams (Eds.), *Neuropsychological assessment of neuropsychiatric disorders* (pp. 121–145). New York: Oxford University Press.

Yulis, S. (1970). Performance of normal and organic brain-damaged subjects on the Canter Background Interference Test as a function of drive. *Journal of Consulting and Clinical Psychology, 34,* 184–188.

Zuelzer, M. B., Stedman, J. M., & Adams, R. (1976). Koppitz Bender Gestalt scores in first grade children as related to ethnocultural background, socioeconomic class, and sex factors. *Journal of Consulting and Clinical Psychology, 44,* 875–876.

BGT Scoring for Cases Presented in Chapter 5

Case 5.1

Error	Figure
Rotation	3, 4
Overlapping Difficulty	6
Simplification	1
Fragmentation	3, 8
Retrogression	A, 8
Perseveration, Type B	1, 2
Collision	2, 6
Impotence	A, 8
Closure Difficulty	A, 4, 7
Angulation Difficulty	2

Total errors: 10
Test diagnosis: Organic brain dysfunction
Diagnosis: Vascular Dementia

Case 5.2

Error	Figure
Rotation	2
Overlapping Difficulty	7
Simplification	A, 5, 6
Retrogression	7
Perseveration, Type B	1
Closure Difficulty	A, 4, 8
Impotence	7 (expressions of inability to correct errors)
Cohesion	7

Total errors: 8
Test diagnosis: Organic brain dysfunction
Diagnosis: Inpatient adolescent with "positive evidence of neurological impairment"

Case 5.3

Error	Figure
Simplification	A, 4, 6, 7, 8
Fragmentation	2, 3, 5
Retrogression	7, 8
Perseveration, Type B	2
Angulation	2
Cohesion	A

Total errors: 6
Test diagnosis: Organic brain dysfunction
Diagnosis: Delirium due to toxic metabolic disturbance

Case 5.4

Error	Figure
Perseveration	
Type A	3
Type B	All except A
Collision	2 & 3, 5 & 6
Closure Difficulty	A, 7, 8
Cohesion	A

Total errors: 4
Test diagnosis: No brain dysfunction
Diagnosis: No psychiatric diagnosis

Case 5.5

Error	Figure
Simplification	1
Perseveration, Type B	3 (extra row)
Collision Tendency	1 & 2, 2 & 3, 3 & 4
Closure Difficulty	A, 4, 7, 8
Cohesion	A

Total errors: 5
Test diagnosis: Organic brain dysfunction
Diagnosis: Cognitive Disorder with seizures

AUTHOR INDEX

SUBJECT INDEX